THE
'BOOK OF BOOKS'

THE
'BOOK OF BOOKS'

William R. Kimball

College Press Publishing Company, Joplin, Missouri

All scriptures quoted, unless otherwise noted, are from the Holy Bible, New International Version, Copyright © 1978 by New York International Bible Society.

Other versions include:

The New King James Version, Copyright © 1979, 1980, 1982, Thomas Nelson, Inc., Publishers. Used by permission.

The King James Version.

The New American Standard Bible, Copyright © 1971, Lockman Foundation.

Library of Congress Catalog Card Number: 86-071101
International Standard Book Number: 0-89900-211-0

"The Bible is not only the book of God but also the god of books." - John Ruskin

Dedicated to my students, whose appetite for learning has helped make this work possible.

THE BIBLE

The charter of all true liberty.
The forerunner of civilization.
The moulder of institutions and govern-
ments.
The fashioner of law.
The secret of national progress.
The guide of history.
The ornament and mainspring of litera-
ture.
The friend of science.
The inspiration of philosophies.
The textbook of ethics.
The light of intellect.
The answer to the deepest human heart
hungerings.
The soul of all strong heart life.
The illuminator of darkness.
The foe of superstition.
The enemy of oppression.
The uprooter of sin.
The regulator of all high and worthy
standards.
The comfort in sorrow.
The strength in weakness.
The pathway in perplexity.
The escape from temptation.
The steadier in the day of power.
The embodiment of all lofty ideals.
The begetter of life.
The promise of the future.
The star of death's night.
The revealer of God.
The guide and hope and inspiration of
man.

Bishop Anderson

TABLE OF CONTENTS

Chapter   Page

Foreword   *13*

Section I

IS THE BIBLE THE WORD OF GOD?

11

Section II

HOW DID WE GET THE BIBLE?

Section III

HOW TO STUDY YOUR BIBLE

FOREWORD

The relationship of many towards the Bible reminds me of the telling story of the circuit-riding preacher. He was making his monthly rounds through the backwoods of Kentucky when he stopped at an isolated farmhouse along the way. As he was hitching his horse to the post, the farmer came out and invited him in for some cool lemonade. As they were talking religion, the farmer's wife thought she'd impress the preacher with her spirituality. She called one of her children to her side and said, "Billy Jo, you run and fetch the book which Mommy loves so dearly—the one she reads all the time—you know the book, son." In a moment the boy reappeared and proudly handed her a thumb-worn copy of the Sears catalog—much to the woman's embarrassment!

Though we may laugh at the homespun humor in this story, it contains a sobering note of reality. We can each sigh an air of relief that we've avoided such embarrassing exposure, but the real life relationship of many to the Bible is aptly characterized by this woman's testimony.

Multitudes of churched and unchurched people possess at least a copy of the Bible, but their real life relationship is closer to apathetic neglect than responsive reverence. Though an expensive, gold-gilded family Bible respectfully opened to a familiar passage may seemingly occupy a place of importance in some households, the actual relationship of its owners to its contents often belies the setting. To many, the Bible is little more than a religious heirloom or an object which possesses little practical relevance for their lives.

Rather than being "the book we love so dearly," it often serves as a religious dust collector. It certainly does not occupy the strategic place of practical importance in the life of its owner which it rightfully deserves. To many, the Bible holds only a marginal place of religious reverence, at best. Though many may not openly reject it or deny its divine inspiration, their silent disregard for its importance is just another form of rejection.

On a more positive note, the relationship of others towards the Bible can be better reflected in the parting words of Sir Walter Scott, a dedicated Christian and noted British novelist and poet. As he lay on his deathbed, it is said that he cried out to his secretary, "Bring me the Book!" Of course, the summons caused considerable consternation for his secretary when she surveyed the countless volumes of books on his library shelves. She replied, "Dr. Scott, which book?" "The Book!" said Scott, "the Bible!"

As he lay on the threshold of eternity, Scott's deathbed request expressed the heartfelt sentiments of millions concerning the supreme place of importance which this book played in their lives.

Which story do we identify with? Which character is truer to life? Do we truly esteem the Bible as precious? Is our real relationship supported by our candid conduct and confession? In viewing our lives against the backdrop of these stories we should

ask ourselves, "How precious is the Bible to me?" "Does my
response live up to my real relationship with it?" If the Bible
is the Word of God, what should my response be to it?" These
are not only questions which unbelievers should ask, but
believers as well. Many Christians have never honestly considered these questions. Though we don't want to become Bible
idolators by deifying the Bible as an object of worship, we do
want to exalt the Bible as the only inspired Word of God. We
want to restore it to its rightful place of prominence in the lives
of Christians.

This book is written for both Christians and non-Christians
alike. For Christians harboring lingering questions about the Bible's reliability and place of importance, this book can birth
fresh confidence. For those who already possess a deep-seated
reverence for the Bible, the contents of this book will only reinforce that appreciation. And for those sincere skeptics who
question its reliability and inspiration, it provides the powerful
proofs of divine authorship, accuracy, and authority, and can
serve as a catalyst for stimulating a deeper relationship with the
Bible.

Hopefully, the results of reading this book will mirror the
experience of the missionary who offered a Bible to a
stonemason who was building a wall. He did not want the Bible,
but finally accepted it. When the lady left, the man removed a
stone from the wall and placed the Bible in a hollow space. He
then continued building the wall around it, laughing to think
how he had fooled her. Not many years after this, there was a
violent earthquake which caused many buildings and walls to
collapse. When the demolition crews were removing the debris,
one of the workers joked, "Perhaps there is a treasure in
there." As he cleared away some stones, there, in the hollow
where the mason had placed the Bible several years before, the
workman found the tattered "treasure". He took it home and
read it, and was led to love it and to serve God. Indeed, he had
found a great treasure.

Like the stonemason's experience, the Bible is often like a hidden treasure whose riches are waiting to be discovered. It is the purpose of this book to duplicate the workman's experience in the lives of all who read its pages. My prayer is that some readers will find the preciousness of the Bible enhanced, that some will joyfully rediscover a long lost relationship with it, and still others will discover for the first time that the Bible is not just another book, but THE Book—the Book of Books!

Section I

Is the Bible the Word of God?

INTRODUCTION

Arguing in Circles

Is the Bible the Word of God? This is a commonly asked question. Bible-believing Christians maintain that it is, but many contend that it isn't. It is a controversy which has seesawed for centuries without being satisfactorily resolved in the minds of many.

One of the primary reasons why this controversy has persisted is because Christians have often been unable to provide conclusive proofs for the Bible's divine inspiration and infallibility. Many people reject the Christian argument that the Bible is the inspired Word of God on the grounds that this claim is shallow, simplistic, and intellectually unconvincing.

Often, the sole defense the church has been able to mount is a form of merry-go-round logic which argues in hopeless circles: "I believe the Bible is the Word of God because the Bible says that it is the Word of God; and because the Bible says it is the

Word of God, I believe the Bible is the Word of God."

This line of reasoning may be a sufficient faith response for Christians, but it is quite unconvincing for most unbelievers. Though absolutely true and non-negotiable as far as Bible believers are concerned, this argument does not present an air-tight case for the scriptures' infallibility, authority, and divine inspiration as far as many sincere skeptics are concerned—they demand more convincing proof.

Christians have a responsibility to "always be ready to give a defense to everyone who asks you a reason for the hope that is in you, with meekness and fear" (I Pet. 3:15, NKJV). Like the Minutemen militia who were ready to grab their musket and powder horn from over the fireplace hearth at a moment's notice to rush to the aid of their country, Christians must also be armed with the same resolute readiness to sufficiently support the truth at all seasons. This is no less true of our defense of the Bible.

The Battle for the Bible

One of the most pressing, contemporary challenges confronting the church today is the need to uphold the Bible as God's infallibly inspired revelation to mankind. This is especially true in light of the current climate of conflict being waged between the forces of darkness and the forces of light.

Whether men and women recognize it or not, the entire human race is engaged in a warfare. A spiritual power struggle is being waged behind the scenes for the souls of men. On the one side of this tug-of-war stands God and His forces of righteousness, and on the other side stands the malevolent forces of Satan. The stakes in this conflict are high. At issue is the eternal destiny of each of us. Though this scenario may seem melodramatic, it is none the less accurate.

But what complicates this conflict is the fact that the battlelines are not always clearly drawn. They are not even well defined within the church, let alone in secular society. Many Christians do not recognize the enemy's strategies or major areas of conflict. There are so many spiritual skirmishes, smokescreens, and diversionary maneuvers being executed that it is often hard to pinpoint the precise heart of the conflict or respond in the proper manner. The scriptures declare that, "If the trumpet makes an uncertain sound, who will prepare himself for battle?" (I Cor. 14:8, NKJV). Too often, uncertain sounds call God's people to irrelevant battlefields when the real battles are overlooked.

One of the fiercest battles being fought, not only on the frontiers of the kingdom but even within the ranks of the soldiers of Christ, is the battle over the Bible. The firefight over whether the Bible is the inspired Word of God is the battle cry of our day. It is this decisive conflict which has a dramatic impact upon all other related battles.

This controversy has intensified in recent years on a scale never before witnessed in human history. The reason is simple. Since the absolutes of God's Word provide the sole basis of authoritative truth for victoriously confronting falsehood, Satan has stepped up his attacks against the Bible's reliability and relevancy. Because the Bible establishes God's absolute truth and reveals His redemptive plan for the human race, Satan has unleashed all of his forces in a desperate attempt to thwart its authority in the earth and sidetrack humanity. If the bulwarks of God's Word buckle and fall, the corresponding result will be like the domino theory upon all other related attempts to defeat error. Therefore, it is absolutely imperative that its truths be upheld. All of our spiritual defenses, arguments, and aggression are impotent without the authority and backing of God's truths contained in the Bible.

The Spirit of Our Age

The very spirit of our age is a subtle reflection of his endeavors. The rising tide of secular humanism is his attempt to submerge our society in a sea of moral relativity and situational ethics. He knows that, apart from God's Word, society's moral fabric becomes increasingly frayed and gradually degenerates into an amoral society devoid of absolutes.

The western world is awash in a popular, humanistic philosophy which exalts the rights of man and ignores, or outright rejects, the moral absolutes of God's Word. We live in an age which panders to self-indulgence and "do-your-own-thingism". It is a period much like the ancient period of Judges in Israel's history where "everyone did what was right in his own eyes" (Judges 21:25, NKJV) and answered to none. This is a fitting commentary on our times. It is an age when men deify their own desires, regardless of the consequences, in defiance of God, for pleasure of self. Because of this, the moral and ethical absolutes of God's Word have often been discarded in favor of a world view which says, "All truth is relative, and what's truth to you may not be truth to me. It really doesn't matter what you believe, so long as you like what you believe." But the inherent weakness is "that if it's true that it doesn't matter what you really believe, then the corollary is equally true: what you believe doesn't really matter either." But the problem is that what you believe does matter. It not only has a dramatic impact upon one's present existence, but upon his relationship to eternity as well.

Removing the Ancient Landmarks

God has not only established physical laws in the universe to govern our temporal existence, but spiritual laws which govern our eternal destiny as well. If you violate either, you pay a detrimental price. A man who climbs to the top of the Empire State Building and defiantly claims that he will successfully challenge the law of gravity by leaping off of the ledge will inevitably end up as a grease spot on the pavement below. So too, those who defy the absolutes of God's spiritual laws will meet inevitable loss and ruin.

God is not silent in warning us. The scriptures caution men,

"Do not remove the ancient landmark" (Prov. 22:28, NKJV). In the Old Testament, the ancient landmarks represented boundary stones which marked a landowner's limits of authority and property rights. In a similar view, the Bible sets the spiritual boundaries, moral definition, and divine direction for men. It is God's established truth in the earth. It defines the limits of man's authority, establishes the guidelines for moral and ethical conduct, and marks the borders between righteousness and unrighteousness.

Without the landmarks of God's Word, mankind loses moral and spiritual definition and direction. If you remove the absolutes of God's Word, man becomes like a rudderless ship, tossed to and fro and driven aimlessly in a sea of meaninglessness and confusion. The Bible has been likened to a divine roadmap for eternity. However, without its counsel and guidance, man is hopelessly lost. Those who seek to point the way without its guiding light become the proverbial blind leading the blind into the ditch.

On Rock or Sand?

When the authoritative truths of the Bible are stripped away as a basis for governing the destiny of men, man is left to his own unstable devices. He is without a secure foundation. Jesus dramatized this in a simple parable. He characterized two categories of men. He did so by illustrating a wise builder who built his house upon a rock, and a foolish builder who built his house upon the sand. The farsighted builder was he who "hears my sayings and does them" (Luke 6:47, NKJV). The shortsighted builder was he who foolishly ignored the need for the fundamental place of the Word of God. When the inevitable winds of adversity arose and the storms of life assaulted both houses, the wise man's weathered the tempest, while the foolish man's was washed away by the storm.

So too, when men fail to anchor their lives upon the reliable bedrock of God's Word, they have no secure foundation. Those who reject the authority of God's Word and choose to build

23

upon the shifting sands of human reason, man-made religion, and the wisdom of the world are doomed to disappointment. Those who strive to structure their lives on anything contrary to God's Word are like a man wallowing in a quagmire of quicksand; the more they struggle for stability, the deeper they sink.

This is precisely why the Bible is being so fiercely contested, mocked, and maligned. Satan desires to drown mankind in a sea of deception. If he can destroy the Bible's credibility in the eyes of men and undermine their confidence in its truths, he will succeed in removing absolutes from the earth. Without God's truths, there are none. They won't come from our courts, our professions, our schools, out of the halls of the Congress, the philosophies of men, or the laws of society. They come, ultimately, from the revelation of God's Word.

The Enemy Within

What makes our need to respond so critical is not only the vicious attacks from without, but the divisive attacks from within. Not only are the secular critics legion, but liberal voices within the structures of Christendom are also attacking the Bible's divine authority, accuracy, and authorship on an unprecedented scale. It may come as a shock to many, but even among the mainline evangelicals, the statistics concerning the extent of those who deny the Bible as the only inspired Word of God are alarming.

Several years ago, Western Reserve University mailed out a questionnaire to 10,000 clergymen in five major U.S. denominations. They received a reply from 7,442 of them. The question which they asked was simply phrased, "Do you believe the Bible to be the inspired Word of God?" The statistical breakdown of those who flatly responded "No!" was:

82% of the Methodists
89% of the Episcopalians
81% of the United Presbyterians

24

57% of the Baptists
57% of the Lutherans

The results of this poll are sobering and should serve to alert Bible-believing Christians to the seriousness of the battle that is raging.

The Best Defense...

The attacks of modern liberalists within the church, coupled with the relentless criticisms from without, are a present threat which Christians can ill afford to ignore. We cannot complacently assume the posture of the proverbial ostrich who sticks her head in the sand and hopes that the danger will go away.

The psalmist raises a penetrating question: "When the foundations are being destroyed, what can the righteous do?" (Psalms 11:3). Well, we can't afford to sit idly by and do nothing. We must act. We must establish the foundations of our faith. We must rise to the Bible's defense.

It is said that "the best offense is a good defense," but the opposite is equally true. We need to go on the offensive in defending the Bible. Our aggressiveness should mimic the actions of some French Christians at the University of Caan. During the sixties, in the midst of student riots, some Chinese Communist students took over the campus. They set up a table and began distributing copies of the little red-book containing the thoughts of Mao Tse Tung. Behind them flew a banner with the words, "Read the little red-book of Chairman Mao." The French Christians did not retreat in the face of the challenge but went on the offensive. They contacted a Bible society, asking them to send little red bound copies of the New Testament. When they arrived, they set up their own table, got a Chinese Christian to man it, and unfurled their own banner which said, "Read the little red-book by Jesus Christ!" We must respond accordingly. We need to take the same initiative and boldly exalt the Bible before men as the inspired revelation of Christ's redemptive plan for mankind.

We should realize that multitudes are caught in the middle of this crossfire over the Bible. However, our readiness to staunchly defend the Bible as the inspired Word of God can be the deciding factor in whether they are won over or fall victim to the deceptive propaganda of those who oppose it.

We do not have to succumb to intimidation from those who deny the Bible's divine accuracy and reliability, or those who have sincere doubts about its inspiration. We need not fear the challenge to confidently take the offensive, for when all the evidence is in and weighed in a just balance, the burden of proof falls more heavily on the shoulders of those who seek to disprove it as the only infallibly inspired Word of God than those who seek to prove it.

1

THE ULTIMATE GROUNDS
OF ACCEPTANCE

A Variety of Objections

For a variety of reasons, many remain skeptical and unconvinced concerning Christian claims about the Bible's trustworthiness and divine authorship. While some of the questions are, on the surface, both reasonable and justifiable, others are based upon willful ignorance and blind opposition.

Many have written off the Bible as the infallible Word of God without taking the time to seriously examine the facts. Some harbor deep reservations about the Bible simply because they have not been confronted with sufficient proofs to the contrary. Others reject its divine authorship without sacrificing a token respect for the Bible as a noble piece of ancient literature or a great religious masterpiece. Still others challenge the Bible's reliability on superficial grounds. Their opposition is often based upon well worn arguments, sweeping generalizations, mindless objections, and preconceived prejudices rather than the sound foundation of reason, truth, and reality.

A Call to Reason

An absolutely essential requirement for those examining the proofs presented in this section is an attitude of openness and intellectual integrity. Though many of those who hold intellectual doubts about the Bible are sincere skeptics with legitimate questions, others are intellectually insincere. They are willfully opposed to the Bible regardless of the weight of evidence which can be accumulated in its behalf. This category of critics avoid any Bible proofs like the plague. Even when substantial proofs can be mustered in defense of the Bible, they obstinately refuse to consider them. Like the response of the three monkeys, "they don't want to hear any facts, see any facts, or speak about any facts." Though they strongly defend their intellectual integrity and maintain their rejection is based purely upon rational grounds, their resistance is not a matter of the mind, but the will. What really stands in the way are not mental roadblocks at all, but the stubborn barriers of willful disbelief. This group doesn't have a mental problem but a heart problem. Those who reject the Bible after having been confronted with convincing proofs of its divine inspiration generally do so because they don't want to respond to the moral and spiritual implications.

Their typical reaction reminds me of the rich Chinese merchant who returned from a business trip to England. He had purchased a powerful microscope which he proudly displayed to his friends. They were curious to see how it worked, so he took a tiny bit of rice and placed it under the lens. When the grain of rice was magnified, he recoiled in horror. He saw thousands of microscopic creatures crawling all over it and part of his religion was to eat no animal life. What was he to do? He loved rice. So he simply smashed the microscope to pieces. This was an easy way out of the dilemma.

His action may seem foolish, but no more foolish than the

reaction of those who reject the convincing proofs of the Bible because the spiritual implications are distasteful. Their reaction is just as intellectually unsound and unreasonable.

If a person approaches this issue with a mental mindset which obstinately refuses to honestly consider the proofs presented, he or she will be wasting their time. Though I respect the genuine mental reservations a person may have (Lord knows I've had my own), a person must seriously challenge any bias against the Bible which is not based upon reason or a careful examination of the facts. If a person will review the information presented with an open and intellectually honest attitude, he will see that the evidence in support of the Bible's inspiration and infallibility are overwhelming and conclusive.

The Missing Ingredient

It is one thing to dogmatically contend that the Bible is the inspired Word of God; we can even substantiate this claim with many convincing arguments. However, all of our proofs will amount to the tenth part of nothing apart from a faith response. As one perceptive scholar put it:

> Ultimately this question of the authority of the Scriptures is a matter of faith and not of argument . . . you may convince a man intellectually of what you're saying, but still he may not of necessity believe in and accept the authority of the Scripture.[1]

The missing ingredient is faith. When all is said and done, the Bible is a book which must ultimately be accepted by faith not just passive mental agreement. Being intellectually persuaded alone is insufficient grounds for allowing the Word of God to truly profit a person's life. When speaking of Israel's unbelief,

---

1 **Decision**, "Authority of the Scriptures" (June, 1963), C. Martyn Lloyd-Jones.

the scriptures declare that, "the Word did not profit them, not being mixed with faith" (Hebrews 4:2, NKJV). The Bible and faith are like the two ingredients in five minute epoxy—unless the resin is combined with the hardening compound, it will not take hold and set up. So too, the Word cannot effectively take hold in our lives without the addition of corresponding faith.

Many powerful proofs can be rallied in defense of the Bible, but a person must ultimately come to a place of responsive faith in it, its message, and its author—Jesus Christ. Though the following proofs can help stimulate intellectual confidence in the Bible, a person must exercise a rational faith which acts upon the logical facts presented in order for the Word of God to have its intended effect upon our lives. Though some may mock this qualification as a "blind leap of faith", it is not a blind leap at all; it is a sensible, open-eyed faith which clearly sees the facts and acts accordingly. You don't have to commit intellectual suicide to exercise faith in God. You don't have to rely on blind faith, but an intelligent, reasonable, objective faith.

It has been said that, "You can lead a horse to water, but you can't make him drink." How true! The proofs presented can intellectually lead a person to the waters of faith, but that person must drink for himself. However, it has also been said, "Though you can lead the horse to water and can't make him drink, you can salt the oats." Hopefully, this book will intellectually "salt the oats" and produce a deeper thirst to partake—in faith—from the living waters of God's Word.

2

THE BIBLE'S INDESTRUCTIBILITY

Against All Odds

The indestructible character of the Bible gives strong support to its divine preservation. The Bible has weathered the test of time. It has successfully withstood the repeated attacks of atheistic philosophers, the schools of higher criticism, modernists, liberal theologians, rationalists, humanists, scientific skepticism, Communists, and every conceivable brand of critic.

In spite of the relentless assaults against the Bible, it has not only survived, but has consistently triumphed over all its enemies. "There is not an arrow in the quiver of the devil but has been fired at the Bible and has failed." In fact, the Huguenots likened the Bible's survivability to an anvil surrounded by three blacksmiths. Beneath the picture they inscribed the words, "The more they pound and the more they shout, the more they wear their hammers out!" In keeping with the Huguenot poem, the Bible has outlasted all of its opponents:

Last eve I paused beside a blacksmith's door,
And heard the anvil ring the vesper chime;
Then looking in, I saw upon the floor,
Old hammers, worn with beating years of time.

"How many anvils have you had," said I,
"To wear and batter these hammers so?"
"Just one," said he, and then, with twinkling eye,
"The anvil wears the hammers out, you know."

And so, thought I, the anvil of God's Word,
For ages skeptic blows have beat upon;
Yet, though the noise of falling blows was heard,
The anvil is unharmed—the hammer's gone.

Notorious Opponents

For example, the Emperor Diocletian ruthlessly attacked Christianity. In A.D. 303, he issued an imperial edict demanding that every copy of the Bible be burned. He butchered so many Christians and destroyed so many Bibles that he rejoiced that he had exterminated Christianity. To celebrate his triumph, he struck a coin which carried the inscription, "The Christian religion is destroyed and the worship of the gods restored." However, only ten years later, Emperor Constantine embraced Christianity and shortly thereafter, commissioned Eusebius to prepare fifty copies of the Bible at governmental expense.

Voltaire, the infamous French atheist, confidently proclaimed that "In one hundred years the Bible will be an extinct book." During the same year, the British Royal Museum purchased an ancient manuscript copy of the Greek New Testament (the Codex Sinaiticus) from the Russian government for the hefty sum of $510,000. In comparison, a ninety-two volume, first edition set of Voltaire's writings were auctioned off a few years ago from the Earl of Dudley's library. The leather-bound set sold for a paltry 8 cents a copy! What makes Voltaire's prophecy so ironical is the fact that only fifty years after his death, the Geneva Bible Society was using his house and his printing press to publish an avalanche of Bibles! His house later became the Paris headquarters for the British and Foreign Bible Society.

Thomas Paine, the noted author of the "Age of Reason," also predicted that the Bible would be out of print within his lifetime. He declared that, "When I get through, there will not be five Bibles left in America. Within one hundred years, Bibles will be found only in museums or in musty corners of second-hand bookstores." After a lifetime of opposition, Paine's dying words left a sobering tribute to Christianity's triumph: "I would give worlds, if I had them, if the 'Age of Reason' had never been published. O Lord, help me! Christ, help me! Stay with me! It is hell to be left alone."

It Lives On

Paine has long since passed from the stage of human history, but the Bible lives on. As H. L. Hastings wrote:

> "This book outlives its foes. If you could gather all the books written against it, you could build a pyramid higher than the loftiest spire. Now and then a man goes to work to refute the Bible, and every time it is done it has to be done over again the next day or the next year. And then, after its enemies have done their worst, some of its professed friends torture and twist and mystify and misrepresent it. Surely it is no fool of a book if it lives through all that! Infidels for eighteen hundred years have been refuting and overthrowing this book, and yet it stands today as solid as a rock. Its circulation increases, and it is more loved and cherished and read today than ever before. Infidels, with all their assaults, make about as much impression on this book as a man with a tack hammer would on the Pyramids of Egypt. . . . The hammers of infidels have been pecking away at this book for ages, but the hammers are worn out. . . . If this book had not been the book of God, men

33

would have destroyed it long ago. Emperors and popes, kings and priests, princes and rulers have all tried their hand at it; they die and the book still lives.''[1]

You can confiscate, mutilate, ban, and burn the Bible, but it survives. It not only endures, but it thrives in the face of opposition. The destructive energy generated against it has often served as a catalyst to stimulate its power, popularity, and propagation. This cannot be said of any other work. Someone once remarked, ''Burn a book and you will light the whole world.'' Though this statement has not held true of other works, it has held true for the Bible. Burn the Bible, and its flames of truth will only rise higher.

William Tyndale, an early Reformer and translator of the Bible, was martyred in 1536 because he translated and distributed copies of the Bible. His work was strongly opposed by the ecclesiastical authorities. His Bibles were hunted down, confiscated, and publicly burned in order to keep them out of the hands of the common people. But nothing the authorities did could check the circulation of his Bible translation.

Edward Halle relates an amazing incident about the Bishop of London, showing how God overrode the opposition of men to promote the Bible's circulation. On a visit to the Continent, Bishop Tonstall (an opponent of Tyndale) met a London merchant named Augustine Packington in Antwerp. This merchant was also friendly to Tyndale, having brought many of his English New Testaments into England. The Bishop told Packington that he desired to buy as many copies of Tyndale's new translation as he could. The merchant told him that he was well acquainted with the merchants who were handling the new Bibles and that he could buy them in large quantities.

The bishop, thinking that he had God by the toe, when indeed he had (as after he thought) the devil by the fist, said: ''Gentle Master Packington, do you diligence and get them,

1 Cited from **The Greatest Book In The World,** by John W. Lea, pp. 17, 18.

and with all my heart I will pay for them, whatsoever they cost you; for the books are erroneous and naughty, and I intend surely to destroy them all, and to burn them at Paul's Cross.'' Augustine Packington came to William Tyndale and said: ''William, I know thou art a poor man, and hast a heap of New Testaments and books by thee, for the which thou hast both endangered thy friends and beggared thyself; and I have now gotten thee a merchant, which with ready money shall dispatch thee of all that thou hast, if you think it so profitable for yourself.'' ''Who is the merchant?'' said Tyndale. ''The bishop of London,'' said Packington. ''Oh, that is because he will burn them,'' said Tyndale. ''Yea merry,'' quoth Packington. ''I am the gladder,'' said Tyndale; ''for these two benefits shall come thereof: I shall get money of him for these books, to bring myself out of debt, and the whole world shall cry out upon the burning of God's word. And the overplus of the money, that shall remain to me, shall make me more studious to correct the said New Testament, and so newly to imprint the same once again; and I trust the second will much better like you than ever did the first.'' And so forward went the bargain: the bishop had the books, Packington had the thanks, and Tyndale had the money.

Bishop Tonstall purchased thousands of the so-called ''heretical'' New Testaments and had them burned by the Cross at St. Paul's. The money he paid for the English New Testaments was used to print more Testaments. The effect of burning the Word of God was the opposite of what the Bishop expected. Instead of suppressing its popularity or distribution, it only increased their desire for reading the Word and stimulated the printing of more Bibles! The attempts of critics to suppress the Bible is as futile as the man who kicks over an anthill in an effort to destroy it. All he succeeds in doing is aggitating the ants to swarm out to recolonize and re-establish themselves once again.

Critics can level their strongest broadsides against the Bible, but history has consistently proved that it will have about as much detrimental effect as shooting an air-rifle at the Rock of Gibraltar.

No matter what the argument, no matter what the attack, the Bible has triumphed. As Bernard Ramm commented:

> No other book has been so chopped, knived, sifted, scrutinized, and villified. What book has been subject to such a mass attack as the Bible? with such venom and skepticism? with such thoroughness and erudition? upon every chapter, line and tenet? . . . A thousand times over, the death knell of the Bible has been sounded, the funeral procession formed, the inscription cut on the tombstone, and committal read. But somehow the corpse never stays put.[2]

It always rises again.

When the Bible's indestructibility is viewed against the historical backdrop of such violent opposition, we can only conclude that, if it had been any other book, it would have been utterly annihilated long ago. But its very endurance and survival gives strong, silent testimony to its divine nature and providential protection. Its very existence bears witness to the passage, "All men are like grass, and all their glory is like the flowers of the field; the grass withers and the flowers fall, but the word of the Lord stands forever" (I Pet. 1:24, 25).

Though millions upon millions of Christians have died in the faith, they have left behind an indelible testimony of the Bible's enduring popularity and its triumph against all opposition. In the underground labyrinth of the catacombs, snaking almost 600 miles beneath the city of Rome, lie the burial vaults of several million Christians. For ten successive generations of relentless persecution, Christians had fled to the sanctuary of the catacombs to escape their tormentors. There they lived, died, and were eventually interred. On the walls of those dark

---

2 Bernard Ramm, **Protestant Christian Evidences**, pp. 232, 233.

tunnels are thousands of Christian inscriptions, but the one which best exemplifies their irrepressible faith is the one which reads, "The Word of God is not bound." During 300 years of violent opposition, they had found that the scriptures cannot be destroyed or silenced because they are the living Word of God.

It Lives

Generation follows generation —yet it lives.
Nations rise and fall —yet it lives.
Kings, dictators, presidents come and go —yet it lives.
Hated, despised, cursed —yet it lives.
Doubted, suspected, criticized —yet it lives.
Condemned by atheists —yet it lives.
Scoffed at by scorners —yet it lives.
Exaggerated by fanatics —yet it lives.
Misconstrued and misstated —yet it lives.
Ranted and raved about —yet it lives.
Its inspiration denied —yet it lives.

Christians of all generations have consistently discovered the indestructible nature of the Bible and have confidently concluded that, "The tooth of time gnaws all books but the Bible . . . nineteen centuries of experience have tested it. It has passed through critical fires no other volume has suffered, and its spiritual truth has endured the flames and come out without so much as the smell of burning" (W. E. Sangster). When all has been said and done and the forces of opposition have extended their last round against the Bible, it will still be standing strong. As W. F. Griffin Thomas concluded: "When the dust of the battle dies down, we shall hear all sixty-six books declare with the Apostle Paul, 'Do thyself no harm, for we are all here'!"

3

ITS ENDURING POPULARITY

How Much Is It Worth?

I remember when I was in high school watching an episode of the old Twilight Zone series which left a lasting impression. It was about a gang of thieves who had devised a foolproof crime which would guarantee that they would never get caught. The robbery involved stealing an armored car carrying a large shipment of gold bullion. One of the masterminds was a scientist who had invented time capsules into which the gang would retire for several hundred years. In these time capsules, they would long outlive the authorities and, when they emerged, any remembrance of them or their crime would have long been forgotten.

After pulling off the heist, they escaped to a prearranged hideout in a remote part of the desert. They drove the armored car into a cave, camouflaged the entrance, and each climbed into their waiting capsule to sleep off the centuries in suspended animation.

After the time had passed, they awoke. Now they were free and filthy rich — so they thought. What they had not planned for were the unpredictable factors of time. During their sleep, the truck, in which they planned to drive out of the desert, had deteriorated to the point that it was undrivable. What is more, they had only stored a couple canteens of water. They had no choice but to hike out of the desert by foot.

They each gathered a couple bars of gold, what little water they had, and started their trek across the desert. Because of the unexpected turn of events, coupled with their greed, the tension between the gang members started to mount. Soon, the water was running out and they began fighting over the precious drops of liquid. Murder set in, and they killed each other off until only one was left. The lone survivor staggered on across the burning desert until he came to the edge of a highway where he collapsed from exhaustion and died of thirst.

Shortly after, a hovercraft came streaking down the highway. The driver saw the body of the thief lying on the shoulder of the road and pulled alongside. A man and his son stepped out of the vehicle. As they approached the body, the boy noticed the corpse clutching a bar of shining metal. He had never seen anything like it, and asked his father what it was. The father reached down, pried the ingot out of the thief's hand, and carefully examined it. He then told his son, "I believe it is called gold. It used to be worth a lot many years ago, but it's worth almost nothing now since they've learned how to manufacture it."

The point of the story is obvious, and it's more than "crime doesn't pay." Things seldom hold their value for long. Time has a way of devaluating many things and diminishing their appeal and popularity. However, this is not true of the Bible.

I recently came across an interesting tidbit of information which humorously underscores the popularity of the Bible. According to librarians in Milwaukee, Wisconsin, four out of five people picked up for stealing books from the public library are stealing the Bible! All joking aside, whether purchased or purloined, the Bible remains the all-time best seller of human history. No other book can even come close in volume of sales and circulation, and the Bible continues to outdistance all competitors under the sun.

Not only has the Bible remained invincible against the repeated attacks of its critics, but its appeal has not been tarnished by time or persecution. Critics may come and critics may go, but its worldwide popularity has never diminished. As James Douglas commented:

> A cynical man of science long ago sneered at the Bible as "a collection of rude imaginings of Syria," as "the worn-out old bottle of Judaism into which the generous new wine of science is being poured." The cynical savant is dead, but the Bible is still alive, for it is the Book of Books. The old wines of science grow sour in their cellars, and its new vintages have their day. But the Bible shows no signs of senility. Its youth is eternal. When our men of science and their theories are forgotten, the Bible will remain what it has been for mankind for two thousand years, the one universal book of wisdom, of truth, of sublimity, and of consolation.

Neither has it become obsolete or irrelevant to the masses. Even in the face of the ever-changing ebb tide of humanity, it retains its enduring popularity.

Solomon once wrote, "Of making many books there is no end" (Eccl. 12:12). Millions of books have been written since the Bible, but it is a rare exception if it stays around for very long, even it it finds a niche on the New York Times "Best Seller List." In fact, the average book has a maximum shelf life of only five years. Only a handful of literary works over a hundred years old are still read, and then only by a few specialists, English majors, playwrights, or scholars. In fact, of all the new books published in 1859, only five were still to be found in 1959:

Darwin's "Origin of the Species," Dickens' "Tale of Two Cities," Eliot's "Adam Bede," Mills' "Essay on Liberty," and Tennyson's "Idylls of the King." Of the more than 50,000 books published over 300 years ago, only about 60 are still in print. If the Lord tarries, how many current titles will still be around a hundred years from now? One for sure: the Bible.

In comparing the Bible's enduring popularity to other noted works, G. Campbell Morgan noted:

> Homer has been translated into about twenty different languages. Shakespeare has been translated into about forty different languages. Leaving out all others, there are two books, so far as I know, that have gone out into over one hundred translations. Those are John Bunyan's "Pilgrim Progress" and "The Imitation of Christ," by Thomas a Kempis. The only two which have reached the three figures are those dependent upon the Bible. They are the offspring of the Bible. . . . The Bible in its entirety, or parts of it, has been translated into just over *one thousand* languages of human speech.

Though the above quote is somewhat dated, it substantiates the fact that there is absolutely no book that even comes close to comparing with the circulation and popularity of the scriptures.

Current Statistics

The Bible was the first major book printed by Johannes Gutenburg's press in 1456. Since that time, over 7 billion have been printed!

According to statistics compiled by the United Bible Society, which is the parent group of 103 Bible societies around the world, 7,111,665,848 had been distributed as of 1985. Just in the year 1985 alone, 548,754,501 Bibles were distributed worldwide. In that year, 14,838,012 were distributed in the African continent, 302,480,147 in the Americas, 220,568,892 in Asia and the Pacific, and 10,867,450 in Europe. At the current rate, over a half a billion Bibles are being distributed worldwide each year.

The Gideon Bible Society began distributing Bibles in motels, hotels, prisons, college campuses, the armed forces, and convalescent homes free of charge in 1908. Since then, they have distrbuted over 350,000,000 copies of either portions of the Bible or the Bible in its entirety in 55 languages in 134 countries. Their current rate of distribution is 1 million copies in 55 languages every 15 days!

These figures are staggering and attest to the enduring demand for the Bible. But what is even more incredible is the fact that there are other Bible societies whose statistics are not even available.

The Bible has been read by more people and published in more languages than any other book. There is absolutely no other book that even comes close to the circulation of the scriptures. In fact, on February 5, 1970, a microfilm packet containing Genesis 1:1 in sixteen languages and a complete RSV Bible was deposited on the moon by Apollo 14 LEM Commander Edgar Mitchell. According to the United Bible Society, as of 1985, the Bible has been translated, in its entirety or in part, in 1829 distinct languages or dialects. In that year, they were involved in 544 translation projects of which 21 languages were receiving the translated Word for the first time. And what is even more amazing is the fact that new languages are being reported each year. In 1984 alone, 23 were reported.

The Bible's enduring popularity throughout the ages testifies of the universal reverence and respect which it rightfully deserves as the inspired, authoritative Word of God. As Bernard Ramm stated, "After 1900 years, the Bible is still loved by millions, read by millions, and studied by millions."[1] It remains the most important, widely read, memorized, and influential book in the world.

---

1 Bernard Ramm, **Protestant Christian Evidences,** p. 283.

4

ITS UNITY

Not a Book But a Library

The Bible is not just one book, but a collection of books. It is a library containing sixty-six books in all. But what makes the Bible so extraordinary is the fact that all of these books fit together in perfect agreement. Each individual book is like a distinctive piece of a complicated jig-saw puzzle. They are unique by themselves, yet, when pieced together, they each contribute a portion to the overall picture presented in the Bible. This incredible depth of unity gives strong support to the divine Architect behind its design.

The Power of Unity

Have you ever heard the story of the farmer and his twelve quarreling sons? It is a revealing lesson on the power of unity. It seems that the sibbling rivalry had escalated to the point that they were constantly bickering or brawling in all-out donnybrooks. The farmer became so exasperated with the situation that he gathered his sons together for a much needed object lesson on unity.

Starting with the eldest, he handed each a small stick. He then told them to break it if they could. Well, each of the easily snapped their stick. With that the eldest son said, "Pa, what did ya have us do that for?" The father replied, "You'll see in a minute, son." He then gathered twelve similar sticks and wrapped them in a bundle. He handed it to the eldest and said, "Break this." He grunted and groaned, but try as he would, he couldn't break the bundles. Each of the sons tried in turn, but they all failed. When they were done, the farmer said. "Now boys, the lesson is like the sticks I gave you. When you stand by yourself, you are weak. But when you come together in unity, you form an unbreakable band of strength."

With this simple example, the farmer forcefully illustrated the power in unity. So, too, the individual books of the Bible manifest the same powerful unity. By themselves, they generally present a weak and often unconvincing argument for the Bible's divine inspiration. To the ignorant and the profane, they may even seem to be in conflict with one another. But when joined together, they form an unbreakable bond of unity which presents a powerful proof of the Bible's divine authorship and harmonious construction.

A Unity in Spite of Diversity

What makes the issue of unity so amazing is the fact that the Bible is such a complex book involving many diverse factors. The Bible maintains a consistent continuity of message in spite of the fact that it incorporates so many complex ingredients.

For example, the individual books were not written at the same time. A Bible symposium was not convened in order for the various authors to compare notes, synchronize the story line, eliminate potential discrepancies, and come up with a unified end-product.

The Bible gradually evolved over a 1600-year period, covering sixty generations. Sometimes centuries elapsed between the authoring of books. During this extended period, empires rose and fell, languages changed, and the conflicting cross-currents of humanity often shifted their course. But none of those external factors had an adverse effect upon the overall continuity of the Bible.

Over forty authors contributed to its overall composition. These men came from many varied occupations and stations in life. They included **kings** (David), **a fisherman** (Peter), **a Pharisee and scholar** (Paul), **a tax collector** (Matthew), **a physician** (Luke), **a prime minister** (Daniel), **a military general** (Joshua), **a statesman and political leader** (Moses), **a prophet** (Jeremiah), **a priest** (Ezekiel), **a poet** (Solomon), **a king's cupbearer** (Nehemiah), **a teacher** (Ezra), and **a shepherd** (Amos).

It was penned under many different circumstances and conditions. The books run the entire gamut of human emotions and moods. Some of the authors wrote during times of **great emotional distress** (Jeremiah), some during periods of **depression and discouragement** (David), and others during **intense joy** (Paul), **righteous indignation** (Jude), **rapturous revelation** (John), **remorse and melancholy** (Solomon), **romantic love** (Solomon), **fiery rebuke** (Jeremiah), or **heartfelt anguish** (Hosea).

The books were written from a variety of geographical locations including three different continents (Asia, Africa, Europe). Paul wrote as a prisoner from Rome, Luke wrote during missionary travels through Asia Minor and Greece, James wrote from Jerusalem, Moses wrote while wandering through the Sinai wilderness, Daniel wrote from the courts of Babylon, and Jeremiah wrote from a dungeon.

Books were written during seasons of political turmoil and spiritual unrest, during times of peace and prosperity, during times of financial upheaval, and during times of war and natural disasters.

What is more, the Bible is a linguistic composite of three languages. Most of the Old Testament was written in ancient Hebrew, the language spoken by the Israelites prior to their Babylonian captivity; a few portions of the Old Testament are written in Aramaic (Chaldee); and the New Testament was written in the common Greek language of the first century.

It also covers hundreds of controversial subjects, and involves a variety of literary styles including history, poetry, law, prophecy, philosophy, theological apologetics, biographies, and personal correspondences. And yet, it has maintained an overall unity. As F. F. Bruce confirmed:

> The writers themselves were a heterogeneous number of people, not only separated from each other by hundreds of years and hundreds of miles, but belonging to the most diverse walks of life. In their ranks we have kings, herdsmen, soldiers, legislators, fishermen, statesmen, courtiers, priests and prophets, a tent-making Rabbi and a Gentile physician, not to speak of others of whom we know nothing apart from the writings they have left us. The writings themselves belong to a great variety of literary types. They include history, law (civil, criminal, ethical, ritual, sanitary), religious poetry, didactic treatises, lyric poetry, parable and allegory, biography, personal correspondence, personal memoirs and diaries, in addition to the distinctively Biblical types of prophecy and apocalyptic. . . . For all that . . . there is a unity which binds the whole together. [1]

The Central Theme—The Central Figure

What is more, the central theme of the Bible is harmonious. Above all else, the Bible is not primarily concerned with a system of ethics, religious ordinances, the history of Israel, or

---

1 F. F. Bruce, **The Books and the Parchments**, p. 88.

the history of the human race, for that matter. It is true it is intimately concerned with history, as viewed from a divine perspective, but more properly it deals with HIS STORY—the story of God's redemptive plan for mankind through the death, burial, and resurrection of Jesus Christ. The Bible either points to His coming to save men, or His coming again to judge men.

He is the central figure of the Bible. The contents of all the books ultimately revolve around Him. Like a scarlet thread weaving its way throughout a patchwork quilt, Jesus is interwoven throughout the pages of the Bible. It is He who gives a living, organic unity to the Bible and its unfolding message. Even Christ bore personal witness to this fact when He said, "Study the scriptures because you think that by them you possess eternal life. These are the scriptures that testify about me" (John 5:39).

The following overview of the Bible confirms this:

The Old Testament

Genesis	**Creator and Seed of the woman**	Genesis 1:1; 3:15
Exodus	**Lamb of God for sinners slain**	Exodus 12:3,4,13
Leviticus	**High Priest**	Entire Book
Numbers	**Star out of Jacob**	Numbers 24:17
Deuteronomy	**Prophet like unto Moses**	Deut. 18:15
Joshua	**Captain of the Lord's Host**	Joshua 5:13-15
Judges	**Messenger of Jehovah**	Judges 3:15-30
Ruth	**Kinsman Redeemer**	Ruth 3:13
I & II Samuel	**Despised and Rejected King**	I Sam. 16-19
Kings & Chronicles	**Lord of Heaven and Earth**	Entire Books
Ezra	**Our Restoration**	Entire Book
Nehemiah	**Our Strength**	Nehemiah 8:11
Esther	**Our Mordecai**	Chapter 10
Job	**Risen and Returning Redeemer**	Job 19:25; 25:6
Psalms	**The Blessed Man**	Psalm 1
	The Son of God	Psalm 2:7
	The Son of Man	Psalm 8:4,5,6
	The Crucified One	Psalm 22
	The Risen One	Psalm 23
	The Coming One	Psalm 24

49

	The Reigning One	Psalm 72
	The Leader of Praise	Psalm 150
Proverbs	Our Wisdom	Chapter 4
Ecclesiastes	The Forgotten Wise Man	Eccl. 9:14,15
Song of Solomon	"My Beloved"	Song of Sol. 2:16
Isaiah	Our Suffering Substitute	Isaiah 53:3-10
Jeremiah	The Lord Our Righteousness	Jer. 23:6
Lamentations	The Man of Sorrows	Lam. 1:12-18
Ezekiel	The Throne Sitter	Ezekiel 1:26
Daniel	The Smiting Stone	Dan. 2:34
Hosea	David's Greater King	Hosea 3:5
Joel	The Lord of Bounty	Joel 2:18,19
Amos	The Rescuer of Israel	Amos 3:1
Obadiah	Deliverer upon Mount Zion	Verse 17
Jonah	Buried and Risen Savior	Entire Book
Micah	The Everlasting God	Micah 5:2
Nahum	Our Stronghold in the Day of Wrath	Nahum 1:7
Habakkuk	The Anchor of Our Faith	Hab. 2:4
Zephaniah	He is in the midst for judgment and cleansing	Zeph. 3;5,15
Haggai	The Smitten Shepherd	Haggai 2:6,7
Zechariah	The Branch	Zech. 3:8
Malachi	The Sun of Righteousness	Malachi 4:2

The New Testament

Matthew	The King of the Jews	Matt. 2:1
Mark	The Servant of Jehovah	Mark 1:1,2
Luke	The Perfect Son of Man	Luke 3:38; 4:1-13
John	The Son of God	John 1:1
Acts	The Ascended Lord	Acts 1:8,9
Romans	Our Righteousness	Romans 3:22
I Corinthians	The Firstfruits from among the dead	I Cor. 15:20
II Corinthians	He is made sin for us	II Cor. 5:21
Galatians	The End of the Law	Gal. 3:10,13
Ephesians	Our Armor	Eph. 6:11-18
Philippians	The Supplier of every need	Phil. 4:19
Colossians	The Preeminent One	Col. 1:18
I Thessalonians	Our Returning Lord	I Thess. 4:15-18
II Thessalonians	The World's Returning Judge	II Thess. 1:7-10

I Timothy	The Mediator	I Tim. 2:5
II Timothy	The Bestower of Crowns	II Tim. 4:8
Titus	Our Great God and Savior	Titus 2:13
Philemon	The Father's Partner	Verses 17,19
Hebrews	The Rest of Faith and Fulfiller of Types	Heb. 9:11;4:9;12:1
James	The Lord of Sabaoth	James 5:4
I Peter	The Theme of Old Testament Prophecy	I Pet. 1:10,11
II Peter	The Longsuffering Savior	II Peter 3:9
I John	The Word of Life	I John 1:1
II John	Target of the Antichrist	Verse 7
III John	Personification of Truth	Verses 3,4
Jude	Believer's Security	Verses 24,25
Revelation	King of Kings and Lord of Lords	Rev. 19:11-16

A Simple Test

In spite of this multitude of contributing factors, the Bible is a single, unified book with a single, unfolding theme. A unity of such scope and magnitude gives strong, silent testimony to its divine authorship and design. No other secular or religious work can equal such an accomplishment.

To illustrate the significance of this feat, Josh McDowell relates the story about a personal encounter he had with a salesman for the Great Books of the Western World series.[2] This set includes the works of many great thinkers who had an influence on the shaping of western civilization. According to Mr. McDowell, they talked for five minutes about the Great Books of the Western World series, and an hour and a half about the Book of Books—the Bible. To demonstrate just how great this book is, he proposed a test which would involve ten authors, all from one walk of life, one generation, one place, one time, one mood, one continent, one language, and just one controversial subject to see whether they would totally agree! He asked the salesman if they would agree. He paused for a moment and replied, "No! They would be a conglomeration."

---

2 Josh McDowell, **Evidence That Demands a Verdict**, pp. 19, 20.

The inevitable result of such a test would be a hopeless hodgepodge of conflicting opinions and perspectives. Yet the Bible is an harmonious book covering many complex and controversial subjects. When all of these factors are taken into consideration, the only plausible explanation for the Bible's unity is the fact that a sovereign, all-knowing, all powerful God was behind its construction and composition.

5

THE FULFILLMENT OF
BIBLICAL PROPHECY

A Perfect Score

Each year brings a new round of predictions from secular soothsayers, fortune tellers, astrologers, and self-appointed prophets concerning the future. Individuals like Jeanne Dixon give their annual list of prognostications, and each year ends with a worse than dismal success rate. History is filled with so-called seers such as Nostradamus, Mother Shipton, Edgar Cayce, and Jeanne Dixon whose prophecies are coveted by many, yet the actual accuracy of their predictions is notoriously inaccurate. A few of their prophecies may seem to have been fulfilled, but in their hit-or-miss approach, they miss far more than they hit. However, this cannot be said of biblical prophecy. Its accuracy rate is perfect. The Bible is still batting 1000.

The issue of prophetic fulfillment is another pivotal proof supporting the accuracy and divine authorship of the Bible. In

fact, it is one of the most arresting evidences. Critics may scoff
at the claim of personal experience and explain away a variety of
other proofs which are offered in support of the Bible, but they
hit the wall when attempting to refute the fulfillment of biblical
prophecy. The evidence is too overwhelming.

The Bible is saturated with specific prophecies concerning
nations, cities, historic events, and individuals. But what lends
such overwhelming credibility to the divine origin of these prophecies is the fact that hundreds have been literally fulfilled in
the most minute detail. Unlike secular predictions or extra-
biblical prophecies which are often so absurdly vague or
generalized that almost any conceivable situation could be
pointed to as a fulfillment, biblical prophecy is precise and
unfailing in its fulfillments. An example is Isaiah's prophecy
concerning the eventual conquest of Babylon by Cyrus, king of
Persia. Over 150 years before the days of Cyrus, Isaiah called
him by name and predicted that he would repatriate the Jews
and help them rebuild their temple in Jerusalem (II Chron.
36:22, 23; Ezra 1:1-4; Isaiah 45:1-6).

Tyre

Some of the more outstanding prophetic fulfillments focus
upon the destiny of cities and nations. Since God is sovereignly
in control, He can determine their fate and foretell their future.

A classic example of the many remarkable fulfillments
which could be cited centers upon Ezekiel's prophecies concerning the fate of the ancient city of Tyre. The prophecy is given in
Ezekiel 26:3-5, 7, 12, 14, and 21. This prophecy includes the
following details: 1) many nations would rise against her (verse
3); 2) she would be leveled and turned into barren rock (verse 4);
3) fishermen would spread their nets in the midst of her (verse
5); 4) Nebuchadnezzar, the king of Babylon, would capture her
(verse 8); 5) the debris of Tyre would be thrown into the sea
(verse 12); 6) and she would never be rebuilt again (verse 14).

These specific predictions were fulfilled to the letter:
Nebuchadnezzar did capture the old mainland city of Tyre in

573 B.C. after a thirteen-year siege. When he finally took the city, he discovered that the Phoenician inhabitants had withdrawn to a fortified island lying about a half mile offshore. Other nations participated in her downfall. For 241 years, the mainland city of Tyre remained as Nebuchadnezzar found it. But in 332 B. C., Alexander the Great laid siege to the island city of Tyre. To reach it, his engineers used the debris from the old city to construct a causeway across the narrow stretch of water to the island on which the new city had been relocated. Thus, the prediction that the city would be scraped clean, turned into a barren rock, and its debris thrown into the sea was accurately fulfilled.

What is more, the glory of ancient Tyre has never been restored. Many cities have been repeatedly razed to the ground yet rebuilt upon their former ruins, but Tyre has remained essentially in the same desolate condition which it was left in when it was finally destroyed in A.D. 1291. All that exists is a small fishing village where Lebanese fishermen spread their nets in accordance with Ezekiel's prophecy. Several specific things were predicted about Tyre and each was literally fulfilled. One scholar calculated the mathematical probability of this happening at 1 in 75,000,000 or 7.5×10^7 [1]

Sidon

Another remarkable fulfillment centers upon Sidon, the sister city of Tyre. The prophet Ezekiel predicted that blood would flow in her streets and she would suffer the sword on every side (Ezekiel 28:23). He did not predict her utter extinction as he had for Tyre. Sidon has been leveled many times during the last two millennia, but she has always been rebuilt and exists today. However, she has suffered from more persistent bloodshed and warfare than almost any other city in history! From the repeated sieges of the Crusades, to the conflicts between the Druses and

---

1 Peter W. Stoner, **Science Speaks**, p. 80.

the Turks, to the assaults by the British and the French, to the current street battles between the Moslems, Palestinians, and the Christian militias, Sidon is a city of bloodshed and violence.

Babylon

Another incredible fulfillment involves the kingdom of Babylon, one of the most glorious and prosperous empires of the ancient world. Isaiah and Jeremiah gave a series of prophecies concerning her fate (Isa. 13:19-22; 14:23; Jer. 51:26, 43). In these prophecies, the following facts were given: 1) Babylon would be utterly destroyed like Sodom and Gomorrah (Isa. 13:19); 2) it would never be inhabited again (Isa. 13:20; Jer. 51:26); 3) wild beasts would occupy the ruins (Isa. 13:21,22); 4) she would be covered with swamps of water (Isa. 14:23); 5) Arab nomads would not pitch their tents there (Isa. 13:20); 6) her stones would not be used for other construction projects (Jer. 51:26); 7) and men would not pass by the ruins (Jer. 51:43).

Babylon was conquered in 538 B. C. Since then, the condition of Babylon bears silent testimony to the fulfillment of all these predictions. The site of ancient Babylon is a barren desert wasteland which is uninhabited and rarely frequented by visitors. Even nomadic Bedouins do not bring their flocks to graze there because the vegetation is so sparse. The ruins uncovered by archaeologists have remained where they lay for centuries without being cannibalized for building materials. Desert creatures infest the ruins and the southern reaches where the Euphrates drains into the Persian Gulf has been a vast swampland for centuries.

Egypt

Along with Babylon, Egypt was one of the greatest powers of the ancient world. However, a number of prophecies predicted her gradual downfall and decline (Jer. 46:19; Ezek. 29:15; 30:16). Yet, unlike Babylon, she was not threatened with extinction. Ezekiel prophesied that she would become "the lowliest of kingdoms and will never again exalt itself above the other nations" (Ezek. 29:15). As the centuries passed, Egypt has deteriorated into a backward, impoverished, and weak power which is not even a faint reflection of her former glory. These are just a few examples of the prophetic fulfillments concerning nations and cities. Many others could be given regarding Israel, Edom, Moab, Philistia, Gaza, Samaria, Jerusalem, and Palestine.

The Messianic Prophecies

Probably the most striking series of prophetic fulfillments involves the multitude of Messianic predictions concerning Christ. One, in particular, is the famous 70 week prophecy of Daniel the prophet (Dan. 9:24-27). In 538 B.C., he foretold of the coming Messiah. He indicated that it would occur 483 years after the Persian emperor released the Jews and gave them permission to rebuild Jerusalem. This was precisely fulfilled, to the year, with the advent of Christ's public ministry.

Besides this, the Old Testament contains over 300 specific prophecies which were literally fulfilled by Christ. In fact, one scholar numbered them exactly at 332.[2] I have selected 40 examples of over 300 of these Old Testament prophecies related to Christ:

Born in Bethlehem (Micah 5:2 / Lk. 2:4-7); **He would be presented with gifts** (Ps. 72:10 / Matt. 2:1,11); **Herod would kill the children** (Jer. 31:15 / Matt. 2:16); **born of the tribe of Judah** (Gen. 49:10 / Lk. 3:23,33); **born of a virgin** (Isa. 7:14 / Matt. 1:18,24,25); **referred to as Immanuel** (Isa. 7:14 / Matt. 1:23); **He would be a king** (Ps. 2:6 / Matt. 27:37); **He would be a prophet** (Deut. 18:18 / Matt. 21:11); **He would be a priest** (Ps. 110:4 / Heb. 3:1; 5:5,6); **He would have a special anointing of the Holy Spirit** (Isa. 11:2 / Matt. 3:16,17); **He would be preceded**

---

2 Floyd Hamilton, **The Basis of the Christian Faith**, p. 160.

by a messenger (Isa. 40:3 / Matt. 3:1,2); **entered Jerusalem on a donkey** (Zech. 9:9 / Lk. 19:35-37a); **rejected by His own people** (Isa. 53:3 / John 7:5,48); **betrayed by a friend** (Ps. 41:9 / Matt. 10:4); **betrayed for 30 pieces of silver** (Zech. 11:12 / Matt. 26:15); **silver thrown into the temple** (Zech. 11:13b / Matt. 27:5a); **money used to purchase a potter's field** (Zech. 11:3b / Matt. 27:7); **forsaken by His disciples** (Zech. 13:7 / Mk. 14:50); **His friends stood afar off** (Ps. 38:11 / Lk. 23:49); **people shook their heads at Him** (Ps.109:25 / Matt. 27:39); **wounded and bruised** (Isa. 53:5 / Matt. 27:26); **smitten and spat upon** (Isa. 50:6 / Matt. 26:67; **mocked** (Ps. 20:7,8 / Matt. 27:31); **didn't answer His accusers** (Isa. 53:7 / Matt. 27:12-19); **He fell under the cross** (Ps. 109:24,25 / Lk. 23:26); **hands and feet pierced** (Ps. 22:16 / Lk. 23:33); **crucified with thieves** (Isa. 53:12 / Matt. 27:38); **made intercession for His persecutors** (Isa. 53:12 / Lk. 23:34); **He committed Himself to God** (Ps. 31:5 / Lk. 23:46); **lots cast for His garments** (Ps. 22:18 / Jn. 19:23,24); **He suffered thirst** (Ps. 69:21 / Jn. 19:28); **given gall and vinegar to drink** (Ps. 69:21 / Matt. 27:34); **bones weren't broken** (Ps. 34:20 / Jn. 19:33); **His side pierced** (Zech. 12:10 / Jn. 19:34); **His heart was broken** (Ps. 22:14 / Jn. 19:34); **darkness covered the earth** (Amos 8:9 / Matt. 27:45); **people stared at Him** (Ps. 22:17 / Lk. 23:35); **He asked why He was forsaken** (Ps. 22:1 / Matt. 27:46); **buried in a rich man's tomb** (Isa. 53:9 / Matt. 27:57-60); **ascended to God** (Ps. 68:18 / Acts 1:9).

Since nobody but God has the power to predict or manipulate the fulfillment of prophecy before the fact, the Bible's many prophetic fulfillments lend strong support to its divine authorship, accuracy, and authority.

In closing, though the prophetic dimension is not limited to the Bible, no other literary work of history, whether religious or secular, can duplicate the unique quality of foretelling, accuracy, and fulfillment found in biblical prophecy. As Wilbur Smith stated:

> Whatever one may think of the authority of and the message presented in the book we call the Bible, there is world-wide agreement that in more ways than one it is the most remarkable volume that has ever been produced in these some five thousand years of writing on the part of the human race. It is the only volume ever produced by man, or a group of men in which is to be found a large body of prophecies relating to individual nations, to Israel, to all the peoples of the earth, to certain cities, and to the coming of One who was to be the Messiah. The ancient world had many different devices for determining the future, known as divination, but not in the entire gamut of Greek and Latin literature, even though they use the words prophet and prophecy, can we find any real specific prophecy of great historic event to come in the distant future, nor any prophecy of a Saviour to arise in the human race. . . . Mohammedanism cannot point to any prophecies of the coming of Mohammed uttered hundreds of years before his birth. Neither can the founders of any cult in this country rightly identify any ancient text specifically foretelling their appearance.[3]

This unique fact attests to the Bible's divine origin and inspiration.

---

3 Wilbur Smith, **The Incomparable Book,** pp. 9, 10.

6

THE LAW OF COMPOUND PROBABILITIES

"A More Sure Word"

The scriptures claim that, "we have also a more sure word of prophecy" (II Pet. 1:19, NKJV). As we've already seen, the fulfillment of biblical prophecy is a powerful proof of the Bible's reliability. But just how sure is the word of prophecy? Just how dependable is the Word of God? Is there any scientific way of determining the Bible's reliability?

The answer is a resounding "Yes!" There is a mathematical law in science which can help us find out. It is called "The Law of Compound Probabilities." It is one of the most profound proofs of the Bible's divine accuracy and inspiration. Simply stated, the Law of Compound Probabilities is a mathematical law which is used to calculate the probability of a specific set of conditions, requirements, or qualifications being fulfilled. Basically, it is a way of figuring the odds. It is commonly used in the market place to determine financial projections, in weather casting to forecast the probability of weather conditions, in the insurance industry to calculate insurance tables, in professional athletics, and in political campaigning. Many unconsciously use the essential principle behind this law in their daily lives to estimate a number of things from driving conditions, when the groceries will run out, or the odds in horse racing.

Stoner's Findings

During the 50's, Peter W. Stoner, the Chairman of the Mathematics and Astronomy Department at Pasadena City College until 1953 and Chairman of the Science Division of Westmont College from 1953-57, applied the Law of Compound Probabilities to the area of prophetic fulfillment. He did so to determine the odds of a certain prescribed number of biblical prophecies relating to Christ being fulfilled.[1]

He used the data gathered over a ten-year period and submitted his findings to the American Scientific Affiliation which carefully evaluated his conclusions and stated that,

> The manuscript for "Science Speaks" has been carefully reviewed by a committee of the American Scientific Affiliation members and by the Executive Council of the same group and has been found, in general, to be dependable and accurate in regard to the scientific material presented. The mathematical analysis included is based upon principles of probability which are thoroughly sound and Professor Stoner has applied these principles in a proper, convincing way.[2]

His calculations were so convincing that they ruled out coincidence, chance, or human manipulation in the fulfillment of biblical prophecy.

The Law Illustrated

To illustrate how this principle works in layman's terms,

---

1 Peter W. Stoner, **Science Speaks**, pp. 99-112.
2 H. Harold Hartzler, Ph.D., Secretary-Treasurer, **American Scientific Affiliation.**

suppose 1 in 10 men has green eyes. According to this statistical average, you would need 10 men to find 1 green-eyed man. Suppose 1 in 10 green-eyed men has red hair; you would now need 100 men to find 10 which are green-eyed and 1 who is green-eyed and red-haired. Suppose 1 in 10 green-eyed, red-haired men is pigeon-toed. You would then need 1,000 men, of whom 100 are green-eyed, 10 are green-eyed and red-haired, and 1 is green-eyed, red-haired, and pigeon-toed. Let's compound the problem a little more. Suppose 1 in 10 green-eyed, red-haired, pigeon-toed men is Irish. To fulfill this requirement, you would need 10,000 men of whom 1,000 are green-eyed, 100 are green-eyed and red-haired, 10 are green-eyed, red-haired, and pigeon-toed, and 1 is a green-eyed, red-haired, pigeon-toed Irish man. Suppose 1 in 10 green-eyed, red-haired, pigeon-toed Irish men is left-handed. You would then need 100,000 men, of whom 10,000 are green-eyed, 1,000 are green-eyed and red-haired, 100 are green-eyed, red-haired, and pigeon-toed, 10 are green-eyed, red-haired, pigeon-toed, and Irish, and 1 is a green-eyed, red-haired, pigeon-toed Irish man who is left-handed. This series of ingredients helps illustrate the Law of Compound Probabilities. Every time you add a chance factor or new qualification, you increase the difficulty of fulfillment.

Let's put it another way. If I stood up and boldly proclaimed that there was going to be an earthquake in California in the future, it would not be a very impressive prediction considering the earthquake regularity in that state. At least I have a better than average chance of being right. However, if I added another chance factor to this and compounded the difficulty of my prophetic prediction, the odds are increased that I will be wrong and my prediction won't be fulfilled.

For example, if I stood up and said there's going to be a future earthquake in California in the month of November, then I'm compounding the chance that I am going to be proved wrong. If I declared that there is going to be a future earthquake in California on Tuesday, November the 12th, at 12:34 p.m., its epicenter will be in downtown San Francisco, measuring 8.3 on the Richter scale, 29,000 people will die, and the Golden Gate

Bridge will collapse into the bay, I greatly increase the chances that I will be proved to be a false prophet.

So, in a prophetic light, every time we add a factor, statistic, circumstance, or event, it increases the mathematical odds that the prophecy will not be fulfilled because it becomes increasingly more difficult.

The Prophecies Related to Christ

Dr. Stoner applied this law to one lone individual coming on the stage of human history and fulfilling, to the tee, a series of prophetic requirements. What he wanted to calculate was the odds of someone fulfilling a specified number of Messianic prophecies related to Christ.

No man in history who has ever come into this world has ever had more written about Him prior to His birth than Jesus Christ. As we have seen, there were over 300 specific prophecies related to His life. Hundreds of years before His birth, holy men of God wrote pertinent facts concerning His birth, life, death, and resurrection. His fulfillment of these prophecies is His divine credentials that He is who the Bible says He is. He validates the Bible's accuracy.

However, Bible critics have written Christ off by arguing that the prophecies related to Him were simply the result of coincidence or chance occurrences. Given enough time, so they reason, if you have any set of facts, predictions, or factors, they are bound to be fulfilled.

In the face of such an argument, Dr. Stoner employed the Law of Compound Probabilities to see if this claim was justified. Dr. Stoner's basic objective was to determine what the chances would be of one lone individual stumbling through history and accidentally fulfilling over 300 prophecies. He started conservatively with only eight Messianic prophecies. For example, what would be the odds of someone literally fulfilling these eight prophecies:

1. **He would be born in Bethlehem** (Micah 5:2; Matt. 2:1).
2. **He would be born of a virgin** (Isa. 7:14; Matt. 1:18).

3. **He would be betrayed for 30 pieces of silver** (Zech. 11:12, 13; Matt. 26:15).
4. **He would be smitten and spat upon** (Isa. 50:6; Mk. 14:65).
5. **He would be crucified with thieves** (Isa. 53:12; Matt. 27:38).
6. **His hands and feet would be pierced** (Ps. 22:16; Jn. 20:27).
7. **They would cast lots for His garments** (Ps. 22:18; Mark 15:24).
8. **He would be buried in a rich man's tomb** (Isa. 53:9; Matt. 27:57-60).

How Many Silver Dollars?

I will spare you the complicated and confusing mathematical computations, but Stoner calculated the odds of someone fulfilling only eight of the Messianic prophecies at 1×10^{17}. This is a 1 followed by 17 zeros!

How can we put this figure into relatable terms? Just how big is this number? Well, if you had 1×10^{17} silver dollars, you could carpet the entire state of Texas 2 feet deep in neatly stacked piles. If you specially marked just one of them, blindfolded a man and told him to wander around the great state of Texas sloshing through silver dollars until he felt that he could reach down and successfully pick that one specially marked silver dollar, the odds of him picking the right silver dollar on the first try would be equivalent to a man fulfilling only 8 prophecies. But, we must remember that Christ fulfilled over 300 prophecies!

Dr. Stoner then computed the odds of one individual fulfilling just 16 prophecies related to Christ. He calculated the odds at 1×10^{45} power, or a 1 followed by 45 zeros. The sun is 93 million miles from earth; however, if you had this many silver dollars, you could build a stellar ball so enormous that it would extend 30 times farther out than the sun.

Suppose you could construct a special space shuttle which could travel through this massive ball of silver dollars. Let's say you equip an astronaut with cosmic scuba gear, blindfold him, thoroughly stir that specially marked silver dollar into this ball, and instruct him to pick that one silver dollar. The odds of him picking that one silver dollar on the first try is 1 x 10^{45}, or the equivalent of one individual fulfilling just 16 prophecies. But remember, Jesus fulfilled over 300!

Electrons and the Universe

Dr. Stoner then went for broke and calculated 48 prophecies which computed out at 1 x 10^{157}. The computers began to overload and burn out at this point. This figure is so astronomical and beyond human comprehension that there's not even a name for it. This will give you an idea what this number looks like:

$$1 \text{ x } 10^{157} = 10,000,000,000,000,000,000,$$
$$000,000,000,000,000,000,000,000,000,000$$
$$000,000,000,000,000,000,000,000,000,000,$$
$$000,000,000,000,000,000,000,000,000,000,$$
$$000,000,000,000,000,000,000,000,000,000,$$
$$000,000,000,000,000,000.$$

Keep in mind that, according to the reckoning of our decimal system, every time you add an additional zero you increase the previous figure ten times.

How can we better comprehend these odds? Well, forget silver dollars—they're just too big! Let's try another approach. First, what is the smallest thing in the universe? An atom? No. There are parts which make up an atom called electrons which spin around the nucleus of an atom like a miniature solar system. There are smaller things such as protons, neutrons, and sub-atomic particles, but an electron is more familiar to most of us.

How small is an electron? An electron is so small that it is only 2.5 x 10^{15} quintillionth of an inch long. If you devoted yourself to counting just a single file of electrons one inch long, you would have to count 250 per minute, day and night, for 19 million years! To count the number in just one cubic inch of electrons, you would have to count 250 per minute, day and night, for 19 million years, times 19 million years, times 19 million years. It has been said that there are more electrons in a grain of sand than there are leaves on all the trees in the world.

Now, what is the largest thing we know? The universe. The diameter of our universe is 12 billion light years across. I've always wondered what's on the other side of the boundary line.

What is a light year? It's not when you're having a good year. A light year is "the distance traveled in one year at a constant velocity of 186,000 miles per second." Keep in mind that our universe is 12 billion light years across!

Let's look a little closer. There are 60 seconds in a minute, 1,440 minutes in a day, and 86,400 seconds in a day. So, at the uninterrupted speed of light, you would travel 16 billion, 70 million miles in one day! In a year, you would travel over 6 trillion miles, and our universe is 12 billion light years across.

Our sun is so large that you could put a million earths, like B. B.'s in a basketball, inside of it. Yet, there are stars which are so large that you could place a million suns the size of ours in them! One star named Zeta Aurigae is ten million times larger than our sun. Some stars are so enormous that the light radiated by ours, in comparison, would be like the flicker of one match burning on a lone prairie night. Their energy output is equal to 20 billion suns. There are over 100 billion stars in our galaxy, and billions of other galaxies just like our own. In fact, the number of stars visible to the naked eye on a clear night would be the equivalent of what a microscopic protozoan would see around it. The heavenly bodies which can be visibly seen by man are like a single drop of water in the endless sea of the universe.

To give you a better idea of the size of our universe, consider the following illustrations. If the thickness of this page of paper which you are reading equaled the distance of the earth to the sun (93 million miles), the distance to the nearest star (4½ light years) would equal a stack of paper 71 feet high. The diameter

67

of just our Milky Way Galaxy (100,000 light years across) is the equivalent of a 310 mile stack of paper, while the edge of our universe is equal to a stack of paper 31 million miles high! If you constructed a scale model of the universe, with our earth represented by a ball one inch in diameter, our nearest star (Alpha Centauri) would have to be positioned nearly 51,000 miles away.

Now, suppose that you could travel at the speed of light. We are talking star drive, "warp 10 Scotty," hyperspace. If somehow you could be converted into a pure beam of light so that you could travel out into space on an intergalactic beam of light, you would travel around the earth 7½ times in one second.

Let's say, after a few warm-up orbits, you decide to become a space voyager and set off in exploration of the frontiers of deep space. In 1¼ seconds you would pass the moon. In 7½ minutes you would pass the sun. In six hours, you could look out your porthole and see Neptune in a flash. 14 hours later, you would bid farewell to the last lonely outpost of our solar system—Pluto. Now you are on the threshold of the vast, cold expanses of our universe. In 4½ years, you would reach our nearest neighboring star, Alpha Centauri. In 100,000 years, traveling at 186,000 miles per second, you would finally leave our galaxy—the Milky Way. Buy before you reach our nearest neighboring galaxy, you would have to travel for another 6 billion light years before you would reach what astronomers refer to as the edge of space. So you see that our universe is quite large.

However, if you had 1×10^{157} electrons to work with, you could make a cosmic ball of electrons so large it would be as big as our known universe. In fact, you would have so many electrons that if there was some way to mass produce these balls, you could make them at a rate of 500 a minute, day and night, for 6 billion years, 10^{10} times over! Now, specially mark one of these electrons, if you could see it, and we are dealing with the odds of one individual fulfilling only 48 prophecies. Yet Christ fulfilled over 300 specific prophecies!

How sure is biblical prophecy? How reliable is the Bible? It is reliable beyond any conceivable shadow of doubt. The Law of Compound Probabilities proves the divine authorship of the scriptures and shows that it could not, by any stretch of the imagination, be a product of human manipulation or devising. It is God's infallible Word.

7

ITS SCIENTIFIC ACCURACY

Who Is Outdated First?

Unlike other religious writings, the scriptures entertain no fanciful ideas about science and the physical universe. For example, the Vedas, which are the Hindu scriptures, teach that the moon is approximately 150,000 miles higher than the sun and shines with its own light, that the earth is flat and triangular, and that earthquakes are caused by elephants shaking themselves under it.

What is more, though many almost deify the sacred cow of science as an infallible and authoritative oracle, it has never been exact, consistent, or fault-free. Libraries are filled with scientific books and journals whose current positions will be discarded as obsolete in a few years. It reminds me of the story told by Dr. Walter Stewart, who questioned some students coming out of a seminar at the Institute for Advanced Study at Princeton. When he asked "How did it go?", one of the students replied, "Wonderful. Everything we knew about physics last week isn't true!"

Many of the cherished scientific concepts and practices of yesterday have proven unsound by subsequent discoveries. From Ptolemy's theory that the earth was flat or the earth was the center of the universe, to the belief that blood leeching cured certain diseases or cow dung poultices would prevent infection, all are ridiculed today. Science has always been in an ever-changing state of flux, redefinition, and even self-contradiction. But the Bible's scientific statements are absolutely reliable and trustworthy and never need to be updated or revised.

It is a common myth and misconception that the advancements of modern science and scholarship continue to discredit the Bible as an inaccurate and antiquated book whose scientific references are out of touch with reality. Though the Bible is not a textbook on science, nor was ever intended to be, when it speaks about scientific matters, its statements are backed by the infallible authority of the omniscient God who created the universe and controls all the physical laws of science undergirding it. These include those which are presently known, and those which remain unknown to man. The truth is that the steady progress of science has not undermined the Bible's accuracy in the least. The Bible doesn't contain the slightest shred of scientific irregularity or error. In fact, not a single scientific fact has ever disproved a biblical statement.[1]

The established truths and principles of science are not only in complete harmony with the scriptures, but the Bible has been consistently ahead of its time in setting forth scientific truth, often centuries before the so-called discoveries of modern science. Many scientific truths were quietly concealed within its pages and only came to light within the last few hundred years.

Scientific References and Allusions

The Bible's anticipation of scientific discoveries is another

---

1 Henry M. Morris, **The Bible Has the Answers,** p. 3.

72

convincing proof of its divine authorship and accuracy. Many of the established principles of modern science were stated as biblical fact long before scientists confirmed them through the process of experimentation. For example, in the realm of astronomy, men have tried to count the number of stars for centuries. On a clear night, you can see only about 1,160 stars. If you could survey the whole celestial sphere, only about 3,000 stars would be visible to the naked eye. About 150 years before Christ, Hipparchus calculated the number of stars at 1,022. Ptolemy, the father of modern astronomy, gave the number as 1,056. Tycho Brahe cataloged 777, and Kepler counted 1,005. They arrived at these tallys before the invention of the telescope in the 17th century. These figures seem foolish to modern man who has since discovered that there are over a hundred million stars just in our galaxy, and over a hundred million galaxies just like our own. However, 600 years before Christ, the prophet Jeremiah revealed that the number of stars was innumerable when he wrote, "the host (stars) of heaven cannot be numbered" (Jer. 33:22, NKJV).

Only a few hundred years ago, men believed that the earth was flat and that anyone who dared sail too far out from land would eventually drop off the edge of the earth or be swallowed by great sea monsters. However, nearly 2,200 years before 15th century explorers discovered that the world wasn't flat after all, Isaiah the prophet established this fact. In referring to God's rulership, Isaiah stated, "He sits enthroned above the circle of the earth" (Isa. 40:22). The Hebrew word for "circle" (chuwg) in this verse actually means "sphericity" or "roundness."

Other scientific references include: **the gravitational field around the earth** (Job 26:7); **the hydrologic cycle** (Ecc. 1:7); **the principle of evaporation** (Ps. 135:7); **the meteorological circulation of the atmosphere** (Ecc. 1:6); **the principle of mass-energy equivalents** (Heb. 1:3; Col. 1:17); **the law of progressive entropy** (Ps. 102; 25-27); **the immensity of the universe** (Job 22:12; Isa. 55:9; Jer. 31:37); **the principle of blood circulation** (Lev. 17:11); **the law of conservation of mass and energy** (II Pet. 3:7); **the** source of earth's energy (Gen. 1:14,17; Ps. 19:6); the concept of atomic disintegration (II Pet. 3:10); and the rotation of the earth (Job 38:12,14). These are but a few of many scientific allusions in the scriptures. The Bible avoids the technical jargon and scientific terminology of today in describing scientific phenomena, but its general references are absolutely accurate and indicate the divine source behind its composition.

The Laws of Thermodynamics

Though it is not the purpose of this chapter to tackle the ongoing controversy of creationism versus evolutionism, it should be stressed that the theory of evolution, and that's all it is, violates two of the most fundamental laws of physical science. These two laws are clearly established by the Bible. They are the First Law of Mass Energy Conservation, or the First Law of Thermodynamics, and the Second Law of Energy Decay, or the Second Law of Thermodynamics. These laws deal with the principle of energy which includes all the phenomena of the physical universe.

The first law states that nothing is presently being created or destroyed. It is the most important, basic law of all physical science. This law holds that though matter may change in size, state, and form, its total mass remains constant. This law was only demonstrated quantitatively by science about a hundred years ago. However, the Bible anticipated the scientific discovery of this law about a thousand years ago when it confirmed the fact that creation is no longer going on. Contrary to the foundational premise underlying the theory of evolution, nothing new is evolving through a continual process of evolutionary creation. New forms of creation are no longer taking place. The Bible reveals that the present universal system is the finished result of God's original creation: "Thus the heavens and the earth were completed in all their vast array. By the seventh day God had finished the work he had been doing; so on the seventh day he rested from all his work" (Gen. 2:1,2; see also Ex. 20:11; Heb. 4:3).

The second law states that everything in an ordered system, left to itself, always tends to become downgraded and disorganized. It is also known as the Law of Entropy (meaning disorder, randomness). Like a clock left to itself, it gradually winds down and loses energy and momentum. Everything steadily deteriorates, wears out, and eventually dies. Although the total amount of energy remains unchanged, it is gradually transferred or altered through the process of deterioration so that its availability and usefulness is decreased. In any closed mechanical system, large or small, complicated or simple, the inbuilt energy is continually winding down. Our universe is running down, not building up. Thus, the theory of evolution and the Second Law of Thermodynamics are hopelessly incompatible. This principle is clearly indicated by scriptural as well as experiential fact: "In the beginning you laid the foundations of the earth, and the heavens are the work of your hands. They will perish, but you remain; they will all wear out like a garment. Like clothing you will change them and they will be discarded. But you remain the same, and your years will never end" (Ps. 102:25-27). The Bible reveals that this very law is the direct result of the decaying process of sin and its effect upon the entire creation (Rom. 8:21, 22).

Contray to the scientific hypothesis of evolution, the existence of this law, of necessity, implies that all things were originally created in a perfect state. This in turn, leads us to the inevitable conclusion, which is supported by the scriptures, that "In the beginning, God created the heavens and the earth" (Gen. 1:1). As Henry Morris noted:

> But this law certainly testifies equally as well to the necessary truth that the universe had a definite beginning. If it is growing old, it must once have been young; if it is wearing out, it must once have been new; if it is running down, it must first have been "wound up." In short, this law of energy degeneration leads us to an affirmation of the necessary truth of the existence of a Creator, and a

definite creation which took place in the past but which, according to the law of mass and energy conservation, is not continuing in the present.[2]

Mass Energy Equivalence

Another corollary principle intimately associated with the Laws of Thermodynamics is the Principle of Mass and Energy Equivalence. This is a truth which has only come to light in our 20th century, primarily through the pioneering efforts of Einsteinian physics, which have revolutionized our understanding of physical laws. Basically, this truth established the fact that matter is simply another form of energy. When mass is converted to energy in the form of an atomic explosion, we have a tremendous release of energy.

Matter is simply another form of energy known as atomic energy. Atoms are the building blocks of our material universe. But what is so amazing is that enormous amounts of energy are needed to maintain the configuration of atoms and the terrific motions and the forces associated with their various atomic particles. Scientists do not understand what these unknown forces are, but the Bible declares that it is God: "But in these last days he has spoken to us by his Son, whom he appointed heir of all things, and through whom he made the universe. The Son is the radiance of God's glory and the exact representation of his being, sustaining all things by his powerful word" (Heb. 1:2-3a). This passage reveals that "all things" are actually kept together by the power or energy of God. He is the upholder of all things in the universe, and manages and maintains all matter in our physical universe.

The fact that He is the unseen, sovereign force behind the scenes is also brought out in Colossians 1:17 which states that "He is before all things, and in him all things hold together." The concept of mass energy equivalence is also amplified in

2 Henry M. Morris, **That You Might Believe,** p. 27.

Hebrews which declares that, "Through faith we understand that the worlds were framed by the word of God, so that things which are seen were not made of things which do appear" (Heb. 11:3, NASB). Our material universe is not purely matter. It is actually created out of something which is not apparent. The word "worlds" used in this verse literally means "world-times" in the Greek. Many view it as a biblical allusion to the scientific view of the universe involving the space-time continuum of mass and time. This concept is an integral facet of the Theory of Relativity dealt with so comprehensively by Einstein. According to this verse, our material universe was not formed by chance out of preexistent, chaotic matter, but was created out of nothing apparent or visible to us. It was brought forth through the omnipotent energy of the Word of God!

The Testimony of Great Men of Science

In our scientific age, the masses have been led to the widespread belief that science and Christianity are as incompatible as oil and water—that scientists and the scriptures are as diametrically opposed as black and white. However, this is a mistaken impression. It might come as a surprise to learn that many of the greatest scientific minds and scientific discoveries were the product of men who had an unshakable faith in the infallibility of the Bible. In fact, the very origin of modern science rests upon the fundamental truths of the scriptures, and the fact that there is an omniscient, omnipotent God who created and designed an ordered universe. It was this basic belief which prompted men like Newton, Faraday, and Kelvin to search for scientific laws to explain this order.

There are thousands of eminent scientists from both the past and present who are Bible-believing Christians. Some of these include: **Johann Kepler** (1571-1630), the founder of physical astronomy and formulator of the Ephemeris Tables; **Francis Bacon** (1561-1626), the one primarily responsible for the "scientific method"; **Robert Boyle** (1627-1691), the father of modern chemistry; **John Ray** (1627-1705), the father of

English natural history; **Sir Isaac Newton** (1642-1727), credited with the discovery of the laws of gravity, the formulation of calculus, and the invention of the reflecting telescope, along with many other scientific developments; **Sir William Herschel** (1738-1822), one of history's greatest astronomers and inventor of the Global Star Catalog; **Michael Faraday** (1791-1867), one of the most outstanding physicists of all time who excelled in the field of electromagnetism and invented the electric generator; **George Cuvier** (1769-1832), the founder of the science of comparative anatomy; **Samuel F. B. Morse** (1791-1872), celebrated as the inventor of the telegraph, who wrote "the nearer I approach to the end of my pilgrimage, the clearer is the evidence of the divine origin of the Bible"; **Joseph Henry** (1797-1878), the discoverer of the principle of self-induction and the inventor of the electromagnetic motor and the galvanometer; **Matthew Maury** (1806-1873), the founder of the modern sciences of hydrography and oceanography; **Louis Agassiz** (1807-1873), the father of glacial geology; **Gregor Mendel** (1822-1884), the father of genetics; **Louis Pasteur** (1822-1895), one of the great men of medicine and formulator of the germ theory of disease and responsible for the development of pasteurization, vaccination, and immunization; **Joseph Lister** (1827-1912), the founder of antiseptic surgery; **William Ramsey** (1852-1916), a noted chemist responsible for the discovery of argon and other inert gasses; and **George Washington Carver** (1864-1943), one of the world's great black scientists and agricultural chemists who was noted for his work on the humble peanut, who, when testifying before the Senate Agriculture Committee on the value of the peanut, was asked what the Bible said about peanuts, replied, "The Bible does not teach anything regarding the peanut. But it told me about God and God told me about the peanut."

These are only a few of history's renowned men of science who were devout Christians and outspoken advocates of the Bible's infallibility and inspiration. Today, there are many Bible-believing scientists who support the scriptures. The Creation

78

Research Society has a membership of over 700 top scientists, in a variety of fields, who embrace the Bible's divine inspiration. The American Scientific Affiliation has hundreds of credentialed scientists, and the Bible-Science Association includes both laymen and scientists who have lent their talents to defending the Bible's divine accuracy and authorship.

In closing, the absolute confidence which many of the world's greatest scientific minds have placed in the Bible's reliability and revelation that God was the creator of an ordered universe was underscored by an encounter which Sir Isaac Newton had with a scientific skeptic. Sir Isaac Newton had a replica of our solar system made in miniature. In the center was the sun with its retinue of planets revolving around it. A scientist entered Newton's study one day and exclaimed, "My! What an exquisite thing this is! Who made it?" "Nobody!" replied Newton to the questioner who was an unbeliever. "You must think I am a fool. Of course somebody made it, and he is a genius." Laying his book aside, Newton arose and laid his hand on his friend's shoulder and said: "This thing is but a puny imitation of a much grander system whose laws you and I know, and I am not able to convince you that this mere toy is without a designer and maker; yet you profess to believe that the great original from which the design is taken has come into being without either designer or maker. Now tell me, by what sort of reasoning do you reach such incongruous conclusions?"

Time Is on Our Side

The fact is that modern science does not pose a threat to Christianity or the Bible. It is not a foe, but an ally. The steady progress of science only works to vindicate the Bible's reliability rather than discredit it. The premature conclusion of many that "science undermines the Bible" continues to prove itself a fallacy. It should more appropriately be rephrased, "science supports the Bible." The yearly advances of scientific study will increasingly confirm the scriptures' accuracy. Time is on our side.

Whether we are talking about the truths of science or the truths of God's Word, truth is absolute and mutually compatible. As scientific knowledge increases, the evidence in favor of the Bible's scientific accuracy, infallibility, and divine inspiration also mounts. As Sir Charles Marston stated:

> The newest knowledge cannot be said to be drawing us away from the Bible; on the contrary it is bringing us back to it. Our foremost scientists are feeling and finding their way through a vast undergrowth of materialistic facts towards a world horizon much more in harmony with Holy Scripture. And it has further become clear that the leaders of Science a generation ago both overestimated and overemphasized the limited knowledge of their time, and neglected to look beyond it. Because education reflects the beliefs of leading minds of the previous generation, and not those of the present, so today we are suffering from those miscalculations. But in the light of facts not then observed, or whose significance had been overlooked, scientists of the present have ceased to overestimate human knowledge; on the contrary they are emphasizing human ignorance. So called Miracles are no longer being laughed at, they are being recognised.[3]

The Bible, too, is being recognized as authoritative, not only in the realm of spiritual truth, but in the realm of science.

---

3 Cited from **Explore the Book,** J. Sidlow Baxter, p. 124.

8

THE TESTIMONY OF GREAT MEN AND WOMEN

When Stanley, the noted British explorer, began his exploratory trek across the continent of Africa, he started out with seventy-three books weighing 180 pounds. After he had traveled three hundred miles, he was obliged to discard some of the books to alleviate the burden of his porters. As he pressed deeper and deeper into the heart of Africa, his library continued to dwindle. One by one, the excess weight was cast off until only one book remained - the Bible. It is reported that during that epic journey, Stanley read his Bible through three times. His story is a living acknowledgment of the reverence which he placed on the Bible as the Book of Books. He stands in a long line of great historical figures who staked their reputations and sacred honor upon the absolute accuracy and authority of the Bible.

Poets, Politicians, Philosophers, Scholars, and Scientists

George Washington   "It is impossible to rightly govern the

world without God and the Bible.''
Patrick Henry - "This is a Book worth all other books which were ever printed."
John Quincy Adams - "So great is my veneration for the Bible that the earlier my children begin to read it the more confident will be my hope that they will prove useful citizens of their country and respectable members of society. I have for many years made it a practice to read through the Bible once every year."
Thomas Jefferson - "The Bible is the cornerstone of liberty. . . . The studious perusal of the Sacred Volume will make better citizens, better fathers, and better husbands."
Andrew Jackson - "That book, sir, is the rock on which our republic rests."
Abraham Lincoln - "I believe the Bible is the best gift God has ever given to man. All the good from the Savior of the world is communicated to us through this book."
Robert E. Lee - "The Bible is a book in comparison which all others are of minor importance. In all my perplexities and distress the Bible never failed to give me light and strength."
Ulysses S. Grant - "Hold fast to the Bible as the sheet anchor of your liberties; write its precepts on your heart and practice them in your lives. To the influence of this Book we are indebted for the progress made, and to this we must look as our guide in the future."
Horace Greeley - "It is impossible to mentally or socially enslave a Bible-reading people."
W. H. Seward - "The whole hope of human progress is suspended on the ever growing influence of the Bible."
Daniel Webster - "There is no solid basis for civilization but in the Word of God. . . . If we abide by the principles taught in the Bible, our country will go on prospering; but if we and our posterity neglect its instructions and authority, no man can tell how sudden a catastrophe may overwhelm us and bury all our glory in profound obscurity. . . . If religious books are not

widely circulated among the masses in this country, I do not know what is going to become of us as a nation. If truth be not diffused, error will be; if God and His Word are not known and received, the devil and his works will gain the ascendency; if the evangelical volume does not reach every hamlet, the pages of a corrupt and licentious literature will; if the power of the Gospel is not felt throughout the length and breadth of the land, anarchy and misrule, degradation and misery, corruption and darkness, will reign without mitigration or end.''

William McKinley - ''The more profoundly we study this wonderful Book and the more closely we observe its divine precepts, the better citizens we will become and the higher will be the destiny of our nation.''

Theodore Roosevelt - ''If a man is not familiar with the Bible, he has suffered a loss which he had better make all possible haste to correct.''

Woodrow Wilson - ''A man has deprived himself of the best there is in the world who has deprived himself of this, a knowledge of the Bible. When you have read the Bible, you will know that it is the Word of God, because you will have found it the key to your own heart, your own happiness, and your own duty.''

Herbert Hoover - ''The whole of the inspiration of our civilization springs from the teachings of Christ and the lessons of the Prophets. To read the Bible for these fundamentals is a necessity of American life. . . . We are indebted to the Book of books for our ideals and institutions. Their preservation rests in adhering to its principles. The study of the Bible is a rich post-graduate course in the richest library of human experience.''

J. Edgar Hoover - ''Inspiration has been the keynote of America's phenomenal growth. Inspiration has been the backbone of America's greatness. Inspiration has been the difference between defeat and victory in America's wars. And this inspiration has come from faith in God, faith in the teachings in the Sermon on the Mount, and faith in the belief that the Holy Bible is the inspired Word of God.''

Douglas MacArthur - "Believe me, sir, never a night goes by, be I ever so tired, but I read the Word of God before I go to bed."

Dwight D. Eisenhower - "To read the Bible is to take a trip to a fair land where the spirit is strengthened and faith renewed."

John Ruskin - "Whatever merit there is in anything that I have written is simply due to the fact that when I was a child my mother daily read me a part of the Bible and daily made me learn a part of it by heart."

Ronald Reagan - "I was pleased last year to proclaim 1983 the 'Year of the Bible'. But, you know, a group called the ACLU severely criticized me (sued him) for doing that. Well, I wear their indictment like a badge of honor. I believe I stand in pretty good company."

Sir Isaac Newton - "There are more sure marks of authenticity in the Bible than in any profane history."

Queen Victoria - "That book accounts for the supremacy of England."

Charles Dickens - "The New Testament is the very best book that ever was or ever will be known in the world."

Immanuel Kent - "The existence of the Bible, as a book for the people, is the greatest benefit which the human race has ever experienced. Every attempt to belittle it is a crime against humanity. . . . The Bible is an inexhaustible fountain of all truths. The existence of the Bible is the greatest blessing which humanity ever experienced."

Victor Hugo - "England has two books, the Bible and Shakespeare. England made Shakespeare but the Bible made England."

Thomas Huxley - "The Bible has been the Magna Charta of the poor and oppressed. The human race is not in a position to dispense with it."

Goethe (the universal and most highly cultivated of poets) - "I consider the Gospels to be thoroughly genuine; for in them there is the effective reflection of a sublimity which emanated from the Person of Christ; and this is as Divine as ever the Divine ever appeared on earth. . . . Let mental culture go on advancing, let the natural sciences progress in ever greater extent and depth, and the human mind widen itself as much as it desires; beyond the elevation and moral culture of Christianity, as it shines forth in the Gospels, it will not go.''

Jean Jacques Rousseau - ''The majesty of the Scriptures strikes me with admiration, as the purity of the Gospel has its influence on my heart. Pursue the works of our philosophers with all their pomp of diction, how mean, how contemptible are they, compared with the Scriptures.''

Sir William Jones - ''The Bible contains more true sensibility, more exquisite beauty, more pure morality, more important history, and finer strains of poetry and eloquence, than can be collected from all other books in whatever age or language they may be written.''

Sir William Herschel - ''All human discoveries seem to be made only for the purpose of confirming more and more strongly the truths contained in the sacred scriptures.''

Sir Walter Scott - ''Within this wondrous volume lies the mystery of mysteries; happiest they of human race to whom their God has given grace to read, to fear, to hope, to pray, to lift the latch, to find the way; and better had they ne'er been born who read to doubt, or read to scorn.''

William E. Gladstone - ''There is but one question of the hour: how to bring the truths of God's Word into vital contact with the minds and hearts of all classes of people. . . . I have known ninety-five of the world's great men in my time, and of these eighty-seven were followers of the Bible. The Bible is stamped with a Specialty of Origin, and an immeasurable distance separates it from all competitors.''

William Lyon Phelps (called the most beloved professor in America - of Yale University) - ''I thoroughly believe in university education for both men and women, but I believe a knowledge of the Bible without a college course is more valuable than a college course without the Bible.''

Thomas Carlyle - ''The Bible is the truest utterance that ever came by alphabetic letters from the soul of man, through which, as through a window divinely opened, all men can look into the stillness of eternity, and descern in glimpses their far-distant, long-forgotten home.''

Charles A. Dana - ''The grand old Book still stands; and this old earth, the more its leaves are turned and pondered, the more it will sustain and illustrate the pages of the Sacred Word.''

Matthew Arnold - ''To the Bible men will return because they cannot do without it. The true God is and must be preeminently the God of the Bible, the eternal who makes for righteousness, from whom Jesus came forth, and whose spirit governs the course of humanity.''

Napoleon Bonaparte - ''The Bible contains a complete series of facts and of historical men, to explain time and eternity, such as no other religion has to offer. . . . What happiness that book procures for those who believe it! What marvels those admire there who reflect upon it! . . . The Bible is no mere book, but a living creature, with a power that conquers all that oppose it.''

Haile Selassie - ''Today man sees all his hopes and aspirations crumbling before him. He is perplexed and knows not whither he is drifting. But he must realize that the Bible is his refuge, and the rallying point for all humanity. It is here man will find the solution of his present difficulties and guidance for his future action, and unless he accepts with clear conscience the Bible and its great message, he cannot hope for salvation. For my part, I glory in the Bible.''

John Calvin - ''The Lord does not shine upon us, except when we take his Word as our light. . . . Unless God's Word illumine the way, the whole life of men is wrapped in darkness and mist, so that they cannot but miserably stray.''

Martin Luther - ''A man's word is a little sound, that flies into the air, and soon vanishes; but the Word of God is greater than heaven and earth, yea, greater than death and hell, for it forms part of the power of God, and endures everlastingly. . . . The Bible is alive, it speaks to me; it has feet, it runs after me; it has hands, it lays hold on me.''

John Wesley - ''I have a thought, I am a creature of a day, passing through life as an arrow through the air. I am a spirit come from God, and returning to God: just hovering over the great gulf; till, a few moments hence, I am no more seen; I drop into an unchangeable eternity! I want to know one thing - the way to heaven; how to land safe on that happy shore. God himself has condescended to teach the way; for this very end He came from heaven. He hath written it down in a book. O give me that Book! At any price, give me the Book of God!''

Charles Spurgeon - "Many books in my library are now behind and beneath me. They were good in their way once, and so were the clothes I wore when I was ten years old; but I have outgrown them. Nobody ever outgrows Scripture; the book widens and deepens with our years."

These are but a random sampling of the many quotes that could be listed. Though not all of the above individuals were saved, their candid confessions do reveal the depth of personal esteem which they placed upon the Sacred Scriptures. Their comments are another contributing support for the Bible's claim that it is the authoritative Word of God.

9

THE SACRIFICE OF MILLIONS

The Ultimatum

When the Khmer Rouge toppled the Cambodian government in the mid-70's, they unleashed a reign of terror upon that tiny nation rarely rivaled in history. In a country of approximately seven million people, they ruthlessly murdered over three million. Theirs was a radical brand of agrarian Communism which violently opposed the intelligentsia, modernization, and any form of religion.

They especially targeted the Christian minority during their purge. On a search-and-destroy sweep through the countryside, they stumbled upon a small hamlet with a Christian congregation. The cadre officer in charge sat at a table with a Bible lying in front of him. The soldiers gathered all the villagers together, lined up those who claimed they were Christians, and ordered them to renounce Christ by spitting upon the Bible if they wanted to live. If they refused, they would be taken out and shot. Given the ultimatum, they stepped forward one by one, picked up the Bible, and spit on it. The young officer smiled approvingly as each villager recanted.

Finally, the lot fell upon a young woman. She, too, stepped forward, looked down at the spit-smeared Bible, picked it up, and clutched it to her breast. She then looked around the room and said, "I will not renounce Christ or the words of life in this little book you hate so much. If I did, I would truly lose my life!" With those words the guards grabbed her, dragged her out, and shot her in the back.

To the Cambodian peasant girl, the Bible was a book worth dying for. How many would follow in her footsteps when faced with the same choice? It might surprise you, but tens of millions have done so. She, like many others, had concluded that if the Bible was worth living for, it was also worth dying for.

The fact that countless millions of Christians have laid down their lives in defense of the Bible is another significant support of its divine authenticity. Christians have suffered martyrdom, mutilation, torture, imprisonment, banishment, and confiscation of properties because of their firm belief that the Bible is the only inspired Word of God. Christians have willingly sacrificed everything considered most precious and dear in this world for their convictions concerning the Bible's reliability. When we consider the millions who were butchered by the Roman emperors, martyred by the Catholic inquisitors, and slaughtered by Communist dictators all because of their faith in Christ and His Word, we can only conclude that the Bible is not just another book.

For example, John Huss was condemned by the Council of Constance and burned at the stake in A.D. 1415 because he advocated Bible study and openly taught that the Bible was the only inspired and reliable message from God to mankind. Thousands of his supporters were exterminated by a Crusade ordered by the pope. William Tyndale was strangled and burned to death in A.D. 1586 because he dared to translate the Bible into the language of the common man.

The Blood of Millions

Throughout the Dark Ages of Roman Catholic supremacy, millions of Christians were brutalized in large part because they exalted the scriptures above the dogmas and ordinances of the church. Inquisitions were established to punish those who read the Bible, and wars were declared at times to eliminate those who rallied behind the Bible.

Many popes issued decrees forbidding Bible reading in the common language of the people, condemned Bible societies, and banned its possession, translation, or distribution under the penalty of mortal sin and death. It was officially forbidden to the people and placed on the "Index of Forbidden Books" list by the Council of Valencia in A.D. 1229. The Council of Trent (A.D. 1545-1563) also prohibited its use and pronounced a curse upon anyone who would dare oppose their decree. Those who resisted were often burned along with their Bibles. For example, Pope Gregory IX forbade laymen from possessing the Bible. Translations found among the Albigenses and Waldenses were burned along with their owners.

Not only did the religious authorities persecute Bible believers, but secular authorities did as well. Charles V, King of the Netherlands, attacked the Lutheran Reformers and, in A.D. 1525, he prohibited the printing or possession of the Bible. His son, Philip II, with the help of the Jesuits, brutally massacred over 100,000 people who had embraced the truth of God's Word:

> Some were chained to a stake near the fire and slowly roasted to death; some were thrown into dungeons, scourged, and tortured on the rack before being burned. Women were buried alive, pressed into too small of coffins, and trampled down with the feet of the executioner.[1]

But what is more, these events were not limited to the medieval past. Even within our lifetime, millions of Christians

---

1 Henry R. Halley, **Halley's Bible Handbook**, p. 789.

have been killed in Communist nations for their belief in Christ and His Word. Christians in the Soviet Union, Red China, and the Eastern Block countries have been tortured, imprisoned in labor camps and sanitoriums, exiled, and murdered en masse. Many believers are hounded and harassed by secret police and arrested because of their beliefs. Their Bibles are often confiscated when found and destroyed. So precious is the Bible in many areas controlled by the Communists that men and women on both sides of the Iron and Bamboo Curtains risk their lives to smuggle Bibles to hungry believers.

These are but a few examples of many which could be extracted from history. They reflect the plight of millions who have willingly surrendered their lives in defense of the absolute conviction that the Bible is the inspired Word of God. The blood of so many bears strong witness to the Bible's divine authority.

10

ITS TRANSFORMING POWER

It Works Well

A Bible skeptic once stated, "You can't possibly ask me to believe in a Book whose author is unknown!" A Christian asked him if the compiler of the multiplication table was known. "No," he answered. "Then, of course, you do not believe in it?" "Why, yes, I believe in it because it has proven to work well in my life." "So does the Bible," was the rejoinder, and with that the skeptic had no rebuttal to make. A fact which skeptics can not gainsay is the reality that the truths of God's Word work powerfully in the lives of those who believe.

Amazing Grace

One of the most profound proofs of the Bible's divine authorship centers upon its dynamic, life-changing impact upon the lives of men and women. Its power is timeless and universal. Its transforming effect transcends every conceivable boundary. It has produced the same revolutionary effect upon the lives of individuals worldwide, in spite of their sex, age, nationality, ethnic origin, cultural heritage, social standing, occupation, intellectual attainmant, religious conditioning, or environment.

An outstanding example of what the Word of God can do in the lives of individuals is reflected in the story of John Newton, a notorious slave trader and libertine who was converted to Christ. Like so many others, his entire conduct, character, and course of life was dramatically altered by the Word of God. It was he who penned the beloved hymn "Amazing Grace." One verse, in particular, says it all concerning the life-changing power of the gospel:

Amazing grace, how sweet the sound
That saved a wretch like me;
I once was lost, but now I'm found,
Was blind, but now I see.

It is a song sung by untold millions who have shared a similar transformation.

Regardless of whether men and women come from the uppermost or the guttermost, the Bible radically changes lives. Like the process of metamorphosis which transforms a caterpillar into a monarch butterfly, the Word of God changes the carnal man into a new creation in Christ. No other book, religious writing, philosophy, organization, theory, self-help program, or cult can accomplish this feat. As A. T. Pierson noted, "While other books inform, and some few reform, this one book transforms."

Its Impact Upon Nations and Societies

The Bible's power not only changes individuals, but its transforming power has revolutionized the course of human history and the destiny of nations and societies. For example, during Queen Victoria's sixty-four year reign over the British Empire, England achieved its greatest progress. When she was asked what the secret of Britain's power and progress was, she humbly picked up a book from a table nearby and said, "This is the secret." The book she held was the Bible.

Though many are familiar with the true story of "Mutiny on the Bounty," there is a chapter of the story which most are unaware of. It bears witness to the powerful effect of the Bible upon societies. When the nine mutineers, along with six native men and twelve Tahitian women, put ashore on Pitcairn Island in 1790, they burned the Bounty and isolated themselves from the rest of the world. One of the sailors began distilling crude alcohol and the little colony was soon plunged into debauchery. After ten years, only one white man remained, surrounded by a few native women and half-breed children. One day as he was rummaging through an old chest from the Bounty, he found a Bible. He began to read it and then instruct the survivors. As a result, the lives of all those in the colony were radically changed. When the USS Topas discovered the Pitcairn colony in 1808, it had been transformed into a prosperous community with no alcoholism, crime, or laziness.

Another striking example of the Bible's dramatic impact upon society is revealed in the often told encounter of Clarence Hall, a World War II correspondent, who chanced upon the small village of Shimmabuke on the island of Okinawa as the American army was sweeping across the island. Hall related his experience as follows:

> Thirty years before, an American missionary en route to Japan had stopped there just long enough to make two converts—Shosei Kina and his brother Mojon. He left a Bible with them and passed on. For thirty years they had no contact with any other Christian missionary, but they made the Bible come alive! They taught the other villagers until every man, woman, and child in Shimmabuke became a Christian.
>
> Shosei Kina became the headman of the village, and Mojon the chief teacher. In the school the Bible was read daily. The precepts of the Bible were law in the village. In

95

those thirty years there developed a Christian democracy in its purest form.

When the American army came across the island, an advance patrol swept up to the village compound with guns leveled. The two old men stepped forth, bowed low, and began to speak. An interpreter explained that the old men were welcoming the Americans as fellow Christians!

The flabbergasted GI's sent for their chaplain. He came with the officers of the Intelligence Service. They toured the village. They were astounded at the spotlessly clean homes and streets and the gentility of the inhabitants. The other Okinawan villages they had seen were filthy, and the people were ignorant and poverty-stricken.

Later I strolled through Shimmabuke with a tough army sergeant. He said "I can't figure it out—this kind of people coming from a Bible and a couple of old guys who wanted to be like Jesus Christ. Maybe we have been using the wrong kind of weapons to make the world over."

The Bible's Potency

So potent are the scriptures that only a few words have been known to lead men and women into this life-changing experience in Christ. This was demonstrated by the experience of Sadhu Sundac Singh who was distributing portions of the gospel on a train in the Central Province of India. At one point, he offered a copy of John's gospel to a man who responded by tearing it up in a rage and throwing the pieces out the window. But the scriptural confetti was caught by the wind and blown across the countryside. Shortly after, a man who was earnestly seeking the truth happened to be walking down the rail line and noticed a little scrap of paper which he picked up. In his own language it bore the words, "The Bread of life." He did not know what the words meant, but it grabbed his curiosity. He asked some friends and they told him that "it is out of the Christian book, but you must not read it or you will be defiled.'' He thought for a moment and then said, ''I want to read the book that contains that beautiful phrase!'' So he purchased a copy of the New Testament. He was shown where the sentence occurred in our Lord's words, ''I am the Bread of life.'' As he read on, the light of the gospel poured into his heart and he came to a saving knowledge of Jesus Christ. It is the life-changing power and potency of the Word of God which alone can save men.

The Living Proof

This fact was dramatically illustrated through an encounter between Harry A. Ironside and a Socialist skeptic.[1] Dr. Ironside, a noted Christian minister, was living in San Francisco at the time. One night he encountered a group of Salvation Army workers holding a meeting on the corner of Market and Grant Avenue. When they recognized Ironside, they invited him to give his personal testimony about his salvation through faith in Jesus Christ.

As he was speaking, he noticed a well-dressed bystander in the crowd diligently taking down notes on a card. When Ironside finished, the man stepped forward, lifted his hat, and politely handed Ironside the card. The card carried his name, which Ironside recognized immediately. The man was a famous socialist who had made a reputation for himself by lecturing against Christianity and in behalf of socialistic causes. Ironside turned the card over and read, ''Sir, I challenge you to debate with me the question 'Agnosticism verses Christianity' in the Academy of Science Hall next Sunday afternoon at four o'clock. I will pay all the expenses.''

Ironside reread the card aloud, then looked the man squarely in the face and said:

> I am very much interested in this challenge. Frankly, I
> am already scheduled for another meeting next Lord's Day

1 Cited from **Standing on the Rock,** by James Montgomery Boice, pp. 61-64.

afternoon at three o'clock, but I think it will be possible for me to get through with that in time to reach the Academy of Science Hall by four, or if necessary I would arrange to have another speaker substitute for me at the meeting already advertised. Therefore I will be glad to agree to this debate on the following conditions: namely, that in order to prove that this gentleman has something worth debating about, he will promise to bring with him to the hall next Sunday two people, whose qualifications I will give in a moment, as proof that agnosticism is of real value in changing human lives and building true character.

First, he must promise to bring with him one man who was for years what we commonly call a "down-and-outer." I am not particular as to the exact nature of the sins that had wrecked his life and made him an outcast from society—whether a drunkard, or a criminal of some kind, or a victim of his sensual appetite—but a man who for years was under the power of evil habits from which he could not deliver himself, but who on some occasion entered one of this man's meetings and heard his glorification of agnosticism and his denunciations of the Bible and Christianity, and whose heart and mind as he listened to such an address were so deeply stirred that he went away from that meeting saying, "Henceforth, I too am an agnostic!" and as a result of imbibing that particular philosophy found that a new power had come into his life. The sins he once loved he now hates, and righteousness and goodness are now the ideals of his life. He is now an entirely new man, a credit to himself, and an asset to society —all because he is an agnostic.

Secondly, I would like my opponent to promise to bring with him one woman—I think he may have more difficulty in finding the woman than the man—who was once a poor, wrecked, characterless outcast, the slave of evil passions and the victim of man's corrupt living, perhaps one who had lived for years in some evil resort, utterly lost, ruined and wretched because of her life of sin. But this woman also entered a hall where this man was loudly proclaiming his agnosticism and ridiculing the message of the Holy Scriptures. As she listened, hope was born in her heart, and she said, "This is just what I need to deliver me from the slavery of sin!" She followed the teaching and became an intelligent agnostic or infidel. As a result, her whole being revolted against the degradation of the life she had been living. She fled from the den of iniquity where she had been held captive so long; and today, rehabilitated, she has won her way back to an honored position in society and is living a clean, virtuous, happy life all because she is an agnostic.

With that, Ironside said:

Now, if you will promise to bring these two people with you as examples of what agnosticism can do, I will promise to meet you at the Academy of Science Hall at four o'clock next Sunday, and I will bring with me at the very least one hundred men and women who for years lived in just such sinful degradation as I have tried to depict, but who have been gloriously saved through believing the gospel which you ridicule. I will have these men and women with me on the platform as witnesses to the miraculous saving power of Jesus Christ and as present-day proof of the truth of the Bible.

Dr. Ironside then turned to the Salvation Army captain, a woman, and said, "Captain, have you any who could go with me to such a meeting?" She promptly replied, "We can give you forty, at least, just from this one corps, and we will give you a brass band to lead the procession!" "Fine," said Ironside.

Turning to the Socialist, he concluded:

Now, sir, I will have no difficulty picking up sixty others from the various missions, gospel halls, and evangelical churches of the city. So if you will promise to bring two such exhibits as I have described, I will come marching in at the head of such a procession, with the band playing "Onward, Christian Soldiers,'' and I will be ready for the debate.

When he finished speaking, the Socialist smiled wryly, waved his hand in a deprecating manner as if to imply, "Nothing doing!'' He had obviously sized up the situation, counted the costs, and saw that the ground rules for the debate were hopelessly stacked against him. It was a classic case of "put up, or shut up.'' He wisely chose the latter. It's one thing to boast about the power of your beliefs, but quite another to demonstrate the power. Such is the transforming influence of the Bible on the lives of men and women.

This is not an isolated phenomenon. Hundreds of millions of "born-again" believers can testify of the transforming reality of the Word of God. Their lives are living proof that the Bible not only changes a man outwardly, but produces a radical, inner transformation of the heart, mind, and soul. Their lives confirm the fact that "If anyone is in Christ, he is a new creation; old things have passed away; behold, all things have become new" (II Cor. 5:17, NKJV). The Word of God does not just change a man cosmetically—it changes his entire life. The witness of hundreds of millions to the reality of this fact provides strong evidence of the Bible's divine nature, power, and authority.

11

THE CONTRIBUTION OF
ARCHAEOLOGY

Seeing the Facts Clearly

When digging in a grave mound at Moundsville, West Virginia in 1838, workmen came upon a chamber containing prehistoric relics, one of the objects being a stone tablet inscribed with hieroglyphics which defied translation and was the subject of controversy for 92 years.

At least sixty linguists studied the characters and claimed to have identified them as Runic, Etruscan, or some other ancient language. But the hieroglyphics were not actually deciphered until 1930 when an American chanced to look at them from an unusual angle and saw that they were English letters which spelled out "Bill Stump's Stone, October 14, 1838."

This humorous story says a lot about how many have viewed the archaeological findings of history. Archaeologists have been rummaging through the dusty attics of ancient civilizations, sifting through the ruins of buried cities, and cataloging the rubble of yesterday's trash heaps for several centuries. Much has come to light as the field of archaeology has gradually developed into a refined science. However, many have ignorantly concluded that the findings have brought irreparable discredit to the Bible's historical accuracy and reliability. Many have been viewing the "Bill Stump Stone" of biblical archaeology from a slanted, ill-informed angle which has inaccurately interpreted the facts.

Friend or Foe?

During the 18th and 19th centuries, it was quite fashionable among the so-called higher schools of criticism to poke fun at the Bible's historicity. Many of the alleged discrepancies and historical errors which were pointed to during this period as irrefutable evidence of the scriptures' fallibility have been resolved in favor of the Bible by subsequent excavations and archaeological research. As William Albright, a world famous archaeologist, stated, "The excessive skepticism shown toward the Bible by important historical schools of the eighteenth and nineteenth centuries, certain phases of which still appear periodically, have been progressively discredited. Discovery after discovery has established the accuracy of innumerable details, and has brought increased recognition to the value of the Bible as a source of history."[1]

Rather than disprove the Bible's historical accuracy, archaeology has accomplished just the opposite. It has served as a friend, not a foe. Archaeological research over the last two centuries has repeatedly vindicated biblical accounts by providing overwhelming support for its historical accuracy, even down to the most minute and seemingly insignificant detail. Archaeologists have uncovered an abundance of evidence from countless "digs" which has consistently corroborated the scriptural records. So much data has been amassed in support of the

---

1 William F. Albright, **The Archaeology of Palestine,** pp. 127, 128.

Bible that it literally fills hundreds of volumes. The archaeological facts unearthed have conclusively proven the trustworthiness of biblical data concerning its references to historical figures, dates, the existence of civilizations and cities, and the accuracy of details and information associated with specific incidents.

In spite of the repeated attempts by critics to discredit its contents, archaeology has consistently verified the absolute reliability of biblical accounts, references, and chronologies. A classic example involves the 19th century critics who mocked the scriptural references to the Hittites.

Though the Bible contains many references to the Hittites, until the beginning of the 20th century, there was no extra-biblical evidence that they existed. For this reason, critics mocked the Bible's historicity and claimed the scriptural references to these people were purely myth or legend. However, about a hundred years ago, Hattusas, the sprawling capital of the Hittites, was discovered northeast of Ankara, Turkey. The archaeologists who unearthed it were amazed by its massive scale. The walls were extremely thick and stood between 32-64 feet high. It has since been shown that the Hittites were one of the strongest and most influential nations of the ancient world. In this case, as in countless others, archaeological scholarship has forever silenced the scoffers and laid to rest their premature criticisms.

The Testimony of Scholars

So irrefutable is the body of evidence that one renowned Jewish archaeologist stated that,

> It may be stated categorically that no archaeological discovery has ever controverted a biblical reference. Scores of archaeological findings have been made which confirm in clear outline or in exact detail historical statements on the Bible. By the same token, proper evaluation of Biblical

THE BOOK OF BOOKS

descriptions has often led to amazing discoveries.[2]
Professor Millar Burrows of Yale University also noted that,

> On the whole . . . archaeological work has unquestionably
> strengthened confidence in the reliability of the scriptural
> record. More than one archaeologist has found his respect
> for the Bible increased by the experience of excavation in
> Palestine.[3]

To these, Sir Frederic Kenyon, a former Director of the British
Museum, added,

> It is therefore ligitimate to say that, in respect of that part
> of the Old Testament against which the disintegrating
> criticism of the last half of the nineteenth century was
> chiefly directed, the evidence of archaeology has been to
> re-establish its authority, and likewise to augment its value
> by rendering it more intelligible through a fuller knowledge
> of its background and setting. Archaeology has not yet
> said its last word; but the results already achieved confirm
> what faith would suggest, that the Bible can do nothing but
> gain from an increase of knowledge.[4]

Ramsay

Not only has the Bible consistently withstood the attempts
of higher critics to disprove its historicity, but the sheer weight
of evidence in support of its unfailing accuracy is so overwhelming that the facts unearthed have been known to convert skeptics who harbored a predisposed antagonism toward the biblical
record.

Such was the case with Sir William Ramsay, who is regarded
as one of the world's greatest archaeologists. He was an intellect
of high moral character and integrity who had been steeped in

---

2 Nelson Glueck, **Rivers in the Desert**, p. 31.
3 Millar Burrows, **What Mean These Stones?** p. 1.
4 Sir Frederic Kenyon, **The Bible and Archaeology**, p. 279.

the liberal German historical schools of the mid-nineteenth century which were highly skeptical of the Bible. Consequently, he was doubtful of the Bible's accuracy and considered its historic record to be fraudulent. He was especially critical of Luke's historical account in the Book of Acts. He was commissioned by the British Museum in 1881 to do research work in the Greek islands and Asia Minor and used this opportunity to disprove the Bible once and for all. Thus, he entered the field of the Middle East with the expressed purpose of archaeologically discrediting the Bible's credibility.

As Earle Rowell noted,

> He had spent years deliberately preparing himself for the announced task of heading an exploration into Asia Minor and Palestine, the home of the Bible, where he would "dig up the evidence" that the Book was the product of ambitious monks, and not the book from heaven it claimed to be. He regarded the weakest spot in the whole New Testament to be the story of Paul's travels. These had never been thoroughly investigated by one on the spot. So he announced his plan to take the book of Acts as a guide, and by trying to make the same journeys Paul made over the same routes that Paul followed, thus prove that the apostle could never have made them as described.[5]

However, over the course of fifteen years of extensive digging for evidence, he was compelled to reverse his original intent and revise his former beliefs in favor of the Bible's reliability. One of the deciding factors in his conversion to Christianity was the fact that when he began his research, he could find no reliable maps of the region. So he turned to Luke's record in Acts and, time after time, found them to be accurate and contradictory of previous critical assumptions.

In 1896, he published a large volume entitled "St. Paul the

---

5 Earle Albert Rowell, **Prophecy Speaks,** p. 195.

Traveler and the Roman Citizen" which sent shockwaves throughout the skeptical community:

> The book caused a furor of dismay among the skeptics of the world. Its attitude was utterly unexpected, because it was contrary to the announced intention of the author years before. The chagrin and confusion of Bible opponents was complete. But their chagrin and confusion increased, as for twenty years more, book after book from the same author came from the press, each filled with additional evidence of the exact, minute truthfulness of the whole New Testament as tested by the spade on the spot. The evidence was so overwhelming that many infidels announced their repudiation of their former unbelief and accepted Christianity. And these books have stood the test of time, not one having been refuted, nor have I found even any attempt to refute them.[6]

On an autobiographical note concerning his conversion, Ramsay reflected:

> I may fairly claim to have entered on this investigation without prejudice in favour of the conclusion which I shall now seek to justify to the reader. On the contrary, I began with a mind unfavourable to it, for the ingenuity and apparent completeness of the Tubingen theory had at one time quite convinced me. It did not then lie in my line of life to investigate the subject minutely; but more recently I found myself brought into contact with the Book of Acts as an authority for the topography, antiquities and society of Asia Minor. It was gradually borne upon me that in various details the narrative showed marvelous truth. In fact, beginning with a fixed idea that the work was essentially a second century composition, and never relying on its evidence as trustworthy for first century conditions, I

---

6 Earle Albert Rowell, **Prophecy Speaks,** p. 197.

gradually came to find it a useful ally in some obscure and difficult investigations.[7]

He also concluded that,

Luke is an historian of the first rank; not merely are his statements of fact trustworthy; he is possessed of the true historic sense; he fixes his mind on the idea and plan that rules in the evolution of history, and proportions the scale of his treatment to the importance of each incident. He seizes the important and critical events and shows their true nature at greater length, while he touches lightly or omits entirely much that was valueless for his purpose. In short, this author should be placed along with the very greatest of historians.[8]

During his lifetime he wrote over twenty books providing archaeological support for the New Testament's accuracy, and his findings helped convert many of his skeptical colleagues.

The Old Testament

On the following pages, we will highlight just a few of the archaeological finds, from both the Old and New Testaments, which have proven the Bible's accuracy. These only represent the tip of the iceberg concerning the vast amount of accumulated evidence unearthed thus far.

Babel: Archaeological digs in the region of ancient Babylon have uncovered huge astrological observatories, which once rose hundreds of feet, which are called ziggurats. One tower in particular which is still standing was, according to Babylonian records, old during Babylon's pinnacle of prosperity. Herodotus, the Greek historian, referred to this structure in about 500 B. C. According to Babylonian legend, this structure

---

7 William M. Ramsay, **St. Paul the Traveler and the Roman Citizen,** pp. 7, 8.
8 William M. Ramsay, **The Bearing of Recent Discoveries on the Trustworthiness of the New Testament,** p. 222.

was originally built by Nimrod. This fact agrees with the biblical record which links Nimrod to the building of ancient Babylon. This is not to say that this specific ziggurat is the actual Tower of Babel, but it is no doubt a replica.

Another significant fact associated with Babel is the biblical statement that before the construction of the Tower, ". . . the whole world had one language and a common speech" (Gen. 11:1). However, after its destruction, the scriptures reveal that God confounded the language of the whole earth (Gen. 11:9). Many modern philologists support the origin for the languages of the world from one common source.

Ebla Tablets: One of the more significant discoveries of recent times (1964-1978) involves over 17,000 clay tablets unearthed in Northern Syria at the ancient site of Ebla. These tablets have shed invaluable light upon the Book of Genesis. The Ebla archives include hundreds of references which help authenticate the Bible's historicity. All of these tablets are dated around 2250 B.C., which is almost 200 years before Abraham.

Some of these tablets include references to personal names which are found in the Bible such as Esau, David, Saul, and Ishmael. Though these are not the same individuals, it does prove that these names were commonly in use during that contemporary period. One of the names is that of Ebla's greatest king called Ebrum. Some scholars believe this is the same man as Eber mentioned in Genesis 10:21,24,25 and 11:14—17. It is from this name that the word "Hebrews" was derived. These tablets also list the five cities of the plain mentioned in Genesis 14 (Sodom, Gomorrah, Admah, Zeboiim, Bela = Zoar). They even list them in the same sequence as that of the Bible.

Sodom and Gomorrah: Extensive excavations in the region south of the Dead Sea have confirmed that it once was a flourishing and well-inhabited area before a catastrophic upheaval buried it in oblivion. Archaeological work in this area has also proven that it was inhabited during Abraham's time, but was abruptly destroyed immediately afterwards and became subsequently uninhabited. This region contains large quantities of asphalt, sulphur, sulphurous gases, and volcanic deposits which lend credence to the biblical account of the fiery conflagration which engulfed the cities of Sodom and Gomorrah. Huge beds of salt deposits also shed light on the account of Lot's wife. In the course of fleeing, she hesitated and was consumed in the destruction. It may be that she was subsequently buried by salt thrown into the air as a result of the catastrophe and, through the process of time, she gradually became fossilized into a pillar of salt. This petrifying process has been demonstrated to occur with numerous victims of Pompeii's volcanic destruction.

Jericho: Excavations conducted at the ancient site of Jericho by John Garstang during 1930-1936 vindicated the biblical account of its destruction. He found strong evidence that the wall was violently destroyed and had fallen outward, contrary to what would be expected had the city been assaulted by siege rams. On this amazing discovery, Garstang commented: "As to the main fact, then, there remains no doubt: the walls fell outwards so completely that the attackers would be able to clamber up and over their ruins into the city."[9] This corresponds perfectly with the Bible's statement that ". . . the wall collapsed; so every man charged straight in, and they took the city" (Joshua 6:20).

King Solomon: Many finds associated with King Solomon's ambitious building projects help vindicate the historical accuracy of the Old Testament. Some of these finds include Solomon's extensive stable complex, his copper smelting furnace at his seaport of Ezion-Geber, and his fortifications at the city of Megiddo.

Added to these are countless other archaeological discoveries which conclusively substantiate the Old Testament's reliability. To this fact, many scholars have attested. For example, William R. Albright, a renowned archaeologist, stated, "There can be no doubt that archaeology has confirmed the

---

9 John Garstang, **Joshua Judges,** p. 146.

substantial historicity of Old Testament tradition."[10] Merrill Unger noted that:

> Old Testament archaeology has rediscovered whole nations, resurrected important peoples, and in a most astonishing manner filled in historical gaps, adding immeasurably to the knowledge of biblical backgrounds.[11]

Henry Morris also stated:

> Problems still exist, of course, in the complete harmonization of archaeological material with the Bible, but none so serious as not to bear real promise of imminent solution through further investigation. It must be extremely significant that, in view of the great mass of corroborative evidence regarding the Biblical history of these periods, there exists today not one unquestionable find of archaeology that proves the Bible to be in error at any point.[12]

And finally, Sir Frederic Kenyon concluded:

> To my mind, the true and valuable thing to say about archaeology is, not that it proves the Bible, but that it illustrates the Bible. . . . The contribution of archaeology to Bible study has been to [illuminate] the Bible narrative, and especially of the Old Testament. . . . The trend of all this increased knowledge has been to confirm the authority of the books of the Old Testament while it illuminates their interpretation. Destructive criticism is thrown on the defensive; and the plain man may read his Bible confident that, for anything that modern research has to say, the Word of our God shall stand forever.[13]

---

10 William F. Albright, **Archaeology and the Religion of Israel,** p. 176.
11 Merril Unger, **Archaeology and the New Testament,** p. 15.
12 Henry M. Morris, **That You Might Believe,** p. 109.
13 Cited from **Know Why You Believe,** by Paul E. Little. pp. 87, 88.

The New Testament

Almost every geographical place mentioned in the Gospels and Acts has been identified, along with many relics and articles of antiquity, which have a direct bearing upon the New Testament. For example, the ruins of Mars' Hill (the Areopagus) where Paul preached to the Athenians still stands (Acts 17), and miniature statues of the goddess Diana (Artemis) have been found in Asia Minor (Acts 19) and even an altar carrying the inscription to "the unknown god" has been located (Acts 17:23, NKJV). Along with these, countless coins, architectural ruins, and stone inscriptions have been discovered which lend direct evidence to the Bible's historical accuracy.

Even though Bible critics have tried time and again to disprove the New Testament's reliability by magnifying its alleged discrepancies and historical inaccuracies, each of their arguments have been brushed aside by research in the field. As we have already seen in Ramsay's verification of the historical accuracy of the New Testament, innumerable archaeological discoveries substantiate his learned conclusion.

An outstanding example involves Luke's narrative of the events surrounding the birth of Christ (Luke 2:1-3). For years, critics contended that Quirinius was not the acting governor of Syria, that there was no Roman census at this early date, and that the populace didn't have to travel to their place of birth for the census enrollment. However, archaeological discoveries prove that the details of Luke's account are absolutely accuratge. The regular enrollment of taxpayers was instituted by Caesar Augustus early enough for the one Luke refers to, people were required to migrate to their hometowns for the census, and Quirinius did, in fact, serve as governor during the time of this enrollment.

Critics have repeatedly faulted Luke for his supposed errors in references and title designations. But as Ramsay discovered, Luke was a consummate historian whose account was accurate in every detail. For example, Bible critics accused Luke of inaccuracy by stating that the towns of Lystra and Derbe were in the region of Lycaonia, and Iconium was not (Acts 14:6). However, in 1910 Ramsay excavated a monument which revealed that Iconium was a Phrygian city. They also criticized Luke for placing "Lysanias the Tetrarch of Abilene" (Luke 3:1) at the beginning of John the Baptist's ministry because only one Lysanias was known to exist and he died in 36 B. C. But an inscription unearthed near Damascus refers to "Freedman of Lysanias the Tetrarch" and dates from between A. D. 14 and 29. Luke was also faulted for designating the civil authorities of Thessalonica (Acts 17:6) as Politarchs. This term was not even in existence in classical literature so skeptics concluded that he was wrong. However, almost twenty inscriptions have since been found bearing this title and five of them are in reference to Thessalonica. Luke also attributes to Publius, the chief man of Malta, the title "chief official of the island" (Acts 28:7). Inscriptions discovered do, indeed confer upon him this very honor of "first man."

Another contributing find which supports Luke's accuracy was a Greek inscription unearthed in Jerusalem in 1871 by C. S. Clermont-Ganneau which reads:

> No foreigner may enter within the barricade which surrounds the temple and enclosure. Anyone who is caught doing so will have himself to thank for his ensuing death.

This warning ties in with Luke's account of Paul's last visit to Jerusalem when he was assaulted by an enraged mob of Jews who were reacting to the false rumor that Paul had unlawfully brought an uncircumcised Gentile into the temple and polluted it. They were responding in accord with the warning posted at the entrance to the temple area which made it off-limits to foreigners under the penalty of death.

Critics have not only tried to undermine Luke's information but many other New Testament details, as well. However, all their attempts have failed as the Bible continues to be vindicated by ongoing archaeological research. To these, thousands of other examples could be added, but time doesn't permit. Suffice to say, archaeology, to date, has been one of the most significant contributors to the Bible's accuracy and will continue to be so in the future. As J. A. Thompson concluded:

> There is something exciting about supplementing the biblical records with information from nonbiblical historians and from the thrilling discoveries of modern archaeology. It is very evident that the biblical records have their roots firmly in general world history. Archaeological discovery supplements, explains, and at times corroborates the biblical story. The happy combination of the biblical records, the nonbiblical histories, and the discoveries of the archaeologists have produced such splendid results to date that we are full of optimism about the future. There is work for many centuries yet to be done. Many sites have yet to be excavated thoroughly and many others remain whose excavation has not yet commenced. If the achievements of the excavator up to the present have yielded such important results, what may not the future hold for us?[14]

14 J. A. Thompson, **The Bible and Archaeology,** p. 438.

12

THE MANUSCRIPT ACCURACY

Just How Circumstantial?

Bible critics love to emphasize that since we do not possess the original, firsthand manuscripts (autographs), that over the ensuing centuries monks, scribes, and assorted clerics have copied and recopied the Bible so many times that the purity of the original text has been hopelessly flawed through human error. Though there is an enormous amount of manuscript evidence available, they dismiss its significance as unconvincing because they are not the original documents. They contend that the existing manuscript evidence is only circumstantial evidence at best and, therefore, inconclusive.

However, circumstantial evidence can provide a potent case in an impartial court of law if it is strong enough. If the police are called to the scene of a violent disturbance and encounter a man in a state of rage, standing over a corpse, grasping a smoking revolver, though no one actually saw him murder the victim, the circumstantial evidence does strongly point in that direction. So it is with the manuscript evidence of the New Testament's reliability. So much evidence is available and in such a close time interval between the actual writing of the original documents that by careful cross-comparing, cross-checking, and cross-referencing, we can precisely determine the accuracy of the New Testament in spite of the ravages of time, transmission and human error. Although none of the original, firsthand manuscripts have survived, there are so many available manuscript documents in existence that we can safely establish the Bible's reliability beyond any reasonable shadow of doubt.

The Overwhelming Amount of Manuscript Evidence

The manuscript evidence supporting the Bible's accuracy is overwhelming. There are over 5,500 Greek manuscripts of the New Testament, over 10,000 of the Latin Vulgate, and at least 9,300 other early versions. A combined total approaching nearly 25,000 manuscript copies or portions of the New Testament are in existence today. And what makes this voluminous amount of manuscript material so amazing is the fact that they were all hand copied before the advent of the printing press through a laborious and time-consuming process.

The New Testament was written during a forty-year period from about A.D. 50-90. The earliest known portions date around A.D. 120; about fifty other assorted fragments date between 150-200 years from the time of original composition. Two of the earliest manuscript copies of almost the entire New Testament are the Codex Vaticanus (A. D. 325) and the Codex Siniaticus (A. D. 350).

The Trivial Amount of Minor Errors

What is more, scholars have pinpointed the copyist errors and have found them to be an insignificant percentage of the overall sum of the New Testament and do not negatively affect a single important fact, doctrine, or rule of faith. The discrepan-

116

cies caused either unintentionally by copyists or intentionally are quite insignificant. As F. J. A. Hort, the great scholar, noted, "Apart from insignificant variations of grammar or spelling, not more than one thousandth part of the whole New Testament is affected by differences of reading."[1]

Their Closeness to the Date of Original Composition

Furthermore, the interval of time between the writing of the original documents and the multitude of manuscript copies that we possess is so short that we can establish the accuracy of transmission over the years:

> The interval, then, between the dates of original composition and the earliest extant evidence becomes so small as to be in fact negligible, and the last foundation for any doubt that the Scriptures have come down to us substantially as they were written has now been removed. Both the authenticity and the general integrity of the books of the New Testament may be regarded as finally established.[2]

To this Henry Morris added:

> This being so, it hardly seems likely that there could have been any significant change in the writings during the relatively short interval between their original composition by the Apostles and their general distribution among the churches by the close of the first century. Any significant alterations would certainly have been quickly discovered and corrected. Men who had known and heard the Apostles were still living in considerable numbers at that time. In fact, John the Apostle himself lived through the end of the first century.[3]

1 B. F. Westcott and F.J.A. Hort, **Volume 2 New Testament In Original Greek,** p. 2.

2 Sir Frederic G. Kenyon, **The Bible and Archaeology,** p. 199.

3 Henry M. Morris, **Many Infallible Proofs.** p. 24.

Ancient Writings Compared to the New Testament

Compared to the amount of other ancient writings in existence, the Bible has more manuscript evidence supporting its reliability and accuracy of translation than many other classical writings combined. As Bruce noted, "There is no body of ancient literature which enjoys such a wealth of good textual attestation as the New Testament."[4]

The New Testament manuscripts also stand apart from other ancient literature in regards to their close proximity to the time of original composition:

> . . . besides number, the manuscripts of the New Testament differ from those of the classical authors, and this time the difference is clear gain. In no other case is the interval of time between the composition of the book and the date of the earliest extant manuscripts so short as in that of the New Testament. The books of the New Testament were written in the latter part of the first century; the earliest extant manuscripts (trifling scraps excepted) are of the fourth century—say from 250 to 300 years later. This may sound a considerable interval, but it is nothing to that which parts most of the great classical authors from their earliest manuscripts. We believe that we have in all essentials an accurate text of the seven extant plays of Sophocles; yet the earliest substantial manuscript upon which it is based was written more than 1400 years after the poet's death.[5]

No other writings of antiquity which have survived come as close as the New Testament to its original date of composition. F. F. Bruce points this out when he compared the textual material of other ancient works with the Bible:

> For Caesar's Gallic War (composed between 58 and 50 B.C.) there are several extant MSS, but only nine or ten are

---

4 F. F. Bruce, **The Books and the Parchments**, p. 178.
5 Sir Frederic G. Kenyon, **The Bible and Modern Scholarship**, p. 4.

good, and the oldest is some 900 years later than Caesar's day. Of the 142 books of the Roman history of Livy (59 B.C.—A.D. 17), only 35 survive; these are known to us from not more than 20 MSS of any consequence, only one of which, and that containing fragments of Books III-VI, is as old as the fourth century. Of the 14 books of the Histories of Tacitus (c. A.D. 100) only four and a half survive; of the 16 books of his Annals, 10 survive in full and two in part. The text of these extant portions of his two great historical works depends entirely on two MSS, one of the ninth century and one of the eleventh. The extant MSS of his minor works (Dialogus de Oritoribus, Agricola, Germania) all descend from a codex of the tenth century. The History of Thucydides (c. 460-400 B.C.) is known to us from eight MSS, the earliest belonging to about A.D. 900, and a few papyrus scraps, belonging to about the beginning of the Christian era. The same is true of the History of Herodotus (488—428 B.C.). Yet no classical scholar would listen to an argument that the authenticity of Herodotus or Thucydides is in doubt because the earliest MSS of their works which are of any use to us are over 1,300 years later than the originals.[6]

Even when comparing the Bible with more recent works such as the writings of Shakespeare, the Bible's manuscript accuracy is unequaled. As John Lea pointed out:

It seems strange that the text of Shakespeare, which has been in existence less than two hundred and eight years, should be far more uncertain and corrupt than that of the New Testament, now over eighteen centuries old, during nearly fifteen of which it existed only in manuscript. . . . With perhaps a dozen or twenty exceptions, the text of every verse in the New Testament may be said to be so far settled by general consent of scholars, that any dispute as

---

6 F. F. Bruce, **The New Testament Documents: Are They Reliable?**, pp.16, 17.

to its readings must relate rather to the interpretation of the words than to any doubts respecting the words themselves. But in every one of Shakespeare's thirty-seven plays there are probably a hundred readings still in dispute, a large portion of which materially affect the meaning of the passages in which they occur.[7]

These facts demonstrate that the extreme care given to the preservation and transcribing of the biblical manuscripts was much more diligently executed than towards any other work of antiquity. If we were to apply the same standard of textual criticism to the Bible as we do to other ancient writings, we would have to conclude, in all fairness, that its accuracy and reliability is unsurpassed. As Benjamin Warfield stated:

If we compare the present state of the New Testament text with that of any other ancient writing, we must . . . declare it to be marvelously correct. Such has been the care with which the New Testament has been copied—a care which has doubtless grown out of a true reverence for its holy words—such has been the providence of God in preserving for His Church in each and every age a competently exact text of the Scriptures, that not only is the New Testament unrivaled among ancient writings in the purity of its text as actually transmitted and kept in use, but also in the abundance of testimony which has come down to us for castigating its comparatively infrequent blemishes.[8]

F. F. Bruce also added:

The evidence for our New Testament writings is ever so much greater than the evidence for many writings of

---

7 John W. Lea, **The Greatest Book In the World**, p. 15.
8 Benjamin B. Warfield, **Introduction to Textual Criticism of the New Testament**, p. 12.

classical authors, the authenticity of which no-one dreams of questioning. And if the New Testament were a collection of secular writings, their authenticity would generally be regarded as beyond all doubt. It is a curious fact that historians have often been much readier to trust the New Testament records than have many theologians. Somehow or other, there are people who regard a "sacred book" as ipso facto under suspicion, and demand much more corroborative evidence for such a work than they would for an ordinary secular or pagan writing. From the viewpoint of the historian, the same standards must be applied to both.[9]

With this, John W. Montgomery concluded: "To be skeptical of the resultant text of the New Testament books is to allow all of classical antiquity to slip into obscurity, for no documents of the ancient period are as well attested bibliographically as the New Testament."[10]

The Apostolic Fathers

Besides the tremendous amount of manuscript evidence in existence, the manuscript evidence of the early church fathers, which contain abundant quotations from the New Testament, also supports its accuracy. So numerous are their scriptural references that if all the New Testament was lost, we could reassemble the New Testament in its entirety from just their quotations![11] Their writings help corroborate the reliability of the New Testament manuscripts.

When you tally the number of biblical citations from just seven of the early fathers including Justin Martyr, Irenaeus, Clement of Alexandria, Origen, Tertullian, Hippolytus, and Eusebius up to the time of the Council of Nicea in A. D. 325, it

---

9 F. F. Bruce, **The New Testament Documents: Are They Reliable?**, p. 15.
10 John W. Montgomery, **History and Christianity**, p. 29.
11 Bruce M. Metzger, **The Text of the New Testament**, p. 86.

amounts to over 36,000 quotations.[12]   And you could add thousands more if you included other church fathers.

So conclusive is the evidence for the exacting accuracy of manuscript translation of the New Testament, coupled with the vast amount of manuscript material in existence, that it gives strong support to its divine authorship and preservation over the last 1,900 years, and helps establish the Bible as the only inspired and infallible Word of God (see Section II, Chapter 2, on "Old Testament Canon" for Old Testament manuscript accuracy).

---

12 Norman L. Geisler and William E. Nix, **A General Introduction to the Bible,** pp. 353-357.

13

THE TESTIMONY OF JESUS CHRIST

When Jesus Speaks . . .

Most of us are familiar with the popular investment brokerage commercial played out in the midst of a large crowd. You know the one which has someone stating, "My broker is E. F. Hutton, and he says. . . ." At that point, everything comes to an abrupt halt as everyone bends an ear to hear what E. F. Hutton said. The commercial concludes with the boast, "When E. F. Hutton speaks, everyone listens." Well, this commercialized hype definitely exaggerates the facts, but when the Lord Jesus Christ speaks, everyone would do well to take heed, for His words are absolutely reliable and authoritative.

One of the most powerful proofs authenticating the Bible as the only inspired Word of God rests upon the infallible testimony of Jesus Christ—the living, incarnate Word of God (John 1:1). In stressing the supreme significance of this proof, Christ repeatedly endorsed the Bible's absolute reliability, and

He did so without qualifications or reservations. In so doing, He put His divine stamp of acceptance and approval on its source of inspiration, its message, its contents, and its infallibility. "Christ's attitude toward the Old Testament was one of total trust: nowhere, in no particular, and on no subject did he place Scripture under criticism. Never did he distinguish truth 'in faith and practice' from veracity in historical and secular matter. . . ." [1] James Boice also stated:

> When we honestly turn to the scriptures to see what we have of the recorded testimony of Jesus Christ, we find that Jesus had and taught the highest of all possible views of the scriptures, regarding it as having come from God, as speaking with his authority, and as binding even upon his own actions. He read scripture in order to conform to it and thus also to conform to the will of the Father in heaven. [2]

His Frequent Use of Scripture

The issue of the Bible's veracity was so important to Jesus that He repeatedly stressed that God was its author and that its contents were absolutely accurate, factual, and authoritative. His unqualified support for the Old Testament is proven by the fact that He repeatedly taught from it, quoted from it, and referred to its reliability (see Matthew 21:42; 22:29; John 7:38). Whether He was challenging Satan, correcting the authorities, instructing the crowds, or discipling His followers, His statements were saturated with quotations from the Old Testament. Whether comforting His supporters or debating His religious adversaries, the final court of appeals which Christ consistently resorted to with the words, "Is it not written . . . ?" was the Word of God. Even though He took issue with the oral traditions which the Jewish scribes had added to the written

---

1 Harold Lindsell, **The Battle for the Bible**, p. 44.
2 James Montgomery Boice, **Standing on the Rock**, p. 49.

Word, He never denied the Old Testament's divine inspiration at any point.

As far as Christ was concerned, the ultimate touchstone of truth was the Holy Scriptures. As Leon Morris noted, "It was the only book Jesus ever quoted, and then never as a basis for discussion but to decide the point at issue." Jesus made liberal use of them because He unequivocably accepted their absolute authority. From the commencement of His ministry with His inaugural address in His hometown synagogue of Nazareth taken from Isaiah (Luke 4:18-21 / Isaiah 61:1), to His parting words in fulfillment of biblical prophecy (Ps. 69:21 / John 19:28), Jesus relied on the scriptures.

This reality is substantiated by His use of numerous passages. For example, when challenged of His disrespect and disregard for the scriptures, Jesus revealed His attitude of the Old Testamtent by emphatically declaring, "Do not think I have come to abolish the Law or the Prophets (the basic Jewish divisions of the Old Testament, mine); I have not come to abolish them but to fulfill them. I tell you the truth, until heaven and earth disappear, not the smallest letter, not the least stroke of a pen, will by any means disappear from the law until everything be accomplished" (Matt. 5:17,18; see also Matt. 24:35). When confronting the deceptive manuevers of Satan in the wilderness of temptation, Jesus countered him by stating, "It is written . . ." (Matt. 4:1-11). When referring to His mission on earth which included His life, death, burial, and resurrection, He revealed that it was but a fulfillment of the scriptures: "But how then would the Scriptures be fulfilled that say it must happen in this way? . . . But this has all taken place that the writings of the prophets might be fulfilled" (Matt. 26:54, 56). He also added, "This is what I told you while I was still with you: Everything must be fulfilled that is written about me in the Law of Moses, the Prophets and Psalms. Then he opened their minds so they could understand the Scriptures" (Luke 24:44, 45).

His unqualified acceptance of the entirety of the Old Testament was emphasized during one of His most scathing rebukes against the ecclesiastical authorities. Jesus stated, ". . . and so upon you will come all the righteous blood that has been shed on earth, from the blood of righteous Abel to the blood of Zechariah son of Berakiah . . . (Matt. 23:35; see also Luke 11:51). Since Abel was history's first martyr recorded in the first book of the Bible (Genesis 4:8) and Zechariah was the last martyr mentioned in the last book of the Hebrew Old Testament according to Jewish reckoning (II Chron. 24:21), what Jesus was implying, in effect, was that from the beginning to the end, from Genesis to Chronicles, the Old Testament is God's divinely inspired Word. One of Christ's most all-embracing endorsements of the Old Testament came when He declared that, ". . . the scripture cannot be broken" (John 10:35).

One and the Same

Not only did Christ directly refer to the scriptures as the "Word of God" (Mark 7:13; Matt. 4:4), but He intimately linked the written Word to Himself: "And beginning with Moses and all the Prophets, he explained to them what was said in all the scriptures concerning himself . . . (and) said to them, this is what I told you while I was still with you: Everything must be fulfilled that is written about me in the Law of Moses, the Prophets and the Psalms" (Luke 24: 27,44). In the Gospel of John He added: "You diligently study the Scriptures because you think that by them you possess eternal life. These are the Scriptures that testify about me" (John 5:39).

Jesus and the Bible's Historical Accuracy

Another important pillar supporting the Bible's infallibility centers upon the testimony of Christ. In spite of numerous attempts by skeptics to ridicule its contents and rationalize away its miraculous accounts as being nothing more than a collection

126

of myths, folklore, and fanciful allegories, Jesus repeatedly confirmed its historic accuracy. He did not share the views of higher critics towards the Bible. Jesus consistently placed His divine seal of approval upon the Bible's contents. In fact, He almost seemed to highlight the trustworthiness of those historical figures and accounts which critics mock the most. He personally verified the **Genesis account of the creation of the world** in opposition to the humanistic theory of evolution (Mark 10:6-9), **the historicity of Adam and Eve** (Matt. 19:4, 5), **Abel's murder by Cain** (Matt. 23:35), **Noah and the flood** (Luke 17:26, 27; Matt. 24:37-39), **the destruction of Sodom and Gomorrah and the turning of Lot's wife into a pillar of salt** (Luke 17:28-32), **the existence of Abraham, Isaac, and Jacob** (Matt. 8:11), **the existence of Moses and the burning bush** (Luke 20:37), **the miraculous provision of manna in the wilderness** (John 6:49), **the lifting up of the brazen serpent** (John 3:14), **the existence of King David, King Solomon, and Elijah and Elisha the prophets** (Matt. 12:3; 12:42; Luke 4:25-27), and **the reality of Jonah's deliverance from the belly of a huge fish** (Matt. 12:40). Obviously, Jesus didn't consider this an allegorical fish story, or the other biblical accounts to be the product of legend, folklore, or myth. He entertained no doubts about the factuality of the Bible.

The Accommodation Theory

Some critics have struggled to circumnavigate Christ's evaluation of the scriptures' infallibility by claiming that He was simply accommodating His use of scriptures to the ignorance and superstition of His gullible listeners. They claim that He did so as an expedient means of gaining a receptive audience rather than needlessly alienating the people of Palestine. This theory can be qualified as follows:

> Briefly, this theory states that Jesus, in His reference to the Old Testament, accommodates His teaching to the prejudices and erroneous views of His day. It holds that He

THE BOOK OF BOOKS

did not actually mean that Jonah was really in the 'whale'. It claims that Jesus' purpose was not to question the historical truth, nor to establish critical theories, but to preach spiritual and moral values.[3]

However, a closer examination of this argument shows that it is an anemic one, at best. First of all, if Jesus knew that the Bible was an inaccurate collection of fanciful fairytales and ignorant superstitions and yet taught that it was the infallibly inspired Word of God, then He was guilty of gross deception and, therefore, could not be the guiltless, sinless Son of God. This assumption would pervert the very character, integrity, and deity of Christ. Secondly, if He taught, in all good faith, that it was trustworthy when it wasn't, then we again undermine Him as the omniscient God who is perfect in knowledge and power. Thirdly, if Jesus was manipulatively accommodating Himself to the prejudices of first century Palestine, how will we ever know what He actually believed as absolute truth? How can we ever determine when He was accommodating Himself to a then current prejudice or not? And fourthly, if critics are to be consistent with the accommodation theory, we must ask why Jesus strove to accommodate Himself on some points, but on other seemingly less important points, He strongly challenged the prejudices of the time (Mark 7:1-13)? A careful appraisal of this view shows it for what it is—groundless and indefensible.

The Inevitable Conclusion

On the basis of Christ's infallibility, we believe that the Bible is equally infallible. As James Boice stated, "Jesus Christ as the Son of God speaks to us, not as an errant but as an inerrant, infallible authority. If Jesus is who he claimed to be, and if Jesus taught what we have as his teachings in the Word of God, then we can believe the Bible to be the Word of God because Jesus

---

3 Norman L. Geisler and William E. Nix, **A General Introduction to the Bible**, pp. 59, 60.

believed this to be the case."[4] A rejection of Christ's credibility amounts to a rejection of Christ. A rejection of His words is a rejection of His person, message, and mission. A denial of His claims concerning the Bible's dependability is tantamount to making Christ a colossal liar and a deceiver. For this reason alone, the intellectually honest person can only be led to the inevitable conclusion that the Bible is what Jesus claimed it to be, the infallibly inspired Word of God, even if it contains difficulties and perplexities which have not been satisfactorily settled. As H. C. G. Moule concluded, "He absolutely trusted the Bible; and though there are in it things inexplicable and intricate that have puzzled me. . . . I am going, not in a blind sense, but reverently, to trust the Book because of him."[5]

---

4 James Montgomery Boice, **Standing on the Rock,** pp. 47, 48.

5 John B. Harford and Frederick MacDonald, **The Life of Bishop Moule,** p. 138.

14

THE RESURRECTION FACTOR

The Empty Tomb

Someone with a slightly sick sense of humor once asked me if I knew how many people were dead in the local cemetery When I said, "I don't know," he replied, "All of them." All jesting aside, his answer contained a sobering note of reality. Death has reigned supreme over the entire human race. It inevitably triumphs over all forms of life. There is, however, one notable exception—Jesus Christ. It is true that He was crucified and died and was interred like other men, but the grave could not hold Him.

From obscure gravesites to world famous memorials, tombs all over the earth contain the remains of those who have tasted the sting of death. The great pyramids of Egypt, containing the mummified remains of ancient Egyptian kings, are the world's largest burial vaults. Westminster Abbey in London is the renowned resting place of English royalty and dignitaries. Arl-

131

ington Cemetery in Washington, D. C. is honored as the final resting place of America's fallen heroes. Red Square is revered by Russians for containing the crypt of Lenin. Millions of Chinese journey to the mausoleum of Mao Tse Tung in China's capital to pay homage to their former leader. Mohammed's tomb at Medina is annually memorialized by thousands of devout Moslem pilgrims, and cemeteries around the world contain the private burial plots of deceased loved ones who are cherished by those they left behind. But there is a difference between these resting places and the burial tomb of Christ. They draw visitors and grieving loved ones because of what they contain, while the Garden Tomb of Christ draws visitors from around the world because it is empty.

The Pivotal Proof of Christianity

One of the most compelling arguments for accepting the Bible as the Word of God is because Jesus said so. But what gives such impressive clout to His words is the historical reality of His resurrection from the dead. His resurrection confirms that Jesus is who He claimed to be, and His statements regarding the scriptures' inspiration are absolutely reliable and trustworthy.

The Cornerstone of Christianity

Christ's resurrection is the very cornerstone of Christianity. It is the crowning proof of Christianity, Christ's claims concerning Himself, and the reliability of the Word of God. Without the resurrection, you have lofty ideas and noble words with little substance. Christianity and the teachings of the Bible are hollow without Christ's triumph over death. As Michael Green noted:

> Christianity does not hold the resurrection to be one among many tenets of belief. Without faith in the resurrection there would be no Christianity at all. The Christian church would never have begun; the Jesus-movement would have fizzled out like a damp squib with his execu-

132

tion. Christianity stands or falls with the truth of the resurrection.[1]

Even the Apostle Paul pointed out the ultimate emptiness of Christianity apart from the resurrection when he declared, "And if Christ is not risen, your faith is futile" (I Cor. 15: 17, NKJV).

An Historical Fact

But He did rise from the grave. His resurrection is a solidly substantiated fact of history. As Thomas Arnold, a former Professor of History at Rugby and Oxford and one of the world's great historians, noted:

> The evidence for our Lord's life and death and resurrection may be, and often has been shown to be satisfactory; it is good according to the common rules for distinguishing good evidence from bad. Thousands and tens of thousands of persons have gone through it piece by piece, as carefully as every judge summing up on a most important case. I have myself done it many times over, not to persuade others but to satisfy myself. I have been used for many years to study the histories of other times, and to examine and weigh the evidence of those who have written about them, and I know of no one fact in the history of mankind which is proved by better and fuller evidence of every sort, to the understanding of a fair inquirer, than the great sign which God hath given us that Christ died and rose again from the dead.[2]

Another scholar also concluded, "Indeed, taking all the evidence together, it is not too much to say that there is no

---

1 Michael Green, **Man Alive**, p. 61.
2 Thomas Arnold, **Sermons on Christian Life; Its Hopes; Its Fears, and Its Close**, p. 324.

THE BOOK OF BOOKS

historic incident better or more variously supported than the resurrection of Christ.''[3]

The historic factuality of Christ's resurrection is such an indisputable fact that it is much easier to document its authenticity than more insignificant, historical events or personages which we accept at face value as unquestionably genuine by historians. As Wilbur Smith commented, "Let it simply be said that we know more about the details of the hours immediately before the actual death of Jesus, in and near Jerusalem, than we know about the death of any other man in all the ancient world."[4]

Even Josephus (A.D. 37-100), an eyewitness to the Roman conquest of Jerusalem in A.D. 70 and compiler of one of the most comprehensive histories of Israel, bore witness to the reality of the resurrection:

> Now there was about this time Jesus, a wise man, if it be lawful to call him a man; for he was a doer of wonderful works, a teacher of such men as receive the truth with pleasure. He drew over to him many Jews, and also many of the Greeks. This man was the Christ. And when Pilate had condemned him to the cross, upon his impeachment by the principal men among us, those who had loved from the first did not forsake him, for he appeared to them alive on the third day, the divine prophets having spoken these and thousands of other wonderful things about him. And even now, the race of Christians, so named from him, has not died out.[5]

Though not a Christian, this respected, first century historian provides strong supporting evidence of the historic reality of Christ's resurrection.

---

3 Canon Westcott, cited from **Know Why You Believe,** by Paul E. Little, pp. 51-52.

4 Wilbur Smith, **Therefore Stand: Christian Apologetics,** p. 360.

5 Flavius Josephus, **Antiquities of the Jews,** Book 18, 3:3.

Christ's Self-Witness

Even Christ established the reliability of the resurrection through both pre- and post- testimonies to its reality. On numerous occasions, Jesus informed His disciples of His approaching crucifixion and subsequent resurrection: "We are going up to Jerusalem, and the Son of Man will be betrayed to the chief priests and the teachers of the law. They will condemn him to death and will turn him over to the Gentiles to be mocked and flogged and crucified. On the third day he will be raised to life!" (Matt. 20:18,19; see also 12:38-40; 16;21; 17:9,22,23; 26:32; 27:63; Mark 8:3-31—9:1; 9:10, 31; 14:28, 58; 10:32; Luke 9:22-27; John 2:19-22; 12:34; chapters 14-16).

If any other human being uttered such a preposterous boast that they would rise from the grave three days after they died, men in little white coats would place them in a straitjacket and carry them away to some psychiatric ward for observation. But Christ placed His very credibility on the line when He claimed that He would, indeed, rise again.

> It was this same Jesus, the Christ who, among many other remarkable things, said and repeated something which, proceeding from any other being would have condemned him at once as either a bloated egotist or a dangerously unbalanced person. That Jesus said He was going up to Jerusalem to die is not so remarkable, though all the details He gave about that death, weeks and months before He died, are together a prophetic phenomenon. But when He said that He himself would rise from the dead, the third day after He was crucified, He said something that only a fool would dare say, if he expected longer the devotion of any disciples, unless He was sure he was going to rise. No founder of any world religion known to men ever dared say a thing like that![6]

He "deliberately staked his whole claim to the credit of men upon

6 Wilbur Smith, **A Great Certainty in This Hour of World Crisis**, pp. 10, 11.

his resurrection. When asked for a sign he pointed to this sign as his single and sufficient credential."[7] His testimony, alone, gives sufficient proof of the historic reality of the resurrection.

Post-Resurrection Appearances

Jesus provided His followers with explicit, prophetic indications of His coming crucifixion, but He also made many post-resurrection appearances which proved that His tomb was empty. During a forty-day period from immediately after the resurrection to His ascension to the Father, He made ten distinct appearances; *1)* **to Mary Magdalene in the garden** (John 20:11-18; Mark 16:9); *2)* **to the other women** (Matt. 28:1-10; Luke 24:1-11); *3)* **to the two disciples on the road to Emmaus** (Luke 24:13-35); *4)* **to Peter** (Luke 24:34; I Cor. 15:5); *5)* **to the ten apostles assembled together** (John 20:24, 25); *6)* **to the eleven apostles assembled together** (John 20:26-29); *7)* **to seven of the disciples by the Sea of Galilee** (John 21:1-23); *8)* **to five hundred disciples at once** (I Cor. 15:6); *9)* **to James** (I Cor. 15:7); *10)* **and to the eleven apostles at Christ's ascension** (Acts 1:3-12). Added to these was **Christ's appearance to Paul on the road to Damascus** (Acts 9:3-8; I Cor. 15:8) and **Christ's revelation to the Apostle John** (Rev. 1:12-18). These were all observable, physical appearances by a variety of credible witnesses who spoke with Him, touched Him, and even ate with Him.

New Testament References

The apostles publicly proclaimed that they were eyewitnesses of the genuineness of Christ's resurrection. For example, the Apostle Peter stated, "We are witnesses of everything he did in the country of the Jews and in Jerusalem. They killed him by hanging him on a tree, but God raised him from the dead on the third day and caused him to be seen. He was not seen by all of the people, but by witnesses whom God had already chosen—by

---

7 Benjamin Warfield, **The Person and Work of Christ**, p. 537.

us who ate and drank with him after he rose from the dead. He commanded us to preach to the people and to testify that he is the one whom God appointed as judge of the living and the dead" (Acts 10:39-42). He also defended the integrity of their testimony when he declared, "We did not follow cleverly invented stories when we told you about the power and coming of our Lord Jesus Christ, but we were eyewitnesses of his majesty" (II Pet. 1:16).

The Gospels, Acts, and the epistles are pregnant with references to this testimony; Rom. 1:2, 3; 6:3-9; I Cor. 15:1-58; II Cor. 4:10-14; Gal. 2:20; Eph. 1:19-23; Phil. 2:5-11; Col. 2:12; I Thess. 1:10; 4:14; II Tim. 2:8; Heb. 13:20; and I Peter 1:21. Even the last book of the Bible designates Jesus as "the faithful witness, the firstborn from the dead," and Jesus claims Himself to be "I am he who lives, and was dead, and behold, I am alive forevermore" (Rev. 1:5, 18).

Not only did His immediate band of followers, numbering several hundred, bear witness to the reality of His resurrection, but the post-apostolic fathers, coupled with the early church creedal statements, repeatedly affirm this fact.

In both ecclesiastical history and creedal history the resurrection is affirmed from the earliest times. It is mentioned in Clement of Rome, Epistle to the Corinthians (A.D. 95), the earliest document of church history and so continuously throughout all of the patristic period. It appears in all forms of the Apostles' Creed and is never debated.[8]

The Credibility of Resurrection Witnesses

The number, circumstances, and variety of appearances provide strong evidence that the resurrection was not a figment of the imagination, an elaborate hoax, hallucination, or cleverly manipulated plot. Furthermore, the high moral character and integrity of those witnesses is beyond reproach, and many were

---

8 Bernard Ramm, **Protestant Christian Evidences**, p. 192.

executed for their unwavering defense of the resurrection of Christ. In fact, one of the most convincing proofs of the trustworthiness of their testimony rests in their unswerving dedication to the belief in the resurrection. The skeptical arguments that it was a cleverly manipulated Passover plot, the product of wishful thinking, or the misguided figment of the disciples' imagination is ruled out by the fact that they were so confidently convinced of its historic fact that they sacrificed their lives, their possessions, and their reputations in defense of its certainty. Though others have laid down their lives for various causes, no sane individual willingly surrenders his life for something he knows to be fraudulent. But millions of Christians, throughout the church age, have given their lives in absolute assurance of Christ's triumph over death, hell, and the grave.

For example, Ignatius, a disciple of the Apostle John, wrote:

He was crucified and died under Pontius Pilate. He really, and not merely in appearance, was crucified, and died, in the sight of beings in heaven, and on earth, and under the earth. He also rose again in three days. . . . On the day of the preparation, then, at the third hour, He received the sentence from Pilate, the Father permitting that to happen; at the sixth hour He was crucified; at the ninth hour He gave up the ghost; and before sunset He was buried. During the Sabbath He continued under the earth in the tomb in which Joseph of Arimathaea had laid Him. He was carried in the womb, even as we are, for the usual period of time; and was really born, as we also are; and was in reality nourished with milk, and partook of common meat and drink, even as we do. And when He had lived among men for thirty years, He was baptized by John, really and not in appearance; and when He had preached the gospel three years, and done signs and wonders, He who was Himself the Judge was judged by the Jews, falsely so called , and by Pilate the governor; was scourged, was smitten on the cheek, was spit upon; He wore a crown of thorns and a purple robe; He was condemned; He was crucified in reality, and not in appearance, not in imagination, not in deceit. He really died, and was buried, and rose from the dead. . . .[9]

What makes his words so impressive is the fact that he penned them during his journey from Antioch to Rome to be thrown to the lions in the Colosseum. These were the sober reflections of a man who had dedicated his entire life to the belief in the absolute reliability of the resurrection, and was willing to be martyred for that belief.

The credibility and eyewitness accuracy of the disciples' testimony is so significant that Simon Greenleaf, a former Professor of Law at Harvard University and one of the history's greatest authorities on law, applied the laws of evidence as used in legal jurisprudence to the disciples' testimony and concluded:

> The great truths which the apostles declared, were, that Christ had risen from the dead, and that only through repentance from sin, and faith in Him, could men hope for salvation. This doctrine they asserted with one voice, everywhere, not only under the greatest discouragements, but in the face of the most appalling errors that can be presented to the mind of man. Their master had recently perished as a malefactor, by the sentence of a public tribunal. His religion sought to overthrow the religions of the whole world. The laws of every country were against the teachings of His disciples. The interests and passions of all the rulers and great men in the world were against them. The fashion of the world was against them. Propagating this new faith, even in the most inoffensive and peaceful manner, they could expect nothing but contempt, opposition, revilings, bitter persecutions, stripes, imprisonments,

---

9 Cited from **Who Was Who in Church History**, edited by Elgin S. Moyer, p. 209.

torments, and cruel deaths. Yet this faith they zealously did propagate; and all these miseries they endured undismayed, nay, rejoicing. As one after another was put to a miserable death, the survivors only prosecuted their work with increased vigor and resolution. The annals of military warfare afford scarcely an example of the like heroic constancy, patience, and unflinching courage. They had every possible motive to review carefully the grounds of their faith, and the evidence of the great facts and truths which they asserted; and these motives were pressed upon their attention with the most melancholy and terrific frequency. It was therefore impossible that they could have persisted in affirming the truths they have narrated, had not Jesus actually risen from the dead, and had they not known this fact as certainly as they knew any other fact. If it were morally possible for them to have been deceived in this matter, every human motive operated to lead them to discover and avow their error. To have persisted in so gross a falsehood, after it was known to them, was not only to encounter, for life, all the evils which man could inflict, from without, but to endure also the pangs of inward and conscious guilt; with no hope of future peace, no testimony of a good conscience, no expectation of honor or esteem among men, no hope of happiness in this life, or in the world to come. Such conduct in the apostles would moreover have been utterly irreconcilable with the fact, that they possessed the ordinary constitution of our common nature. Yet their lives do show them to have been men like all others of our race; swayed by the same motives, animated by the same hopes, affected by the same joys, subdued by the same sorrows, agitated by the same fears, and subject to the same passions, temptations, and infirmities, as ourselves. And their writings show them to have been men of vigorous understandings. If then their testimony was not true, there was no possible motive for its fabrication.[10]

His Lasting Influence

Another indirect proof of the resurrection is the unparalleled impact which the living Christ has had upon the world. No other famous personage or religious leader has left this lasting legacy. As the noted church historian Philip Schaff commented:

> This Jesus of Nazareth, without money and arms, conquered more millions than Alexander, Caesar, Mohammed, and Napoleon; without science and learning, He shed more light on things human and divine than all philosophers and scholars combined; without the eloquence of schools, He spoke such words of life as were never spoken before or since, and produced effects which lie beyond the reach of orator or poet; without writing a single line, He set more pens in motion, and furnished themes for more sermons, orations, discussions, learned volumes, works of art, and songs of praise than the whole army of great men of ancient and modern times.[11]

The reason is simple: He is arisen, and continues to exert His divine influence upon the affairs of men throughout the earth.

The Power of This Proof

Once, when conversing with Talleyrand, the Bishop of Autun, someone sarcastically stated, "The Christian religion—what is it? It would be easy to start a religion like that." "Oh, yes," said Talleyrand, "One would only have to get crucified and rise again the third day." No other religion, religious figure, or religious writing can claim this support. As one writer concluded, "Confucius' tomb-occupied, Buddah's tomb-occupied,

---

10 Simon Greenleaf, **Testimony of the Evangelists, Examined by the Rules of Evidence Administered in a Court of Law**, pp. 28-30.
11 Philip Schaff, **The Person of Christ**, n.p.

Mohammed's tomb-occupied, Jesus' tomb-empy.''[12] It is the fact of the resurrection which makes Christianity so unique in comparison to other religions and its claims concerning the Bible so powerful.

In closing, the resurrection factor places an infallible stamp of credibility upon Christ and His authoritative claims about the divine authorship of the Bible. The resurrection is His ultimate credential of divine authority. Furthermore, the evidence pertaining to this historic event is absolutely overwhelming, and the supports we have examined are just a handful of the "many infallible proofs" (Acts 1:3, NKJV) which could be offered in defense.[13]

---

12 G. B. Hardy, **Countdown,** n.p.
13 Josh McDowell, **Evidence That Demands a Verdict,** pp. 203-270.

15

THE SELF-WITNESS
OF SCRIPTURE

Nothing But the Truth

In American courts of law, it is still a time-honored tradition to swear in witnesses by having them recite the familiar oath of honesty: "I swear to tell the truth, the whole truth, and nothing but the truth, so help me God." The witness does this by placing his right hand on the Bible. Somehow, this gesture is supposed to challenge the witness to bring his testimony into the same dimension of truthfulness and absolute honesty as the truths contained in the Holy Bible. However, we are all aware that this courtroom formality does not guarantee that a person will not perjure himself and lie away the world.

There's an old legal adage which states, "He who has himself as a lawyer, has a fool for a client." This axiom may hold up in human terms, but it does not apply to the Bible's self-witness concerning its divine authorship. The deciding difference lies in the fact that the scriptures record God's personally inspired testimony concerning the Bible's reliability. What is more, we must take into account the credibility of the witness involved. The Bible's self-witness is absolutely reliable because it reflects the very character and integrity of God. Though men may perjure themselves and distort the facts, even in the aftermath of swearing on a stack of Bibles, God needs no corroborating support of His honesty. His words are pure and undefiled by dishonesty. When God speaks the truth, we can be confident that it is indeed "the truth, the whole truth, and nothing but the truth," for "It is impossible for God to lie" (Hebrews 6:18).

The Real Author

The Bible's teaching about itself is another support to the Bible's reliability. The Bible makes some very strong claims concerning its divine source of authorship, inspiration, and contents. It repeatedly confirms the fact that God is both the architect and author of its contents. It gives unqualified support for the fact that God was in absolute control of its composition, as well as the sole source of its inspiration. It also guarantees the enduring purity and reliability of its contents, and emphasizes that it was not contaminated, adulterated, or altered by human contact or manipulation. Furthermore, it not only specifies that God inspired the messengers used in writing the Word, but it stresses that the message itself is divinely inspired. These facts are emphasized by the following passages:

"Above all, you must understand that no prophecy of scripture came about by the prophet's own interpretation. For prophecy never had its origin in the will of man, but men spoke from God as they were carried along by the Holy Spirit" (II Pet. 1:20,21).

"All scripture is God-breathed and is useful for teaching, rebuking, correcting and training in righteousness, so that the

144

man of God may be thoroughly equipped for every good work" (II Timothy 3:16,17).

"Heaven and earth will pass away, but my words will never pass away" (Matt. 24:35).

"And the Lord Spoke. . . ."

What is more, the Old Testament is saturated with emphatic declarations that God was the source of its inspiration and authorship. One Bible scholar categorized over 2,600 such claims in the historical books, and 195 claims in the poetic books, to be exact.[1] The divine source of authorship is referred to with such descriptive phrases as "And the Lord said . . . ," "The word of the Lord came unto . . . ," or "The Spirit of the Lord spoke. . . ." Throughout the breadth of the Old Testament, the fact of divine authorship is established. This is particularly true of the prophetic books. As Rene Pache noted in his partial breakdown:

> The prophets, in a peculiarly exact way, identified their message with the Word of God: "Hear the word of Jehovah. The word of Jehovah was addressed to me in these words. The mouth of Jehovah hath spoken. Jehovah spake unto me. Thus hath Jehovah said unto me," etc. We find such expressions in Isaiah 120 times, Jeremiah 430 times, Ezckiel 329 times, Amos 53 times, Haggai 27 times (in 38 verses) and Zechariah 53 times.[2]

New Testament Claims

The New Testament writers also testified of the scriptures' ultimate source of inspiration. They frequently quoted from the Old Testament or definitely alluded to it (see Acts 17:2,11; 18:28; Rom. 1:2; 4:3; 9:17; 10:11; 11:2; I Cor. 15:3, 4; Gal.

---

1 Henry M. Morris, **Many Infallible Proofs**, p. 157.
2 Rene Pache, **The Inspiration and Authority of Scripture**, pp. 81, 82.

THE BOOK OF BOOKS

3:8, 22; 4:30; I Tim. 5:18; II Tim. 3:15-17 as examples). There are over 320 direct quotations from the Old Testament cited in the New, and over 1,000 references. The Apostle Paul affirmed the scriptures' inspiration when he stated, "For everything that was written in the past was written to teach us, so that through endurance and the encouragement of the scriptures we might have hope" (Rom. 15:4). He even claimed that his message and revelations came from God: "I want you to know, brothers, that the gospel I preached is not something that men made up. I did not receive it from any man, nor was I taught it; rather, I received it by revelation from Jesus Christ" (Gal. 1:11,12; see also Rom. 16:25,26; I Cor. 2:13; 14:37; Eph. 3:4,5; and I Thess. 2:13). Even Peter specifically states that Paul's writings were to be compared equally to "the other scriptures" (II Pet. 3:15,16), and links "the words spoken in the past by the holy prophets" to the divine inspiration of "the command(s) given by our Lord and Savior through your apostles" (II Peter 3:2).

In closing, though the self-witness of scripture may not be a convincing proof to many of the Bible's divine inspiration, when we take into account the ultimate source behind the composition, coupled with the integrity of the various authors in cluding Christ Himself, we cannot lightly dismiss this support.

CONCLUSION

We have carefully examined the supporting evidence concerning the Bible's divine authorship and accuracy. It is conclusive and overwhelming. The facts forcefully substantiate the Bible's trustworthiness, accuracy, and divine source of inspiration. The sheer weight of evidence should lead the sincere skeptic to the inevitable conclusion that the Bible is, indeed, the Word of God. With such convincing support in favor of the Bible's reliability, the only sensible and intellectually honest response boils down to accepting this fact. However, it should be stressed that though supporting evidence can help in establishing the Bible's credibility, it is a book which must ultimately be accepted by faith. Intellectual facts can never be an adequate substitute for a faith response. As Merrill Unger emphasized:

> In the first place, the Bible, when legitimately approached, does not need to be 'proved' either by archaeology, geology or any other science. As God's revelation to man,

THE BOOK OF BOOKS

its own message and meaning, its own claims of inspiration and internal evidence, its own fruits and results in the life of humanity are its best proof of authenticity. It demonstrates itself to be what it claims to be to those who believe its message. Since God has made the realization of spiritual life and the apperception of spiritual truth on the basis of faith and not sight, whatever contributions archaeology or any other science might make toward corroborating the reliability of the Bible can never take the place of faith. Scientific authentication may act as an aid to faith, but God has so ordained that simple trust (which glorifies Him) shall always be necessary in dealing with Him or His revealed truth.[1]

As I pointed out in the first chapter of this section, it is not enough to just be intellectually persuaded. Our ultimate response to the Bible, its author, and its message must be more than mere passive mental agreement. Being intellectually convinced is insufficient grounds for the Word of God to have its intended transforming effect upon our lives. On the bottom line, the ultimate grounds of response must be based upon a sincere faith commitment.

As we have previously seen, "the word . . . did not profit them, not being mixed with faith" (Heb. 4:2, NKJV). Faith is essential, but it must be a faith which acts. The Bible cautions us to "be doers of the word, and not hearers only, deceiving yourselves" (James 1:22, NKJV). The world is filled with intellectually convinced people who believe the Bible is the Word of God but have not acted upon that belief. We must give more than lip service to the Bible. We must act upon our belief by humbly surrendering our lives to Jesus Christ and accepting His revelation for our lives contained in the Bible—the Word of God.

---

1 Merrill Unger, **Archaeology and the Old Testament,** pp. 14, 15.

148

Section II

How Did We Get the Bible?

INTRODUCTION

The Bible is a household word recognized by untold millions. But even though the Bible is a book recognized and revered the world over, few have any knowledge of where the word originated. It seems that there was an ancient coastal city overlooking the Mediterranean called Gebal in what is present day Lebanon. However, the Greeks gave it the name Byblos because it possessed the distinctive characteristic of being an important commercial center which carried on a lively trade in papyrus paper imported from Egypt. They did this because in the Greek, the word for "book" was "biblos" (*byblos*). Gebal was noted for its papyrus used in the production of books, and it seemed only fitting to the Greeks to give it this name. Because early copies of the scriptures were written on papyrus, the Book of Books gradually adopted the Greek word for "book," or the Bible.

On a larger note, not only do most not know where the term "Bible" came from, they have very little understanding of where the Bible itself originated or how it evolved into its present form. Many have only the foggiest notion of its development. They assume that it was the product of reclusive monks who collected and edited a bunch of religious writings over the centuries, or that it came from dirty parchments dug up in some remote cave or desert monastery.

About ten years ago, a television mini-series called "Roots" became an overnight success. It was a story about the origins of a young black man who had been captured by slavers in Africa and transported to a plantation in the southern colonies. It traced the struggles of his life and that of his succeeding generations. The story struck a chord not only in America's black community, but in the hearts of many, and sparked a wave of interest among multitudes concerning their own personal roots. Thousands began to research their families' past in order to gain a fuller understanding of how they got here. In a similar vein, this section is directed towards those who share a common desire to understand the unique origins, preservation, and gradual evolution of the Book of Books.

1

THE CANON

What Is Canon?

I once asked a class if anyone knew what the term "canonology" meant. One of the students jokingly replied, "The critical study of ancient field artillery." However, his answer was not quite accurate. The term "canonology" refers to the biblical study of canon. The word "canon" is derived from the Greek word for "reed" (Gr. *kanon*) and means "a cane, rule, or measuring rod." In Old Testament times, the rod was used as a measuring device. This word is now used in a metaphorical sense to characterize the list of writings which are considered as the authoritatively inspired "rule of faith and practice" manifested by the Word of God. It refers to the divinely inspired collection of books in both the Old and New Testaments regarded as scripture. From about A. D. 300 onward, this term has been used for the collection of books considered as sacred scripture.

THE BOOK OF BOOKS

The Church and Canonization

The cataloging of canon was not finalized overnight. The gradual historical process of determining which books met the canonical requirements unfolded over many centuries. Generally speaking, most of the books now considered as sacred canon were commonly accepted as divinely inspired within the consciousness of God's people long before church councils were officially convened to ratify their canonization. However, it should be stressed that the church councils did not create the canon or confer an inspirational status upon the various books of the Bible. As one scholar noted, "The church no more gave us the New Testament canon, than Sir Isaac Newton gave us gravity . . . and similarly He gave us the New Testament canon by inspiring the individual books that make it up."[1]

Ultimately, the individual books comprising the Bible are canonical by virtue of their inspirational authority and not by reason of church decree. As E. J. Young confirmed,

> When the Word of God was written, it became Scripture, and inasmuch as it had been spoken by God, it possessed absolute authority. Since it was the Word of God, it was canonical. That which determines the canonicity of a book, therefore, is the fact that the book is inspired by God.[2]

As F. F. Bruce also added,

> One thing must be emphatically stated. The New Testament books did not become authoritative for the church because they were formally included in a canonical list; on the contrary, the church included them in her canon because she already regarded them as divinely inspired.[3]

The church simply recognized, received, and codified those

---

1 J. I. Packer, **God Speaks to Man**, p. 81.
2 E. J. Young, **The Canon of the Old Testament**, p. 156.
3 F. F. Bruce, **The New Testament Documents: Are They Reliable?**, p. 27.

books that were already inspired from their creation and bore the distinctive marks of divine authority, authorship, and authenticity. They didn't confer inspirational status before the fact but after the fact. The church merely recognized their innate worth and the reality of their existing inspiration. As William Hendriksen pointed out:

> Though the history of the recognition, review, and ratification of the canon was somewhat complicated . . . what should be emphasized . . . is that not because the church, upon a certain date, long ago, made an official decision (the decision of the Council of Hippo, A.D. 393; of Carthage, A.D. 397), do these books constitute the inspired Bible; on the contrary, the sixty-six books, by their very contents, immediately attest themselves to the hearts of all Spirit-indwelt men as being the living oracles of God.[4]

Guidelines for Determining Sacred Canon

The dilemma which faced the church was the question of which books were worthy of canonization. Which books should be accepted as the authoritative Word of God? For most of the books comprising our Bible, this was not a difficult decision, but for others, the final determination was more involved. Over the centuries, many books contended for canonical status. Though some of these were outright forgeries or counterfeit scriptures, others contained traces of religious merit. Others were accepted by Christian churches in certain regions, while not widely accepted in other regions. Therefore, specific rules were gradually adopted for determining which writings met the requirements for sacred canon. Though not officially spelled out, these guidelines were generally understood as a safe barometer of a book's divine authenticity:

1. Does the book possess a definite prophetic and in-

---

4 William Hendriksen, **First and Second Timothy and Titus**, pp. 301, 302.

spirational quality? In short, does it manifest a clear "Thus saith the Lord"?

2. Was the book written by a reputable prophet, authored by an apostle, or a contemporary intimately associated with an apostle? The "apostolicity" (was it written by an apostle or close associate of an apostle?) was the primary consideration of the New Testament works.

3. Was it accepted, collected, preserved, distributed, and read by God's people either in the Old Testament period or New Testament period?

4. Do its contents and message harmonize with the standards of sound biblical teaching? Many of the false writings contained an abundance of fanciful legends, factual inaccuracies, and doctrinal heresies.

5. Does it possess a dynamic, life-transforming power which has a universal impact upon men?

6. Was it endorsed and accepted by successive generations of believers, such as the early church fathers? In other words, there seemed to be a consistent, prevailing witness of the overwhelming majority of the church concerning a book's divine inspiration.

The sixty-six individual books comprising our present Bible have all met these strict standards.

2

THE OLD TESTAMENT CANON

Completed with Malachi

Though no formulized process of canonization of the Old Testament books is known, the evidence indicates that the Hebrew people unquestionably accepted their divine authenticity and inspiration, from the earliest date, with very little controversy. They universally accepted these thirty-nine books as genuine, apart from any official stamp of approval, because they recognized their inherent inspiration and authoritative character.

Since the first writings of Moses, efforts were undertaken by the Jews to preserve their sacred scriptures. The Law was safeguarded by successive generations of priests, Levites, and scribes who appeared to have taken great care in collecting and preserving the various books as they were written until the close of the Old Testament canon.

The closest thing to an official Jewish endorsement of Old

Testament canon can be found in the Babylonian Talmud which confirms the fact that with the completion of the Book of Malachi around the year 425 B. C. the canon was closed on the Old Testament: "After the latter prophets Haggai, Zechariah, and Malachi, the Holy Spirit departed from Israel."[1] The first century Jewish historian, Josephus, also acknowledged this in his writings:

> From Artaxerxes (this refers to the time of the writing of Malachi, mine) until our time everything has been recorded but has not been deemed worthy of like credit with what preceded, because the exact succession of the prophets ceased. But what faith we have placed in our own writings is evident by our conduct; for though so long a time has now passed, no one has dared to add anything to them, or to take anything from them, or to alter anything in them.[2]

Both of these statements clearly indicate that the Jews considered the Holy Spirit's supervision in the writing of the Old Testament to have ceased after the Book of Malachi. With the end of the last of the minor prophets, the Old Testament canon was completed and no additional works were added.

Besides these isolated Jewish supports for the Old Testament canon, Jesus Christ repeatedly offered His unqualified endorsement. This is one of the most convincing supports of the Old Testament's canonicity (see Section I, Chapter 13). Though Jesus challenged the ecclesiastical authorities for their man-made interpretations and traditions which they attached to the scriptures, neither He nor the scribes and Pharisees disagreed about the absolute authority of the Old Testament. Christ contended with them because they put their traditions on the same level of authority as the scriptures.

Though, at various seasons, minor disputes arose over such

---

1 Babylonian Talmud, Sanhedrin, VII-VIII, 24.
2 Josephus, Contra Apion I.

books as the Song of Solomon, Ecclesiastes, Esther, Ezekiel, and Proverbs, they never jeopardized the overwhelming consensus of opinion concerning the canonicity of these books. At the Jewish Canonical Council at Jamnia in A. D. 90, the acknowledgement that these books were sacred scripture was upheld. Though no formal or binding decisions were made, this council helped establish the canonicity of the totality of the Old Testament books as we now know it by recognizing that which had already been accepted for centuries.

The Same Old Testament

The Old Testament canon accepted by the Jews and later by Christ and the early church is exactly the same as the thirty-nine books in our present Protestant Bibles, even though the number of books and sequential order differs (i.e., the Jews do not divide Samuel, Kings, and Chronicles into two books each, they combine Ezra and Nehemiah, they consider the twelve minor prophets as one book, and place Chronicles last instead of Malachi).

Modern Christians have classified the thirty-nine books comprising the Old Testament into four basic divisions: 1) five books of the Law (Genesis—Deuteronomy); 2) twelve of history (Joshua—Esther); 3) five books of poetry (Job—Song of Solomon); and 4) seventeen of prophecy (Isaiah—Malachi). However, the Jews divided the Old Testament into three categories consisting of twenty-four books: 1) the Laws of Moses (the Torah) containing the five books of the Pentateuch; 2) the books of the prophets which also included the historical books (this division includes what the Jews refer to as the Former Prophets: Joshua, Judges, Samuel, and Kings; and the Latter Prophets: Isaiah, Jeremiah, Ezekiel, and the twelve minor prophets); and 3) the "writings" (Kethurim) or poetical writings (Psalms, Proverbs, Job, Song of Solomon [Canticles], Ruth, Lamentations, Ecclesiastes, Esther, Daniel, Ezra-Nehemiah, and Chronicles) which were referred to as the "Psalms" because it is the largest book in this section. Christ alluded to this threefold division when He referred to the Old Testament prophecies related to Himself: "Everything must be fulfilled that is written about me in the Law of Moses, the Prophets and the Psalms" (Luke 24:44). Before the formation of the New Testament, this body of sacred Jewish literature was simply called "The Scriptures."

The Accuracy of Old Testament Texts

In 1631, the King's printers, Robert Barker and Martin Lucas, printed an edition of 1,000 copies of the Bible with the word "not" left out of the seventh commandment. It then read, "Thou shalt commit adultery." Because of this monumental mistake, they were fined a hefty 3,000 pounds. However, when we consider the accuracy of the Jewish copyists in transcribing the Old Testament text, blatant errors of this magnitude cannot be found. Because the Jews held such an intense reverence towards their sacred scriptures, they strove to scrupulously preserve their absolute accuracy with an almost fanatical determination. For hundreds of years, they took great pains to insure the scriptures' accuracy.

The Talmudists and Massoretes

Over the centuries, successive generations of dedicated Jewish scribes strove to insure the accuracy of transcribing their scriptures. Two of the most noted groups of copyists during the New Testament period were the Talmudists and the Massoretes. Both the Talmudists (A.D. 100-500) and the Massoretes (A.D. 500-900) executed such an intense and almost neurotic care in transcribing the sacred texts that we can be confident of the resulting reliability of the Old Testament manuscripts existing today. As William Green commented, "It may safely be said that no other work of antiquity has been so accurately transmitted."[3]

Both companies of copyists followed an intricate system of safeguards which governed the copying of the sacred scrolls against "scribal slips". The earlier Talmudists, for example, rigidly adhered to such disciplines as the required type of writing material, the manner in which it was bound, the mandatory length and width of written columns per page, the color of ink (black) prepared according to a precise recipe, the absolute rule that nothing, not even a word, letter, jot, or tittle be copied from memory, and even the style of dress to be worn during the process of transcribing. So strict were their transcribing disciplines that they were even forbidden to take notice of a king if addressed by him while writing the name of God!

The Massorete scholars followed in the footsteps of their Talmudist forerunners. There were three main systems of Massoretic transmission. They were the Babylonian, the Palestinian, and the Tiberian, but by the tenth century A. D., the Tiberian school rose to the ascendency under the leadership of the family of ben Asher and by the twelfth century, their text became the only recognized form of the Hebrew scriptures. They undertook the laborious task of editing, systematizing, and standardizing the Hebrew text. They developed an official text out of the various manuscripts which had been preserved to their day. They were also responsible for adding vowel signs during the eighth century. This was due to the fact that the Hebrew alphabet consists of consonants and contains no written vowels. They invented vowel signs as a reading help to facilitate proper pronunciation. Their work, known as the Massoretic text, forms the basis for the standard Jewish texts of today. It is accepted as authoritative by both Christians and Jews alike.

Their care in transcribing even surpassed that of the Talmudists. They developed a complicated system of

---

3 William Green, **General Introduction to the Old Testament - The Text,** p. 191.

mathematical cross-checking and grammatical referencing to insure copying accuracy. Each letter was checked and rechecked. If a single mistake was found, the entire page was destroyed. So exacting and meticulous were the Massorete copyists that they counted the precise number of verses, words, and individual letters. They also cataloged the unique alphabetic arrangements and configurations of sentences. They even measured the proscribed space between each letter and calculated the middle word and letter in each book. They constantly compared and cross-checked new copies with these calculations to make sure they agreed. If there was any discrepancy or miscount, they searched until they pinpointed the error and corrected it.

Of the approximately 1,000 Massorete manuscripts in existence prior to the printing of the first Hebrew Bible by movable type in 1488, the oldest dates from A.D. 895. Among these there are almost no variations of significance. Their remarkable agreement attests to the Massorete scribes' exacting diligence in transcribing. As Robert Dick Wilson noted:

> An examination of the Hebrew manuscripts now in existence shows that in the whole Old Testament there are scarcely any variants (differences in textual renderings, mine) supported by more than one manuscript out of 200 to 400, in which each book is found. . . . The Massoretes have left to us the variants which they gathered and we find that they amount altogether to about 1,200, less than one for each page of the printed Hebrew Bible. . . . The various readings are for the most part of a trivial character, not materially affecting the sense.[4]

Though we may consider their scribal behavior to be excessive, it showcases their intense reverence for the scriptures which helped insure the accuracy of the original texts. As Kenyon noted:

---

4 Robert Dick Wilson, **Scientific Investigation of the Old Testament**, pp. 69, 70, 179.

These trivialities, as we may rightly consider them, had yet the effect of securing minute attention to the precise transmission of the text; and they are but an excessive manifestation of a respect for the sacred Scriptures which in itself deserves nothing but praise. The Massoretes were indeed anxious that not one jot nor tittle, not one smallest letter nor one tiny part of a letter, of the Law should pass away or be lost.[5]

Since their transcribing efforts essentially preserve the Old Testament texts endorsed by Jesus Christ as divinely inspired and infallible, we can confidently conclude that their labors have helped guarantee that our existing manuscript copies of the Old Testament are essentially the same as those approved by Christ during the first century. Because of God's preserving power and the Jewish-scribes' reverent attention to editing and detail, the reliability of the Old Testament texts has been protected and maintained through the centuries.

Existing Old Testament Manuscripts

Until the discovery of the Dead Sea Scrolls, the oldest existing manuscript copies of the Hebrew text dated around A. D. 900, making a substantial time gap of 1,300 years between them and the completion of the Old Testament canon in 400 B. C. Surprisingly enough, the very reason why we do not possess the original, firsthand manuscripts (called "autographs") or more older manuscript copies then we do can be directly attributed to the extreme care of the Jewish copyists to preserve the accuracy and purity of the scriptures. Whenever a manuscript showed signs of age or was damaged or accidently defaced, it was promptly buried or burned. The lack of older manuscripts can also be attributed to the relentless persecution to which the Jewish people were subjected by successive empires who overran Palestine. The holocaust of 66-70 A.D. at the hands of the

---

5 Sir Frederic Kenyon, **Our Bible and the Ancient Manuscripts**, p. 38.

Roman legions, culminating with the destruction of Jerusalem, the burning of their temple, and the disbanding of the nation of Israel also resulted in the destruction of countless synagogues and sacred Jewish writings.

The oldest existing Hebrew manuscripts were the product of the Jewish Massoretes (A.D. 500—900) who, as we have seen, diligently supervised the transcribing of the sacred scriptures. The text they completed is referred to as "The Massoretic Text." The oldest of these is **The Cairo Codex** (A.D. 895), prepared by the ben Asher family, which contains both the former and latter prophets. Other Hebrew texts include: **The Codex of the Prophets of Leningrad** (A.D. 916), which contains Isaiah, Jeremiah, Ezekiel, and the twelve minor prophets; **The Codex Babylonicus Petropalitanus** (A.D. 1008), which was transmitted from a revised text of Rabbi Aaron ben Moses ben Asher, is located in Leningrad Russia and represents the oldest complete manuscript text of the Old Testament; **The Aleppo Codex** (A.D. 900 +), considered to be extremely valuable; **The British Museum Codex** (A.D. 950), which contains a portion of Genesis through Deuteronomy; and **The Reuchlin Codex of the Prophets** (A.D. 1105).

The Septuagint

Added to the Massoretic texts which have survived the ravages of time are other sources which help corroborate the accuracy of Old Testament transmission. Of these, the Greek translation of the Old Testament, called the Septuagint, is the most valuable. Due to the prevailing Hellenistic influence of the Greek civilization resulting from the extensive conquests of Alexander the Great (356-323 B.C.) many Jewish people of the Dispersion adopted the Greek language. In about 280 B.C., the curator of the great library in Alexandria, Egypt submitted a request to Ptolemy II Philadelphus (285-246 B.C.) to add the

Hebrew Law to his library collection. Seventy-two Jewish scribes were assembled to translate the Pentateuch into Greek. Over the following years, the remainder of the Old Testament, along with fourteen apocryphal books, were translated from Hebrew into Greek. It has been called the Septuagint because, as legend has it, it supposedly was translated in just seventy days. Others attribute its name to the fact that seventy men translated it. It is commonly designated by the Roman numerals LXX for seventy.

The value of this work lies in the fact that it was in common use and widespread circulation during the time of Christ and the apostles who frequently quoted from it. The evidence is clear that the early church, while rejecting the apocryphal books, did accept the Septuagint as an accurate rendering of the Word of God. It was the Christian churches' wide use of this version which eventually led the Jews to reject this translation in favor of the Hebrew texts preserved by the Talmudists. Because it was translated from the Hebrew texts available during the third century B.C., it helps us establish the accuracy of the Hebrew texts of that time period and the existing Massoretic texts of the ninth century A.D. Extensive textual criticism has shown them to be very close and underscores the accuracy of transmission over the centuries.

Additional Sources

Besides the Septuagint, a variety of additional sources help support the accuracy of Old Testament transmission. These include **The Latin Vulgate,** which was translated by Jerome from Hebrew and Greek into Latin about A. D. 400; **The Syriac Version,** translated from Hebrew about A.D. 200; and **The Samaritan Pentateuch** (400 B. C.), which had been passed down, independent of the Jewish line of transmission, by the Samaritans from the time of Nehemiah. Though these contain minor variations, none of them are major enough to affect a single doctrine or incident in the Old Testament.

Other ancient works contain numerous quotations and references from the Old Testament which help establish its manuscript accuracy. These include **The Jewish Targums** (about A. D. 500); **The Jewish Mishnah** (A. D. 200); **The Jewish Gemaras** (Palestinian, A. D. 200, and Babylonian, A. D. 500); **The Midrash** (100 B. C.—A. D. 300); **The Book of Jubilees; The Book of Ecclesiasticus; The Talmud; The Writings of Josephus and Philo; The Zadokite Fragments,** and many quotations of the Old Testament by Christ and the apostles. All of this lends supporting evidence to the accuracy of Old Testament preservation and transmission over the centuries.

The Dead Sea Scrolls

The discovery of the Dead Sea Scrolls in 1947 is considered to be the most significant manuscript find in modern archaeological history. The announcement of their discovery sent shock waves through both the religious and academic communities. There was initial concern by some that the Dead Sea Scrolls would cast a negative light upon the Bible's reliability, while Bible critics hoped that this is precisely what they would prove once and for all. However, extensive textual study over the last thirty-five years has found just the opposite. They have provided the strongest evidence, to date, concerning the accuracy of the Old Testament texts, and have dramatically pushed back the tides of higher criticism.

The initial discovery of the scrolls was inadvertently made by Muhammed ed Dhib, a Bedouin shepherd boy, who was searching for one of his family's lost goats. As he was wandering around desolate bluffs northwest of the Dead Sea, he stumbled upon a hole in a cliff. Out of curiosity, he tossed in a stone and heard the sound of pottery shattering. He crawled through the cave opening and found several large earthen jars containing leather scrolls.

These scrolls had been providentially preserved in the arid desert climate for nearly 1,900 years. They were the product of a monastic, communal society called the Qumran which lived in the Dead Sea region between 150 B. C. to A. D. 70. Much of their time was spent in an ascetic lifestyle devoted to studying and copying the scriptures while they awaited the apocalyptic return of their expected Messiah. They probably concealed the scrolls in caves to protect them from the approaching Roman legions in A. D. 70. There they remained until accidently discovered 1,900 years later.

The subsequent discovery of additional scrolls in ten other caves in the Dead Sea region comprise a combined total of nearly 40,000 inscribed fragments from which over 500 assorted religious and biblical books have been reconstructed. The leather scrolls are dated between 200 B. C. and A. D. 68. As of this date, all of the Old Testament books except Esther are represented by the finds. Of the scripture fragments, those of Deuteronomy, Isaiah, and Psalms are the longest. The most complete scrolls include two from Isaiah, one of Psalms, and one of Leviticus. One of these is a completed copy of the Book of Isaiah, making this manuscript 1,000 years older than any previously possessed copy. The similarities between it and the Massoretic copies of the tenth century A.D. are striking and overwhelmingly substantiate the accuracy of the oldest manuscript copies of the Massoretic texts in existence. As Robert Boyd confirmed:

> No truth of the Christian faith in these scrolls differs from what we find in the King James Version of the Bible. Christ read from an Isaiah scroll (Luke 4:16-21), and read what we read in our own Bibles. When we quote the Word of God we quote the same truths as Christ when He referred to the Scriptures. What difference we find in the Biblical scrolls is minute. Our King James Version says "waters of Dimon" in Isaiah 15:9. The "Isaiah Scroll" says "Waters of Dibon." The King James Version says "crooked places straight" and the Isaiah Scroll says "hills straight" (Isa. 45:2). The King James Version says "pour down righteousness," and the Isaiah Scroll says "rain down righteousness" (Isa. 45:8). Agreement between the

"Isaiah Scroll," the Hebrew (Masoretic text, mine) text . . . and the text of our King James Version shows the care with which the scribes of old copied Bible manuscripts. "Isaiah" is still the same book it was when it came from the pen of the prophet Isaiah over twenty-seven hundred years ago.[6]

The Dead Sea Scrolls conclusively demonstrate the extraordinary diligence and precision of the Jewish copyists of the sacred scriptures over a thousand year period, and provide us with tremendous confidence in the reliability of our Old Testament texts.

Furthermore, the importance of their discovery has helped defend the Bible's reliability in many areas. As Howard F. Vos confirmed:

> The significance of the Dead Sea Scrolls is tremendous. They have pushed the history of the Old Testament text back 1,000 years (they date during the first two centuries B. C. and the first century A. D.). Second, they have provided an abundance of critical material for research on the Old Testament, comparable to what has been available to New Testament scholars for many years. Third, the Dead Sea Scrolls have provided a more adequate context for the New Testament, demonstrating, for instance, the essential Jewish background of the gospel of John—rather than a Greek background, as scholars have frequently asserted. Fourth, they help to establish the accuracy of the Old Testament text. The Septuagint (Greek Old Testament) has been shown by studies in the scrolls to be more nearly accurate than had previously been thought. Fifth, it has been demonstrated that there were other families of texts besides the Massoretic (traditional), which has served as the text of our Hebrew Bibles for so long. Yet, when all of the evidence is in, perhaps scholars will conclude that the true

---

6 Robert T. Boyd, **A Pictorial Guide to Biblical Archaeology**, p. 171.

text of the Old Testament is in excess of 95 percent of what we have had in the Massoretic text all along.[7]

The Apocryphal Books

As we have previously seen, the translators of the Greek Septuagint included an additional set of books and chapters referred to as the Apocrypha. The word "apocrypha" (Gr. *apokrupha*) means "hidden or concealed." It is applied to those ecclesiastical writings which are secret or mysterious in nature, unknown in origin, spurious, forged, or generally rejected as uncanonical.

These fifteen books include **I Esdras** (referred to as III Esdras in post-Trentian editions of the Latin Vulgate, while the canonical Ezra and Nehemiah are called I and II Esdras ["*esdras*" being the Greek form of Ezra]); **II Esdras** (designated as IV Esdras in the Vulgate), **Tobit; Judith; Additons to the Book of Esther** (it appeared as an appendix to Esther in the Vulgate); **The Wisdom of Solomon** (referred to as "Liber Sapientiae" in the Vulgate); **Ecclesiasticus** (or the Wisdom of Jesus the Son of Sirach); **Baruch; The Epistle to Jeremiah** (in the Vulgate it is attached to Baruch and appears as the sixth chapter of Baruch in most English versions); **The Prayer of Azariah and the Song of the Three Young Men; Susanna** (it follows Daniel as chapter 13 in the Vulgate); **Bel and the Dragon** (it appears as Daniel, chapter 14, in the Vulgate); **The Prayer of Manasseh; The First Book of the Maccabees;** and **The Second Book of Maccabees.**

All of these books were included in Jerome's Latin Vulgate Version. The Roman Catholic Church officially endorsed all of these books except I and II Esdras and the Prayer of Manasseh at the Counter-Reformation Council of Trent in 1546, and includes them in all of their Bible versions. However, Protestants reject them as inspired canon. The Roman Catholic hierarchy endorsed these books at this late date because of the pressure of the Protestant Reformers against many of their unbiblical doctrines, decrees, and dogmas, and because the apocryphal books

---

7 Howard F. Vos, **An Introduction to Bible Archaeology,** p. 52.

169

provided the only semblance of support for a limited number of their teachings, beliefs, and practices (i.e., purgatory, prayers for the dead, etc.).

While some of these works occasionally contain material of literary merit and historical value (i.e., I & II Maccabees), they must, ultimately, be rejected as inspired canon for the following reasons:

1. They were written long after the Old Testament canon was completed in about 400 B.C., and lack the prophetic character which qualifies them as the inspired Word of God.
2. None of the apocryphal writers claim divine inspiration, and some openly disclaim it (i.e., Prologue to Ecclesiasticus; I Mac. 4:46; 9:27; II Mac. 2:23; 15:38).
3. No Hebrew canons include them, though the more liberal Greek Septuagint includes them.
4. Josephus did not include the apocryphal books in his list of canonical books (Contra Apion 1:8).
5. Other Jewish sources such as Philo, a Jewish philosopher from Alexandria (20 B.C.—A.D. 40), quoted extensively from the Old Testament but never quoted from the Apocrypha even though he was obviously intimately acquainted with the Septuagint, which originated in Alexandria.
6. Jewish scholars at the Canonical Council of Jamnia (A.D. 90) did not recognize them.
7. The Palestinian Jews rejected the apocryphal books.
8. Though Jerome (A.D. 340-420) was badgered into hurriedly translating the apocryphal books by two bishop friends who were fond of the books of Tobit and Judith, he did so reluctantly against his wishes. He flatly rejected them as canon and stated that the apocryphal books were in no sense a portion of God's Word. However, after his death, they were added to his translation of the Bible called the Latin Vulgate

THE OLD TESTAMENT CANON

Version. This version formed the basis for all Roman Catholic translations until the mid-twentieth century.

9. The apocryphal books contain numerous historical, factual, and geographical inaccuracies and anachronisms, as well as blatant myths, folklore, and fictitious accounts (i.e., in the Book of Judith [1:1-7], Nebuchadnezzar is called the King of Assyria and states that he reigned in Nineveh even though he was the King of Babylon [Daniel 4:4-6, 30]; in the Book of Baruch, it claims to be written by a man of that name who was the secretary to Jeremiah [1:1]. However, he quotes from the Book of Daniel which wasn't even penned until long after the time of Jeremiah).

10. They teach doctrines which are false, promote questionable ethics, and foster practices which are inconsistent with the accepted standards of biblically inspired teaching (i.e., the books of Judith and Tobit justify falsehood and deception, and make salvation dependent upon meritorious works; Tobit teaches that almsgiving will deliver a person from death [Tobit 12:9; 14:10, 11]; Ecclesiasticus and The Wisdom of Solomon promote an "end justifies the means" morality based upon expediency; The Wisdom of Solomon teaches the creation of the world out of pre-existent matter [7:17]; Ecclesiasticus teaches that the giving of alms will make an atonement for sin [3:3]; and they include writings which justify suicide, assassination, and teach praying for the dead).

11. Jesus and the New Testament writers never quoted from the Apocrypha, even though there are hundreds of quotes and references from almost all of the canonical books of the Old Testament.

12. Many of the early church fathers spoke out against the Apocrypha such as Melito, Origen, Jerome, Tertullian, Cyril of Jerusalem, and Athanasius.

13. No canon or council of the Christian church for the

171

first four centuries recognized or endorsed them as inspired.

14. Luther and the Reformers unanimously rejected their canonicity.
15. Many Roman Catholic scholars, popes, and even some bishops at the Council of Trent rejected their canonical status.

Apocalyptic Literature

Another category of non-canonical writings which competed for scriptural inclusion among the Old Testament books is referred to as the "Apocalyptic Literature". However, these books were not included in the Septuagint, accepted by the Jews, or embraced by the Roman Catholic Church. They were mainly written during the inter-testamental period. Their subject matter deals heavily with the end of the world, the establishment of God's kingdom on earth, and the supposed revelations and purposes of God, hence, the title "apocalyptic," which comes from the Greek word *apokalypsis,* meaning "revelation or unveiling."

They were designed to give comfort to the Jewish peoples who were struggling under the oppressive burden of Gentile kingdoms which had conquered them. They gave hope to the Jews that a day was coming in which God would judge the ungodly, deliver Israel, and establish His glorious kingdom in the earth. They follow the characteristics of the Book of Daniel, but are poor imitations. Some of their distinctive features include: 1) the alleged revelation of God's divine purposes through dreams, visions, or by the seer's journey to heaven to receive insights into the secrets of God's creation and the future; 2) a heavy emphasis on symbolism to convey prophetic predictions; 3) pseudonymity—the anonymous authors used the falsely ascribed name of a reputable prophet to lend legitimacy to their writing. They were compelled to attribute their prophecies to familiar Old Testament saints because, in their day, God was no

longer speaking through the prophets; **4)** pseudo-predictive—
they employed a false predictive element by pretending to be
prophetic works of the distant past which were foretelling
apocalyptic events which would shortly occur.
Some of these apocalypses include: **I Enoch** or **The Ethiopic
Enoch** (200—100 B.C.); **Jubilees** (second century B.C.); **The
Assumption of Moses** (late first century B.C.); **Fourth Ezra** or
Second Esdras and **The Apocalypse of Baruch** (written after the
destruction of Jerusalem in A.D. 70); **Second Enoch** or **The
Slavonic Enoch** (date uncertain); and a variety of writings found
among the Dead Sea Scrolls. Other works which do not truly fall
into the apocalyptic category but contain eschatological
material (material dealing with the study of last things or end
times) include: **The Testaments of the Twelve Patriarchs** (second century B. C.); **The 17th and 18th Psalms of Solomon**
(first century B.C.); and **The Sibyline Oracles.**

3

THE NEW TESTAMENT CANON

The final ratification of the twenty-seven New Testament books universally recognized by all branches of Christianity as being sacred canon did not take as long as its Old Testament counterpart. This was due to the compacted timeframe during which they were written (A.D. 50-90), and the added ingredient of unique external factors which helped expedite the process of canonization. These included the proliferation of counterfeit writings which competed for scriptural status, the rise of heretic sects which demanded that those books which promoted sound, apostolic doctrine be officially established to offset their corruptive teachings, and, in view of the ruthless persecutions unleashed against the church, there was an urgent need to clearly establish which writings were worth dying for and safeguarding from confiscation.

During the first century, the various books which make up our New Testament were written, copied, and circulated among Christian churches scattered throughout the Roman Empire.

Some epistles were specifically written for widely separated regions. Though, as indicated by Paul, the apostles seemed to have encouraged the circulation of their writings among other churches as well as the ones to which an epistle was originally addressed (Col. 4:16; I Thess. 5:27; II Thess. 2:15), it appears that not all the churches shared an equal familiarity with all the books that another region did. Thus, because the means of communication and circulation was laborious and time-consuming, some books were more readily recognized in certain localities than in others. The periodic outbreak of persecution against the church, coupled with imperial edicts ordering the destruction of the scriptures, also hindered the dissemination of certain books and thus rendered them more inaccessible or less familiar to certain regional congregations. Though, as a whole, the church was acquainted with the majority of New Testament works, some of the epistles such as Hebrews, II Peter, II and III John, James, and Jude were not as widely recognized or revered. Because the collection of books considered to be inspired was incomplete and varied from one geographical region of the empire to the next, the process of coming to a universal consensus on canonization took several hundred years to complete. Until the first official councils were convened, the New Testament, as we now know it, went through a gradual evolutionary process of canonization.

The Spurious Writings

Along with the canonical books, many other works were also in circulation during the period encompassing the formulization of the New Testament. Some of these works, though inferior in quality to the New Testament, are reputable Christian writings of the post-apostolic period, while others were fraudulent scriptures, outright forgeries, or apocryphal books. Many of these bogus writings were circulated, sometimes with the falsely attached name of an apostle to lend credence to their illegitimate works. These counterfeit scriptures are called

THE NEW TESTAMENT CANON

"pseudepigraphic writings" (false writings), and contain numerous errors and doctrinal heresies. Due to the spread of these fake epistles, some of which were temporarily used among the eastern churches, the need for an officially sanctioned canon of the New Testament became increasingly urgent. In an indirect manner, these spurious writings actually served as a positive external catalyst to help accelerate the finalization of New Testament canonization.

They include an assortment of "Gospels", "Acts of the Apostles", and epistles. They were first introduced into the mainstream of pseudo-Christian literature during the second century. Their contents consist of many legendary tales, ridiculous miracles, outlandish exploits, and nonsensical narratives about Christ and the apostles. Some of these works were misguided but well-intentioned inspirational supplements to minister to the faithful, some were Roman Catholic forgeries, while others were the product of outright heretics who were attempting to establish a credible basis of support for their teachings. Of these, there are nearly fifty false "Gospels," along with many "Acts" and epistles.

Some of the more familiar ones include: **The Gospel of Nicodemus** (2nd to 5th century), **The Protevangelium of James** (2nd to 5th century), **The Passing of Mary** (4th century), **The Gospel According to the Hebrews** (A.D. 100 +), **The Gospel of the Ebionites** (2nd to 4th century), **The Gospel of the Egyptians** (A.D. 130-150), **The Gospel of Peter** (A.D. 150), **The Gospel of Pseudo-Matthew** (5th century), **The Gospel of Thomas** (2nd century), **The Gospel of the Nativity of Mary** (6th century), **The Arabic Gospel of the Childhood** (7th century), **The Gospel of Joseph the Carpenter** (4th century), **The Apocalypse of Peter** (A.D. 150), **The Acts of Paul** (A.D. 150), **The Acts of Peter** (A.D. 190-200), **The Acts of John** (A.D. 190-200), **The Acts of Andrew** (A.D. 190-200), **The Acts of Thomas** (A.D. 190-200), **The Letter of Peter to James** (A.D. 190-200), **The Epistle to Laodicea** (4th century), and **The Letters of Paul to Seneca** (4th century). These are but a handful of the scores of forgeries and pseudonymous writings which were circulated during the first few centuries of church history.

The Post-Apostolic Writings

Besides these fraudulent works, there were a number of writings attributed to the apostolic fathers which were circulated among the various churches along with our twenty-seven canonical books of the New Testament. Though some scholars lump these works in the same category as the New Testament apocryphal or pseudonymous books, they have been accorded a special status by others. They were written at a very early date in church history, sometimes one generation removed from the apostles, and afford us invaluable insights into the overlapping period of the first century church and the post-apostolic period. Prior to the official ratification of the New Testament, a few of these works vied for an equal status with the scriptures and were temporarily regarded as such in some quarters of Christendom. The value and esteem paid to them by some Christians forced the church to consider very carefully those works which were truly inspired and superior.

These works include: **The First Epistle of Clement to the Corinthians** (A.D. 95) - Clement was a contemporary of Peter and Paul, and was a bishop of the church in Rome. This letter is a gentle exhortation against a feud which had broken out in the Corinthian church. It was valued by many, and was read publicly in many churches. It is included alongside of our present New Testament in the Codex Alexandrinus (A.D. 400); **The Epistle of Polycarp to the Philippians** (A.D. 110) - Polycarp was a disciple of the Apostle John. He penned this epistle to the Philippian church in response to their requests for advice. It is very similar in nature to Paul's writings; **The Epistle of Barnabas** (A.D. 90-120) - This is a general epistle addressed to all Christians and is included in the Codex Sinaiticus (A.D. 350), which attests to the value placed on it by many Christians. It is still uncertain whether the Barnabas of Acts actually wrote this letter; **The**

Epistles of Ignatius (A.D. 100) - He was a disciple of Polycarp. As he was being escorted to Rome to face martyrdom, he wrote a series of seven epistles addressed to the Ephesians, Magnesians, Trallians, Philadelphians, Smyrnaeans, Romans, and Polycarp; **The Papias Fragments** (A.D. 100 +) - Another disciple of John who wrote an **"Explanation of the Lord's Discourse."** This writing survived until the thirteenth century, but only portions can be found in quotations from Irenaeus, Eusebius, and others; **The Didache** (or **"The Teachings of the Twelve,"** about A.D. 100) - Though not actually written by the apostles, it is a church manual of the primitive church which reflects what the unknown author considered those teachings to be. It was denied as canonical at an early date, but is considered to be an extremely valuable writing; **The Shepherd of Hermas** (A.D. 95-140) - It is considered to be the "Pilgrim's Progress" of the early church because of its allegorical treatment of the Christian life. It was read in many churches until the time of Jerome, and is also included in the Codex Sinaiticus; **The Apology of Aristides** - He was an Athenian philosopher who wrote a **"Defense of Christianity"** to Emperor Hadrian in A.D. 125, and another to Antonius in A.D. 137; **Justin Martyr** (A.D. 100-167) - A philosopher converted from the philosophical schools of Greece who also wrote the **"Apologies"** to Emperor Antonius defending Christianity, and a **"Dialogue With Trypho,"** which is a debate with a Jew about the Messiahship of Jesus; **The Second Epistle of Clement,** also known as the **"Ancient Homily"** (A.D. 120-140)—It is uncertain whether Clement of Rome actually wrote this sermon; and **The Epistle of Diognetus** - The anonymous author of this defense of Christianity claimed to be a disciple of the apostles.

Post-Apostolic Quotations

From as early as the beginning of the second century, there are indications that the New Testament began to informally take shape. As we have seen (Section I, Chapter 12), the post-apostolic fathers quoted profusely from the New Testament. The references of these extra-biblical writers, often during seasons of life-threatening persecution, serve as an unofficial endorsement of which books they considered to be authoritative scripture. The writings of these reputable church leaders reveal, at a very early date, which body of books were in general use and recognized as inspired. Their repeated referral to the New Testament books helped narrow the field in determining the canon. Some of these works are: **The Didache** (A.D. 100) - Contains twenty-two quotations from the Gospel of Matthew and includes references to Luke, John, Acts, Romans, Thessalonians, and I Peter; **Papias** (A.D. 70-155) - In his work entitled, **"Explanation of the Lord's Discourse,"** he quotes from John and mentions traditions concerning the origin of Matthew and Mark; **Clement of Rome** (A.D. 95) - In his **Epistle to the Corinthians,** he quotes from, or refers to, Matthew, Luke, Romans, Corinthians, Hebrews, I Timothy, and I Peter; **Ignatius** (A.D. 70-110) - In his seven epistles, he quotes from Matthew, John, Acts, Romans, I Corinthians, Ephesians, Philippians, Galatians, Colossians, James, I and II Thessalonians, I and II Timothy, and I Peter; **Polycarp** (A.D. 110) - In his **Epistle to the Philippians,** he quotes from Philippians and includes phrases from nine other of Paul's epistles and I Peter. His statement that, "I have letters from you, and from Ignatius. I shall send yours to Syria, as you request; and I am sending the letter of Ignatius to you, with others, and the present one of my own" (verse 14) is strong evidence that at the beginning of the second century, churches were already involved in accumulating a body of literature which they considered to be inspired; **The Epistle of Barnabas** (A.D. 90-120) - Includes quotes from Matthew, John, Acts, and II Peter; **Irenaeus** (A.D. 130-200) - Gives over 1,800 quotes from most of the New Testament books; **The Shepherd of Hermas** (A.D. 96-140) - Includes numerous New Testament references; **Justin Martyr** - Gave over 300 quotations from the New Testament books, mentions Revelation, and referred to the Gospels as "The Memoirs of the Apostles"; **Ter-**

tullian (A.D. 160-220) - Gave 3,800 quotes from the Gospels and a combined total of over 7,000 from the New Testament; **Hippolytus** (A.D. 170-235) - Gave more than 1,300 references; **Origen** (A.D. 185-254) - Wrote more than 6,000 works in which he included an astounding 18,000 New Testament quotations!; **Cyprian** - Gave 1,030 quotes; and the Christian historian, **Eusebius** (A.D. 264-340) - Provided us with over 5,000 quotations from all the New Testament books.

Early Canonical Listings

The gradual evolution of our present New Testament canon took shape in stages. Some of the earliest lists of canonical books were compiled in the second century. As F. F. Bruce noted:

> The first steps in the formation of canon of authoritative Christian books, worthy to stand beside the Old Testament canon, which was the Bible of our Lord and His apostles, appear to have been taken about the beginning of the second century.[1]

One of the earliest lists, surprisingly, was not compiled by a Christian but by the heretic Marcion around A.D. 140. His canon was drawn up to serve his heretical self-interests. He drew a distinction between the Creator-God of the Old Testament, which he considered to be inferior to the God revealed in the New Testament. He, consequently, rejected the entire Old Testament, along with those sections of the New Testament which he considered to be tainted with a Judaistic influence. His list included only the Gospel of Luke, though edited of any "Jewishness", because it was the most Gentile of Gospels, and ten of Paul's epistles including Romans through II Thessalonians, and Philemon. He omitted the three pastoral epistles. His partial list did not accurately reflect the overwhelming consensus of other Christians concerning those books which were con-

---

1 F. F. Bruce, **The New Testament Documents: Are They Reliable?**, p. 23.

sidered canonical. However, what makes his list so important is the fact that he had to appeal only to those books which were widely accepted as authoritative scripture in order to support his teachings.

Another early list, dating from the end of the second century, is the "Muratorian Fragment". It was so called because it was first published in Italy in 1740 by Cardinal L. A. Muratori. Though the first part is partially destroyed, it clearly alludes to Matthew and Mark because it refers to Luke as the "third Gospel". It mentions John, Acts, nine of Paul's letters addressed to churches (Romans, I and II Corinthians, Galatians, Ephesians, Philippians, Colossians, and I and II Thessalonians), four letters addressed to individuals (Philemon, Titus, and I and II Timothy), along with Jude, two epistles of John, and the apocalypse of John. His list also includes the pseudepigraphic "Apocalypse of Peter" and "The Wisdom of Solomon". It mentions "The Shepherd of Hermas" as worthy to be read, but qualifies that it should not be included with the prophetic or apostolic writings.

The Old Syriac Version of the Bible, which dates from the middle of the second century, included all the New Testament books except the general epistles (James, I and II Peter, I, II, and III John, Jude, and Revelation). The Old Latin Version, compiled at about the same period, omits Hebrews, James, and II Peter.

Around A.D. 170 Tatian compiled the first fourfold harmony of the Gospels. It is called the "Diatessaron" (meaning a harmony of four parts). At about the same time, Paul's writings were being collected into a group referred to as the "Corpus Paulinum". Shortly after, the epistle to the Hebrews was added to this Pauline group, and the general epistles of Peter, James, John, and Jude, along with the historical book of Acts, were compiled.

Another list composed by Origen (A.D. 185-254), states that the four Gospels, Acts, the thirteen Pauline epistles, I Peter, I John, and Revelation were accepted by all. However, he adds that Hebrews, II Peter, II and III John, James, and Jude, along with "The Epistle of Barnabas," "The Shepherd of Hermas," "The Didache," and "The Gospel According to the Hebrews" were held in dispute by some.

The Formal Ratification of New Testament Canon

The formal ratification of the twenty-seven books comprising our New Testament canon reached the final stages of completion during the fourth century. The last spasmodic surge of persecution against the church was executed under Diocletian. During his reign of terror, he ordered the utter destruction of the Christian scriptures. For ten years, imperial agents hunted down the sacred scriptures and had them publicly burned. Even to possess the scriptures was a treasonable act risking the death penalty. Therefore, this violent persecution placed those books thought to be inspired in a special category of consideration and confronted the church, on an extremely serious note, with the sobering responsibility of determining which books were really worth dying for.

During Diocletian's reign, Eusebius (A.D. 264-340), the noted church historian and Bishop of Caesarea, was imprisoned. However, when Emperor Constantine, who converted to Christianity, succeeded Diocletian, Eusebius became Constantine's confidant and close religious advisor. To help reverse the damage done by Diocletian, Constantine commissioned the writing of fifty Bibles under Eusebius' supervision. Through diligent research, Eusebius was able to determine the general consensus of which books should be included in the New Testament canon. In his Ecclesiastical History, he referred to four categories of books. These included: **1)** those books which were universally recognized; **2)** the disputed books (James, II Peter, and II and III John) which, though included in the twenty-seven books of his New Testament, were still in dispute among some churches; **3)** the spurious books in which he includes "The Acts of Paul," "The Shepherd of Hermas," "The Apocalypse of Peter," "The Epistle of Barnabas," and "The Didache";

and **4)** the counterfeit books of the heretics such as "The Gospel of Peter," "The Gospel of Thomas," "The Gospel of Matthias," "The Acts of Andrew," and "The Acts of John." His New Testament version included the same twenty-seven books which make up our present New Testament.

In A.D. 367, Athanasius, Bishop of Alexandria, gave us the earliest authoritative list of New Testament books which he classified as, alone, being canonical. It was exactly the same as our present New Testament. Both Jerome and Augustine followed suit shortly afterwards in the west. All of these books were accepted in the east, with the exception of II Peter, II and III John, Jude, and Revelation, which were not finally ratified and included in the Syriac Bible until A.D. 508.

For the most part, by the end of the fourth century, the canon was generally established. Two ecclesiastical councils were finally convened in North Africa to officially ratify the canonization of New Testament books. No official church council had been organized until this date because the successive waves of persecution which had been unleashed against the church during the three preceding centuries had hitherto prevented this. But with Constantine's conversion and his "Edict of Toleration," the church was free to come to a general unanimity as to which books were canonical. With the councils at Hippo Regius (A.D. 393) and Carthage (A.D. 397), the church, as a whole, accepted all of the twenty-seven books forming our New Testament.

Though some of the general epistles had been questioned in some geographical regions, they were accepted without controversy in other localities by those who were more intimately acquainted with them. This caution in some quarters was due, in large part, to the hindrances of persecution and the slow means of communication and dissemination which would have permitted a wider sphere of recognition among Christians concerning these lesser known works. The caution exercised by the church in accepting these epistles is a credit to their carefulness, discernment, and discretion. When the church, at large, was finally able to come together to decide once and for all the issue of canonicity, they were able to arrive at a universal recognition of all of our New Testament books, including those handful of letters which had previously been questioned by those less familiar with their contents and origins.

Since the close of New Testament canon at the end of the fourth century, there has never been any serious challenge to the divine validity of these works by either addition or subtraction. Though liberal theologians and numerous Bible detractors have tried to delete some books as being non-canonical, the integrity of our New Testament has stood firm. Though Christian cults such as the Mormons, Christian Scientists, and Jehovah Witnesses have tried to supplement the scriptures by adding their own erroneous writings, they have not been able to successfully circumvent the Bible's closing warning of Jesus which reads, "I warn everyone who hears the words of the prophecy of this book: If anyone adds anything to them, God will add to him the plagues described in this book. And if anyone takes words away from this book of prophecy, God will take away from him his share in the tree of life and in the holy city, which are described in this book" (Revelation 22:18,19; see also Deuteronomy 4:2; 12:32).

New Testament Manuscripts

As we have previously seen (Section I, Chapter 12), the overall manuscript evidence supporting the Bible's accuracy is overwhelming. Of the extant texts (existing texts), there are over 5,400 Greek manuscripts of the New Testament, over 10,000 of the Latin Vulgate, and at least 9,300 other early versions (i.e., Syriac, Coptic, and Armenian). A grand total of over 24,000 manuscript copies or portions of the New Testament are in existence today.

The art and science of textual criticism has helped determine the New Testament's reliability beyond any reasonable shadow of doubt. The massive abundance of manuscript copies in possession have aided textual scholars in establishing the exacting accuracy of manuscript translation and transmission, as well as the divine authorship, accuracy, and preservation of the New Testament over the last 1,900 years!

Manuscript Classifications

The existing Greek New Testament manuscripts fall into the following categories:

1. **Unicals** - These manuscripts were written on fine parchment made from animal skins called vellum. There are over 260 in existence. The unicals refer to manuscript texts written in capital letters. This required a laborious effort from the transcribing copist. Each letter had to be painstakingly executed.

2. **Cursive Scripts** - These were also written on vellum. It was a common writing style, written in a cursive or running, freehand script. The majority of existing Greek manuscripts of the New Testament were written in cursive (over 2,700 in existence).

3. **Minuscules** - Most of the cursive script manuscripts were written in the minuscule form. Around the ninth century, the cursive style was modified to a smaller, running script which linked the letters together and allowed more copy to be written on a page. This helped promote the production of books by expediting the speed in writing and the amount of information which could be placed on a single page. They date from the ninth to fifteenth centuries, and number over 2,600.

4. **Papyri** - Copies of the New Testament refer to manuscripts written on sheets made of pressed slices of paper known as papyrus, derived from a reed-like water plant which grew in the marshy ground of the Nile Delta in Egypt. This writing material was in wide use until the fourth century when it was replaced by the far more durable vellum. Until the fairly recent

discovery of a handful of papyri manuscripts (under 100) which had been preserved in the arid, desert climate of Egypt, all manuscript copies of the New Testament known to exist were written on vellum.

5. **Lectionaries** - These are books containing selected scriptural passages which were read in church services on specific days according to a liturgical calendar. We possess over 2,100 of these.

Ancient Greek Manuscripts

Of the larger extant Greek manuscripts, the most ancient and valuable are in a "codex" form. Around the second century, translators began to compose books consisting of many consecutively numbered pages placed in the same volume. The codex form was a forerunner of the essential format of modern books. These include:

1. **The Codex Vaticanus** (A.D. 325-350) - This extremely valuable Greek manuscript contains most of the New Testament. It has been housed in the Vatican Library in Rome since 1481.

2. **The Codex Sinaiticus** (A.D. 350) - The circumstances surrounding its discovery are quite colorful. It is called the Codex Sinaiticus because it was found at St. Catherine's Monastery at the base of Mt. Sinai by a German scholar named Tischendorf. In 1844, while searching through the monastery's library, he happened to notice in a wastebasket of leaves waiting to be burned some vellum pages with Greek writing. As he examined them closer, he found that they were 43 pages of ancient manuscript texts from the Septuagint Old Testament. This discovery ignited a flame of interest in Tischendorf. He diligently scoured the monastery for further manuscripts, but could find none. In 1853, he returned to resume this search but was again disappointed. Finally, in 1859, he returned for one final search. As he was talking to one of the

monks about the Septaugint copies he had chanced upon fifteen years earlier, the monk told him that he had an ancient copy of it. He delivered it to Tischendorf wrapped in a paper napkin. It was the remaining portion of the manuscript which he had previously discovered. It was eventually obtained by the Imperial Library in St. Petersburg where it remained until 1933 when the Russian government sold it to the British Museum for $510,000. It contains a total of 199 vellum leaves of the Old Testament, the entire New Testament with the exception of Mark 16:9-20 and John 7:53—8:11, the "Epistle of Barnabas," and a portion of "The Shepherd of Hermas" on 148 leaves which measure 15 x 13½ inches. It is one of the most priceless manuscripts in existence.

3. **The Codex Alexandrinus** (A.D. 400) - It appears to have originated from Alexandria Egypt. It contains nearly all of the Bible. It was presented to Charles the I of England in 1627 by the Patriarch of Constantinople. It, too, is kept in the British Museum.

4. **The Codex Ephraemi** (A.D. 400+) - It contains about half of the New Testament and is kept in Paris.

5. **The Codex Bezae** (or Beza, A.D. 450) - It has the Gospels and Acts in both Greek and Latin. It is located in the library of the University of Cambridge.

6. **The Codex Washingtonensis** (A.D. 500) - It contains the four Gospels in the order of Matthew, John, Luke, and Mark, and is kept at the Smithsonian Library in Washington, D.C. It was not discovered until 1906 in Egypt.

7. **The Codex Claromontanus** (A.D. 500+) - This manuscript contains the Pauline epistles.

Ancient Papyrus Fragments

Some of the oldest and most valuable manuscript fragments of the New testament include:

188

1. **The John Rylands Manuscript** (A.D. 130) - This is a tiny fragment of papyrus measuring 3½ x 2½ inches which contains, on one side, John 18:31-33, and on the other side, John 18:37-38. It is the oldest known manuscript of the New Testament. It was discovered in Egypt in 1920, and is located in the Rylands Library in Manchester, England.

2. **The Chester Beatty Papyri** (A.D. 200) - It contains thirty flawed papyrus leaves containing portions of Matthew, Mark, Luke, John, and Acts. Included in the Chester Beatty Collection are 86 leaves containing Romans, Hebrews, I and II Corinthians, Ephesians, Galatians, Philippians, Colossians, and I and II Thessalonians. This collection also has some Old Testament manuscripts such as Genesis, Numbers, Deuteronomy, Isaiah, Jeremiah, Ezekiel, Daniel, and Esther. Scholars consider this body of manuscripts to be the most important textual find since the discovery of the Codex Sinaiticus. This collection is housed in the Chester Beatty Museum in Dublin, Ireland.

3. **The Bodmer Papyrus II** (A.D. 150-200) - This manuscript contains most of John's Gospel, and is located at the Bodmer Library of World Literature.

These extremely rare papyrus manuscripts were discovered as a result of excavations undertaken in the desert of central Egypt by Flinder Petrie around the turn of the century. He and his colleagues, B. P. Grenfell and A. S. Hunt, uncovered ancient rubbish heaps which had been buried beneath the desert sands. They contained numerous papyrus sheets of paper which had been preserved by the dry climate for thousands of years. Over a ten-year period (1896-1906), their excavations at Oxyrhynchus yielded over 10,000 papyrus manuscripts. Most of these were everyday documents such as bills, receipts, grocery lists, certificates, personal letters, diaries, and almanacs, but a few were extremely valuable historical documents which were as old as 2,000 B.C., as well as a few papyrus fragments containing the oldest manuscript texts of the New Testament in existence. The present total of papyrus fragments of the scriptures stands at seventy-six.[2]

Syrian and Latin Versions

Other ancient manuscripts come from the Syrian and the Latin Vulgate line of biblical texts. Of the Syrian, the following are the rarest:

1. **The Old Syriac Version** (3rd century A.D.) - This is an incomplete New Testament containing only the four Gospels.
2. **The Peshito Syriac** (or Peshitta, meaning "simple") - Though originally produced during the second century to replace the Old Syriac Version, no copies of the more than 350 in existence date prior to the fourth century.
3. **The Palestinian Syriac** (A.D. 400-450).

The ancient Latin versions include: **The Old Latin** (2nd century A.D.); **The African Old Latin** (A.D. 400); **The Codex Corbiensis** (A.D. 400-500) containing the four Gospels; **The Codex Vercellensis** (A.D. 360); and **The Codex Palatinus** (5th century A.D.).

The Latin Vulgate (meaning "common") was translated by Jerome between A.D. 366-384. Several of his bishop friends urged him to translate the Bible into the common language of the people which, at the end of the fourth century, was Latin. He spent over thirty-four years at Bethlehem, mostly as a hermit in a cave, where he carried out his scholarly labors. It became the standard Bible version of the Roman Catholic Church until the late sixteenth century and, even after that date, subsequent Catholic translations of the Bible until the mid-twentieth century were based on Jerome's Latin Vulgate Version.

---

2 Bruce M. Metzger, **The Text of the New Testament,** p. 32.

Manuscript Families

Contemporary translations of the New Testament are derived from specific groupings of manuscripts, depending upon the version. They are grouped together into "text-types." These families consist of completed manuscript codices or fragments derived from a common manuscript source or geographical region. Since copies were derived from previous copies, they tend to carry the distinctive marks of that unique family line of manuscripts, including any scribal errors. These distinct family lines tend to perpetuate a textual style.

Some of these families date from an earlier period and are marginally more reliable. However, extensive textual criticism has shown that there is an amazing similarity between manuscript texts, with only the slightest differences, which have not jeopardized or contradicted any doctrinal point or rule of faith.

One of these families includes what scholars commonly refer to as the "Majority Text." This is the majority grouping of existing manuscripts of the New Testament. In fact, there are far more manuscripts in this family than in all the others combined. Between 80-90% of all existing Greek manuscripts come from this text-type grouping. This group is classified as the "Byzantine Family of Manuscripts" (A.D. 500 +) because they originated from the geographical region of the old Byzantine Empire which includes the countries of Turkey, Greece, Bulgaria, Albania, and Yugoslavia. It is from this large body of available manuscripts that the "Textus Receptus" (or "received text") is derived which forms the basis of the King James Bible. Because this family dates later than other available manuscript families not discovered until after the publication of the King James Bible, most scholars tend to textually favor the other, older families.

These other older manuscript families include the "Alexandrian Family" (A.D. 200-400), which contains such important manuscripts as the Codex Vaticanus and the Codex Sinaiticus, as well as the oldest manuscripts in existence (Egyptian papyri);

the "Western Family"(A.D. 200), from the area of the Western Mediterranean; and the "Caesarean Family" of manuscripts. Most modern versions of the Bible base their textual translation on the "Alexandrian Family" of manuscripts.

4

THE EVOLUTION OF
THE ENGLISH BIBLE

The Earliest Origins

The historical origin of the English Bible traces its roots back to the 7th century A.D. It was an outgrowth of the gradual Christianizing efforts which had begun in Britain as early as the second century when it was still occupied by the Roman Empire. The progress of Christianity was slow until the sixth century when Augustine and his monks landed in Southern England in A.D. 596 and began to aggressively preach the Gospel. The Bible they carried to the shores of Britain was the Latin Vulgate, but as the Old English language developed, so did the need for a Bible version in the common language of the Anglo-Saxon people. In fact, the evolution of the English Bible actually paralleled the development of the English language.

At first, the means of communicating the Bible's message to the Britons was limited to pictures, preaching, and poems.

Though the Roman Catholic hierarchy promoted a policy which restricted the reading of the scriptures to the clergy for fear that the common people might misunderstand and misuse the scriptures, some of the more enlightened among the Roman Catholic clergy in Britain took exception.

In A.D. 670, Caedmon, a monk at Whitby, composed in verse form, some lyrical, paraphrased portions of selected Bible narratives in the old English language. During the beginning of the eighth century, another member of the Catholic clergy by the name of Aldhelm, Bishop of Sharborne in Dorset, translated the Psalms into the language of the people. About A.D. 705, Egbert, who was later appointed as the Archbishop of York, translated the Gospels into the Old English for the first time. One of the greatest scholars of his day was Bede (A.D. 674-735). He was a learned monk in the writings of Greece and Rome, and was noted for his authorship of the famous "Ecclesiastical History of the English Nation." Not only was he skilled in medicine, astronomy, rhetoric, and most of the other sciences of his time, but he was deeply devoted to the study of the holy scriptures, as well. Even as he was dying on his deathbed, he was dictating to his scribe an English translation of the Gospel of John. Another contributor to the development of the English Bible was King Alfred the Great (A.D. 849-901). He was both a scholar and a devout Christian who earnestly promoted Bible reading among all the citizens of his realm. He had the Ten Commandments, part of the Psalms, and portions of the Old and New Testaments translated into English. Some Latin versions of the Gospels which have survived from this period contain a word-for-word translation into English written between the lines of Latin. They are called "glosses," or a word-for-word translation without regard to the idiom and usage of the vernacular. Around A.D. 950, a priest named Aldred produced one of these glosses. Towards the end of the tenth century, Aelfric, the Archbishop of Canterbury, translated portions of Genesis through Judges, along with other portions of the Old Testament, into English.

When the Normans invaded England in A.D. 1066 and crushed the Saxons, they ostracized the Anglo-Saxon language from the courts, books, and schools. Their conquest of Britain brought a new tongue which caused a great deal of confusion and resulted in almost no literature being produced until the thirteenth century. Only a handful of manuscripts from this period have survived as portions of the Bible translated into Anglo-Norman French.

However, in spite of the prolonged period of confusion and literary stagnation, there was one notable exception. Around A.D. 1215, an Augustinian monk by the name or Orm translated a poetical version of the Gospels and the Acts called the "Ormulum". After this, there were a couple of minor translation projects, but nothing undertaken on a scale which would provide the common man of England with the entire Bible.

John Wycliffe

The first to do so was John Wycliffe (A.D. 1320-1384). He stands out as one of the greatest pivotal characters in church history and has been referred to as the "Morning Star of the Reformation." He was born in Yorkshire in 1320 during a transition period between the Dark Ages and the dawning of the Reformation. It was a time when several important factors were converging which would act as a catalyst to promote the translation of an English Bible.

He lived during a period of great political and religious upheaval and intrigue. The Roman Catholic Church had sunk to its lowest level of corruption. In her insatiable appetite for wealth and power, she was draining the coffers of Europe and exacting an oppressive tribute from the English peoples. King Edward III finally refused to send an annual tribute to Rome. Wycliffe took a major step towards defying the abuses of Rome by siding with the king.

Wycliffe vigorously opposed the widespread corruption of the Roman Church and saw the scriptures as the surest way of breaking Rome's influence over England. Because of his ardent anti-Catholic stand, a number of papal bulls were issued against him, he was eventually brought to trial for heresy, and was condemned and excommunicated from the Roman Catholic Church. However, none of this deterred Wycliffe.

He strongly advocated that the Bible be placed in the hands of the commoner and soon began to undertake the responsibility of seeing this task accomplished. Through Wycliffe's instrumental efforts and supervision, a complete English translation from Jerome's Latin Vulgate of the New Testament was completed in 1380, and the Old Testament in 1382. Though it is questionable whether Wycliffe actually translated much of this version, it was still called the "Wycliffe Bible" because of his supervision in producing it. Several scholars worked on this joint project, with the bulk of Old Testament translation being undertaken by Nicholas of Hereford. By 1388 John Purvey, Wycliffe's secretary, completed a revised version of the Wycliffe Bible.

Before his death in 1384, Wycliffe organized an order of poor, itinerant priests who roamed all over England preaching and teaching the English Bible to the common people. They were derogatorily known as the "Lollards" (meaning "mutterers"), because they were commonly reciting and memorizing the scriptures in a low voice. This was a practice the church hierarchy found particularly offensive.

The combination of Wycliffe's Bible translation and the efforts of his followers had a tremendous impact upon the nation of England. The established church resisted his efforts and the Parliament enacted laws trying to suppress Wycliffe's translation. One of these laws was the notorious "Constitutions of Oxford," enacted in 1408, which forbade anyone from translating or reading any part of the Bible in the language of the people without the expressed permission of the ecclesiastical authorities. However, in spite of their attempts, the flames of enthusiasm and receptivity among the English people could not be quenched. Even though the people were threatened with severe penalties for reading Wycliffe's translation, the eagerness and public demand for the Bible could not be abated. His efforts only stimulated the growing interest among the common man for the Word of God and encouraged further translating efforts after his death. Though all copies of his Bible were handwritten and it was introduced sixty years before the advent of printing with movable type, the impact of his pioneering efforts cannot be overestimated. He did much to pave the way for the Reformation.

The work of Wycliffe and his followers has left an indelible imprint upon our modern day English Bible. Such familiar expressions as "strait gate," "make whole," "compass land and sea," "son of perdition," and "enter into the joy of the Lord" were the result of his translating efforts. Furthermore, his Bible acted as a cohesive and unifying force by bringing the related tongues and diverse dialects of England together into one language. It served as an indispensable aid for future translating efforts to make the Bible accessible to the English people in a common tongue. Only about 170 copies of Wycliffe's Bible are known to exist today. Of these, less than thirty contain the original translation of 1382, while the rest are copies of Purvey's 1388 revision.

Translating Efforts in Europe

During the fifteenth century, events were taking shape in Europe which would help expedite the development of the English Bible. For centuries, Constantinople, the capital of the Eastern Empire, had been the center of Greek learning. But with its fall to the Moslem invaders in 1453, its Christian scholars were forced to flee westward. They carried with them Greek manuscript copies of the Bible. This exodus led to a renewed interest in Europe in the study of the Greek language, as well as textual studies of the Bible.

One of the practical outgrowths of the renewed interest in biblical studies was the first Greek translation of the New Testament. In 1515, a Dutch Reformer by the name of Desiderius Erasmus began to assemble a Greek New Testament text in the city of Basel. At about the same time, the Roman Catholic Cardinal Ximenes of Spain was in the process of printing another Greek text called the "Complutensium Polyglot" ("Complutensium" for the city in which it was published, and "Polyglot" meaning "many tongues or languages" because it included Greek, Hebrew, and Latin). The development of this Roman Catholic translation of the Greek text catapulted Erasmus into an unofficial race to publish his text before the Catholic version was released. He was forced to hastily compile his New Testament text with those manuscripts which were available. His text was completed in 1516, four years ahead of the "Complutensium Polyglot."

Coupled with the renewal of interest in the classical languages, an intellectual revival and a quest for knowledge was sweeping over Europe. It was a period when nations were emerging from the thralldom of the Dark Ages into the light of the Renaissance and the spiritual emancipation of the Reformation. The sixteenth century witnessed the rise of nationalism, a fresh interest in exploration, discovery, and invention, and a surge of creativity in the arts and sciences. It was a time when the minds of men were throwing off the shackles of religious superstition and intellectual stagnation which had gripped Europe for nearly a millennium. This phenomenon helped promote the increased interest not only in secular fields of study, but in the sacred scriptures, as well.

While work in translating the Bible was steadily progressing in Europe, similar endeavors had lagged behind in England due to the restraints of the "Constitutions of Oxford." By the year 1500, the majority of European countries had the scriptures translated into the vernacular. The invention of Gutenberg's printing press (1454) also helped promote the publication and distribution of the Bible on the continent. England only had a few copies of Wycliffe's Bible in circulation and, by this time, the language which he had employed in his version had become outdated. England was in need of a new translation of the Bible.

William Tyndale

The man who would assume this task was William Tyndale (1494-1536). Tyndale followed in the footsteps of Wycliffe. He, too, was intensely opposed to the papal abuses and widespread corruption which hung over Europe like a thick cloud. He longed for the light of truth to break through and saw the Bible as the instrument to accomplish this task. He felt an urgent need to translate the Bible into the language of the common man in order to open their eyes to the truth.

His burden was epitomized by a heated controversy with a clergyman who said, "We would be better without God's law than the Pope's." To this, Tyndale replied, "I defy the Pope and all his laws," and added, "If God spare my life, ere many years I will cause a boy that driveth the plow to know more of the Scripture than thou dost." This resolve became the all-consuming passion of his life.

Tyndale solicited the support of the Bishop of London, but was turned down. A wealthy merchant by the name of Humphrey Monmouth came to his aid but, after six months, he was compelled to leave England in 1524 because of the prevailing spirit of resistance against his efforts. He never returned. He spent the next year in Hamburg under constant hardships, diligently translating the New Testament. He found a printer in Cologne who was willing to print his Bible and, in 1525, Tyndale published an English New Testament translated for the first time from the Greek texts published by Erasmus instead of the Latin Vulgate. However, due to Roman Catholic opposition, he was forced to flee to Worms in Germany. He was warmly welcomed and by late 1525, he managed to have 3,000 additional copies of the New Testament published.

In 1526, Tyndale arranged to have his Bibles smuggled into England hidden in bales of cotton, sacks of flour, and bundles

of flax. Their underground release excited a great demand
among the British people and ignited a firestorm of controversy
among the ecclesiastical authorities who violently opposed Tyndale's translation. His Bibles were banned and as many as could
be confiscated were destroyed. The Bishop of London,
Cuthbert Tonstall, was especially outraged and bought up as
many copies of Tyndale's Bible as he could lay his hands on and
had them publicly burned at St. Paul's Cross in London.
However, the sight of the sacred scriptures being publicly
desecrated shocked the sensitivities of the people and caused the
church's opposition to backfire. The public's demand for Tyndale's Bible only increased, and nothing the church officials did
could curb its popularity and circulation.

The opposition which Tyndale encountered only encouraged
him in his translating efforts. By 1530, he had published six editions of the New Testament with revisions and improvements in
each successive edition. With the completion of his New Testament, he began work on the Old Testament. By 1530, he had
translated the Pentateuch, and the following year completed
Jonah. He continued working on the translation of the Old
Testament until he was betrayed in 1534 by an English Roman
Catholic pretending to be his friend. He was so unflinching in
his burden that even in his prison cell, awaiting execution, he
once again revised the New Testament and added chapter
headings to the Gospels and Acts. On October 6, 1536, William
Tyndale was condemned to death as a heretic. His dying prayer
was, "Lord, open the King of England's eyes." He was strangled and burned at the stake for his efforts in placing the Bible in
the hands of the average Englishman. His diligent translating efforts would have an enduring impact on subsequent translations. Such was the quality of Tyndale's laborious efforts that
the King James Version utilized about 90% of it. His New
Testament has also formed the basis of almost every other
English version written after his.

Miles Coverdale

After Tyndale's Bible, a series of versions were published in rapid succession. This was due to the fact that England broke from Rome in 1534, and the government began to recognize the practical need of providing the people with a Bible in their own language. In 1535, one year before Tyndale's death, Miles Coverdale, as assistant of Tyndale, published the first complete English translation of the Bible on the continent for distribution in England. It was called the "Coverdale Bible." He did so with the backing of Thomas Cranmer, the Archbishop of Canterbury, and the tacit approval of King Henry VIII. Coverdale's version incorporated Tyndale's incompleted Old Testament (Genesis through II Chronicles), along with his entire New Testament, with only slight modifications. He also included minor revisions based on the Latin Vulgate and Luther's German translation. It was the first English version to use the word "biblia", or Bible. It was also the first to introduce chapter summaries, as well as separate the Apocrypha from the Old Testament books and print them by themselves as an appendix to the Old Testament.

In 1537, two new editions appeared and carried the words of royal sanction on their title pages: "Set forth with the King's most gracious license." Thus, only one year after his death, Tyndale's prophetic plea to the King of England was fulfilled.

Thomas Matthew

In that same year another English version, called the "Matthew's Bible," was released. It was edited by Thomas Matthew, another associate of Tyndale. His real name was John Rogers but because he, too, had been branded as a heretic, he adopted this alias to conceal his identity. His version also carried a royal license for publication from King Henry VIII. Rogers' work was basically a combination of Tyndale's earlier translation of the New Testament and about half of the Old Testament. The remainder of the Old Testament was a revision of the Coverdale

Bible. It was the first complete English version of the Bible to be printed in England.

The Great Bible

Because both the Coverdale and Matthew's Bible included outspoken Protestant marginal notes which offended some of the more conservative bishops and clergy, Thomas Cromwell, the Secretary of State and a close friend of Coverdale, concluded that the Matthew Bible should be revised to make it more generally accepted. Coverdale was commissioned to rid the new translation of any objectional material found in the previous versions of Coverdale and Matthew. In accomplishing this task, he also made extensive use of the Hebrew texts which were then available. The printing was begun in Paris, but with the outbreak of the Inquisition in France and the opposition of the French Inquisitor-General, he was forced to return to England to complete the work. It was released in 1539 under the full sanction of the King and Archbishop Cranmer, and was widely distributed. It was also placed in parish pulpits all over England by royal decree. It was enthusiastically received by both scholar and commoner alike.

It was called the "Great Bible" because of its large size and elaborate decorative touches. In 1540, a second edition was published with a preface by Cranmer extolling the reading of the scriptures. Because of this, subsequent editions were called the "Cranmer's Bible."

In 1539, another revision of the Matthew's Bible was published by Richard Taverner. It was called the "Taverner's Bible." It was not as popular as previous versions and was never reprinted.

Between 1539 and 1560, the momentum which had been mounting in support of Bible translation suddenly ground to a temporary halt. King Henry VIII retracted his previous support for translating the English Bible because he had had Cromwell beheaded for his opposition against the King's anti-Catholic policies and now feared that the Catholic Church would retaliate against his own life. Thus, to placate Rome, he ordered the confiscation and destruction of English Bibles, made it a crime to publicly teach from the Bible, and severely restricted its private reading.

When King Edward VI assumed the throne in 1547, he endeavored to reverse his father's anti-Bible policy and enthusiastically promoted Bible reading. During his short six-year reign, the "Great Bible" was reprinted twice (1549 and 1553), and an official order was issued placing it in every parish church in England. However, no new translation work was undertaken, and with the ascendency of Mary Tudor ("Bloody Mary") to the throne in 1553, an ardent Roman Catholic, a new wave of terror was unleashed against the Protestants in England. Numerous former church leaders such as John Rogers, Archbishop Cranmer, and hundreds more were burned at the stake. The religious atmosphere in England would not be favorable again to Protestantism until Queen Elizabeth came to. power in 1558.

The Geneva Bible

During this period of religious persecution in England, a number of Reformers sought refuge in Geneva, Switzerland. This was the home of one of the foremost theologians of the Reformation, John Calvin, along with Theodore Beza, one of the leading biblical scholars of his day. Both would help to inspire the publishing of the "Geneva Bible." The individual who was primarily responsible for the production of this version was a scholar and English exile who was Calvin's brother-in-law named William Wittingham.

In 1537, Wittingham published the "Geneva New Testament." It was the first English version printed in Roman type, and the first which divided the text into a verse arrangement and to italicize words which were added for clarity of meaning but were not found in the Greek or Hebrew manuscripts. It also included marginal notes promoting Calvinistic theology along with notes opposing the pope, though much milder in form than some earlier versions.

Wittingham and his group of scholars then set about to revise the entire Bible. They exhausted themselves for two years and finally completed the new Geneva Bible in 1560. They dedicated it to England's new queen, Elizabeth I, who had restored a favorable climate for Bible reading and distribution. It became an overnight favorite among the English people and enjoyed an enduring popularity for nearly sixty years. During its lifespan, it went through 160 editions. It was clearly superior to previous English translations, and retained its wide appeal even in the face of the "Bishop's Bible" (1568) and the first few generations of the "King James Version" (1611).

The Bishop's Bible

Even though the Geneva Bible was a better translation than the Great Bible, its marginal notes were still too abrasive and Calvinistic for the tastes of Anglican church leaders. This led to the publication of still another English version called the "Bishop's Bible." It was the result of nine English bishops who collaborated in its production. This team of qualified scholars was headed by Matthew Parker, who acted as editor-in-chief. It was a revision of the Great Bible. After seven years, it was completed and published in 1568. Though it was given a wide circulation, the Geneva Bible maintained its commanding popularity. It replaced the Great Bible as the officially endorsed version in England until the publication of the King James Version in 1611.

The Douay-Rheims Version

With England's return to the Protestant fold under Queen Elizabeth I, many staunch Roman Catholics fled England and settled in Catholic-dominated France where they established a college at Rheims. However, promotion of Bible reading in England and the succession of English translations had created an interest among these English Roman Catholics for a Bible version of their own. In 1582, Gregory Martin published a Roman Catholic version of the New Testament known as the Rheims Version.

After the college was moved to Douai, France, the Old Testament was completed in 1610. It derived its name from the location of their college and was called the Douai Old Testament. The combination of these works has been known as the "Douay-Rheims Version," or simply the "Douay Version."

It was an inferior translation to previous English versions because it depended primarily upon the Latin rather than the Hebrew and Greek texts. It also contained the Apocrypha as inspired canon, and included many marginal notes which attacked the Protestant position and interpreted scriptural passages in conformity to Roman Catholic dogma. The Rheims-Douay Bible, used by Roman Catholics up until the mid-twentieth century, was based upon a revision made by Bishop Richard Challoner between 1749 and 1763. This version is referred to as the "Challoner-Rheims Version."

5

THE KING JAMES VERSION

Background of the King James Version

Towards the end of the sixteenth century, the religious climate of England was still in a turbulent condition. The discord between the Church of England (Anglican) and Rome continued, and feuding flourished within the Anglican Church as the Puritan faction pressed for greater reforms. When reforms were slow in coming, the more radical factions of the Puritans began to abandon the Church of England and form independent churches.

The link between the Anglican Church and the government was still in force, and the ecclesiastical authorities lobbied for legal sanctions against the dissenters. The radical Puritans were officially branded as heretics in 1593 and given the ultimatum to either silence their opposition and worship in the Anglican Church or be banished from England. Many chose the latter, and fled to the continent and the colonies. However, others remained behind to work within the system for reform. What they were waiting for was a new successor to the throne who would be sympathetic to their cause.

One of the principle grievances of the times was the choice of Bible to be used in worship. At this time, three different versions were in circulation, each with a loyal following. The Geneva Bible was the favorite of the common man and the Puritans, the Bishop's Bible and the Great Bible, which it replaced as the official Bible of the Church of England, was backed by the Anglican Church. Though the Geneva Bible was a better translation, the conservative church authorities rejected it because of its marginal notes. King James also opposed the Geneva Bible for the same reason.

With the death of Queen Elizabeth, James I, who had been the King of Scotland for thirty-seven years as James VI, inherited the crown. With his ascension to the throne, the Puritans saw their opportunity to gain a favorable hearing.

A Proposal for a New Translation

In 1603, a Puritan delegation presented King James with a petition of grievances. This prompted the King to call a conference "for the hearing and for the determining of things pretended to be amiss in the Church." The conference was finally convened for three days (January 14-16) in 1604. It was known as the Hampton Court Conference. At this conference Dr. John Rainolds, the spokesman for the Puritan Party and the President of Corpus Christi College, Oxford, submitted a proposal to settle the bickering between the various factions. He proposed a new translation of the Bible without marginal notes which would prove acceptable to all parties involved. Bancroft, the Bishop of London, balked at the proposal, but King James, who harbored an intense dislike of the Geneva Bible, was in favor of the proposal. The resolution of the Hampton Court conference read:

That a translation be made of the whole Bible, as consonant as can be to the original Hebrew and Greek; and this

208

to be set out and printed, without any marginal notes, and only to be used in all Churches of England in time of divine service.

The proposal was given immediate royal backing, and the wheels were put into motion to produce a new translation of the Bible from the original Hebrew and Greek manuscripts. To accomplish this monumental undertaking, fifty-four of the best Hebrew and Greek scholars of the day were secured; however, only forty-seven actually participated in the project. They included Anglican churchmen, Puritans, and laymen. All the scholars were English with the exception of one French scholar by the name of Adrian de Sarevia, who was Canon of Westminster in 1602.

They were divided into six groups: two at Westminster, two at Oxford, and two at Cambridge. Each group was assigned a specific section of the scriptures. Each of the six groups worked on a distinct portion of the scriptures, separately at first. The Westminster group worked on Genesis to II Kings, and Romans to Jude; the Cambridge group revised I Chronicles to Ecclesiastes, and the Apocrypha (even though it was not included); and the Oxford group took Isaiah to Malachi, and the Gospels and Acts.

Guidelines for Its Translation

A specific set of fifteen rules was adopted to govern their translating efforts. The most important included the following:

(1) The Bishops' Bible should "be followed, and as little altered as the truth of the original permit"; (2) the old ecclesiastical words should be retained; (3) there were to be no marginal notes at all, except such as should be needed for the explanation of the Hebrew or Greek words; (4) whenever Tyndale's, Matthew's, Coverdale's, Whitchurch's Great Bible, here named after one of its printers, or the Geneva translation, agreed better with the original text than the Bishop's Bible, it was to be used. It was pro-

vided, too, that a comparison of translations of each individual translator with every other one in each company should be made, and when any book was completed by any group it was sent to all the other scholars outside of the regular list, if they deemed it wise so to do. Thus every man of the entire company of forty-seven passed upon the work of every other man in the company.

When special difficulties arose, outside scholars were consulted. The only marginal notes were those used to clarify Hebrew and Greek words, and to alert the reader's attention to parallel passages. Italics were used for those words not found in the original but inserted to complete the sense.

The Greek Texts Used in the King James Version

None of the older Greek manuscripts, such as the Codex Sinaiticus, Alexandrinus, and Vaticanus, were available to the scholars translating the King James Version. Some had not been discovered, or, in the case of the Codex Vaticanus, it was known to exist in the Vatican Library as early as 1448 but was unavailable because the Roman Catholic Church refused to grant permission to any outsiders to review it until 1867.

The translating team of the King James Bible used the four existing Massoretic texts of the Hebrew for their revisional work on the Old Testament. The text which they relied upon for the New Testament was based upon revisions drawn from Erasmus' 1516 edition of the Greek New Testament which rested upon a half dozen minuscule manuscripts of somewhat inferior quality, none of which dated earlier than the tenth century. However, as Howard Vos noted, "It is remarkable that, with such an impediment, so little of the King James Version can be improved as a result of more recent discoveries—a wonderful tribute to the miracle of textual preservation."[1]

In 1546, Robert Estienne, who was surnamed Stephanus,

---

1 Howard F. Vos, **An Introduction To Bible Archaeology**, pg. 46.

reprinted Erasmus' Greek New Testament. Between that date and 1551, he published four editions. His first two editions (1546 and 1549) were drawn from the Complutensium Polyglot and Erasmus' edition. His third edition (1550) leaned even more heavily upon Erasmus', though it included marginal references to fourteen additional codices, along with the Complutensium Polyglot. In his fourth and final edition (1551), he added numbered verse divisions to his text.

A few years later, Theodore Beza, an associate of John Calvin and one of the foremost scholars of his day, published nine editions of the Greek New Testament (1588-89 and 1598), based upon Estienne's fourth edition. It was this series of successive revisions from Erasmus, to Estienne, to Beza, upon which the translators of the King James Bible primarily relied.

Though the King James Bible is commonly said to have been derived from the Textus Receptus (or received text), technically speaking, this is not the case. Thirteen years after the publication of the King James Version, the Elzevir brothers published a Greek New Testament based primarily upon Beza's text. In the preface of their second edition in 1633, the publisher included the following in Latin: *"Textum ergo habes, nunc ab omnibus receptum: in quo nihil immutatem aut corruptum damus,"* meaning, "The text that you have is now received by all, in which we give nothing changed or perverted." Precisely speaking, the term "Textus Receptus" (the TR or received text) was derived from this publishing note containing the Latin words "Textum . . . Receptum," which was published twenty-one years after the release of the King James Version. However, this later edition of the Elzevir brothers differed almost imperceptibly from the texts of Erasmus, Estienne, and Beza.

Furthermore, it should be pointed out that when we refer to the King James Version as the "received text", we are not saying that it is received from God as preeminent above other Greek manuscripts, but that it was based upon the texts commonly in use at that time.

Its Release and Universal Popularity

The inclusive work of each group was completed in two years and then submitted to a special committee consisting of two members chosen from each group. After nine more months of review and revision, the overall work was presented to a general meeting of all the panels to iron out any remaining differences in opinion. The work was then reviewed by the bishops, Privy Council, and the King.

The new translation was published in 1611. Even though it was not a truly new translation, its title page bore the following:

> The Holy Bible, Conteyning the Old Testament and the New: Newly Translated out of the originall tongues: & with the former Translations diligently compared and revised: by his Majesties speciall Comandement. Appointed to be read in Churches. Imprinted at London by Robert Barker, Printer to the Kings most Excellent Majestie. Anno Dom. 1611.

Furthermore, though it is called the "authorized version" and was appointed to be read in churches, it never received the official sanction of either the King, the Parliament, or the church.

Its universal acceptance was not obtained overnight. It took nearly fifty years before it replaced the immensely popular Geneva Bible. However, in relatively short order it became the preferred Bible in Christendom and has, for the most part, retained that distinction for over 370 years. Since its release in 1611, it has undergone four revisions (1629, 1638, 1762, and 1769). It is the latter revision which is in general use today.

Some of the major reasons why it was such a valuable translation and has experienced such an overwhelming success are:

1. The personal qualifications of the revisers, who were the choice scholars and linguists of their day as well as men of profound and unaffected piety.

2. The almost universal sense of the work as a national effort, supported wholeheartedly by the king, and with the full concurrence and approval of both church and state.

3. The availability and accessibility of the results of nearly a century of diligent and unintermittent labor in the field of biblical study, beginning with Tyndale and Purvey rather than Wycliff, and their efforts to "make a good translation better."

4. The congeniality of the religious climate of the day with the sympathies and enthusiasm of the translators, as the predominant interest of their age was theology and religion.

5. The organized system of cooperative work which followed the precedent of the Geneva translators, while it may have been improved, resulted in a unity of tone in the Authorized version which surpassed all its predecessors.

6. The literary atmosphere of the late sixteenth and early seventeenth centuries paralleled the lofty sense of style and artistic touch of the translators.[2]

The Authorized Version has served as the foundation for righteousness and morality in England. As Stroughton observed:

> There can be no reasonable doubt that the pre-eminence which distinguishes the history of England among the states of Europe for the last three hundred years is to be attributed largely to the wide circulation of this volume, and the Bible reading habits of the people. It has proved a pillar of strength, bearing up and giving stability to the public and private virtue to patriotism, loyalty, obedience, and domestic affection. It is a fountain of light and love,

---

2 Norman L. Geisler and William E. Nix, **A General Introduction to the Bible**, pp. 420, 421.

illuminating the intellect and purifying the heart; the true palladium of our liberties, our peace, and our prosperity.[3]

It has served as the very foundation of religion, language and law within western civilization.

Its quality has been defended by many, of whom Maurice Price commented:

> For almost three centuries the Authorized, or King James, Version has been the Bible of the English speaking world. Its simple, majestic Anglo-Saxon tongue, its clear, sparkling style, its directness and force of utterance, have made it the model in language, style, and dignity of some of the choicest writers of the last two centuries. Added to the above characteristics, its reverential and spiritual tone and attitude have made it the idol of the Christian church, for its own words have been regarded as authoritative and binding. It has endeared itself to the hearts and lives of millions of Christians and has molded the characters of the leaders in every walk of life in the greatest nation of the world. During all these centuries the King James' Version has become a vital part of the English-speaking world, socially, morally, religiously, and politically. Launched with the endorsement of the regal and scholarly authority of the seventeenth century, its conquest and rule have been supreme. No version of private origin, even in the face of advances of scholarship, could compete with it.[4]

The King James Bible has retained its universal popularity and unique literary legacy because of the deep reverence which it has maintained among the English-speaking people of the world. Its majestic style, devotional quality, and literary beauty is unsurpassed and has endeared itself to countless millions. Untold multitudes trace their conversion experience to preach-

---

3 Stroughton, **Our English Bible**, pp. 258, 259.
4 Maurice I. Price, **The Ancestry of Our English Bible**, pg. 282.

ing from this version, and have been made "wise unto salvation" through its study. Even after three centuries, it is still the most preferred, widely read, circulated, and quoted from Bible in existence. It promises to retain its popularity for years to come.

The King James Version Compared With Other Modern Versions

During the 250 years following the publication of the King James Version, the science of textual criticism became progressively refined. As it did so, some scholars had questions about the textual differences which they had found between the Textus Receptus and other texts which had come to light. With the discovery of additional Greek manuscripts which were older than the body from which the King James Bible was drawn, an increasing number of biblical scholars began to call for a new translation of the Bible.

The older manuscripts are primarily from the "Alexandrian Family," and include the Codex Sinaiticus and Vaticanus, which form the basis of such modern translations as the Revised Standard Verson (RSV) and the New American Standard Bible (NASB). In 1881 and 1882, B.F. Westcott and F.J.A. Hort published a Greek text of the New Testament based upon these older manuscripts which were not available to the translators of the King James Version. In 1881, the English Revised Version of the New Testament was published. It used the Greek text of Westcott and Hort. Since that turning point, several translations based upon this text have been released, along with additional Greek texts such as Nextle's text and the United Bible Society Text. The discovery of papyrus manuscripts after the turn of the century has also aided scholars in their textual revisions of the New Testament. Though the Textus Receptus includes a larger number of existing manuscripts (80-90%), most modern scholars prefer relying upon the older texts.

All of this has led to an on-going and sometimes heated

debate over the reliability of the King James Bible. Numerous scholars have expressed their learned opinion in word and print. Generally, the controversy has been handled in a sensible and Christ-like manner while, at other times, it has turned into a mud-slinging contest with each side hurling charges and counter-charges of scholastic ineptitude, mindless bias, and even accusations of heresy against each other.

Each side can field an impressive array of sound arguments for preferring their version. The two schools are basically divided between those who prefer the larger body of manu-scripts, which are in essential agreement among themselves but date no earlier than the fifth century A.D., and those who prefer a smaller body of older manuscripts (10-20%) dating from the third through the fifth century which not only disagree somewhat with the King James Version, but also among themselves. However, the majority of both liberal and conservative scholars side with this latter school.

They do so because of the basic premise that the older the manuscript, the closer it is to the original autographs and, therefore, more reliable. They also consider the Textus Receptus to be inferior because of its later date and indications of editing which makes it less reliable in content and style.

Defenders of the King James Version fall back on the fact that the Textus Receptus is derived from the overwhelming majority of manuscripts in existence, which lends a convincing weight of evidence in its support. They also appeal to the factor of "providential preservation." If, as they reason, we truly believe that God has sovereignly supervised the evolution and preservation of the scriptures, then we must logically conclude that He chose to preserve the true text in the greatest number of manuscripts. They also argue that if this minority body of older manuscripts are original, then why are they so few in number, and how did the majority text become the accepted standard in the first place? They, too, can point to many obvious errors, careless mistakes, discrepancies, and even deliberate editing alterations among the older manuscripts.

The debate continues to rage, with each side offering just as conclusive arguments as the next. However, in weighing these arguments in the balance, we must be careful not to get lost in the verbal smog surrounding this controversy. We must not strain at gnats and swallow camels. On the bottom line, the differences are so trivial, affecting only one word in a thousand, and deal with such minor discrepancies as spelling, the omission or inclusion of a word, and sentence structure, that not a single doctrinal issue or rule of faith has been adversely affected. As one scholar noted, "The real text of the sacred writings is competently exact, nor is one article of faith or moral precept either perverted or lost, choose as awkwardly as you will, choose the worst by design, out of the whole lump of readings."[5]

Since textual scholars have found so little difference between the existing manuscripts, and none which jeopardize any essential points, the controversy over which current Bible translation is the best boils down to a matter of personal preference. When all is said and done, contemporary Christians need not fear the conflicting arguments of textual criticism. We can take absolute confidence in the reliability of our Bible. As Kenyon concluded, "The Christian can take the whole Bible in his hand and say without fear or hesitation that he holds in it the true word of God, handed down without essential loss from generation to generation throughout the centuries."[6]

---

5 C.F. Sitterly, **The International Standard Bible Encyclopedia**, pg. 2955.
6 Sir Frederic Kenyon, **Our Bible and the Ancient Manuscripts**, pg. 55.

6

EVALUATION OF BIBLE VERSIONS

Making the Right Choice

Selecting the right Bible version is a personal decision which should not be taken lightly. It is an important, fundamental decision which confronts each Christian. When people make important purchases such as the choice of a car, the selection of a home, or even the type of bed they sleep upon, they usually take the time to carefully check out the product first to make sure they're not buying a "lemon" or something that doesn't suit their needs. The discerning shopper does not make impulsive choices. So should it be with the process of selecting the right Bible version for you.

Because of the contribution of dedicated biblical scholars, we have at our disposal an impressive array of Bible translations and paraphrases from which to choose. Some are valuable as a primary reading or study Bible, while others are useful as secondary study aids or supplementary reading helps. However, the high caliber of scholarship which has gone into most available versions should give those who are cautious about selecting a quality version of the Bible a great deal of confidence.

The following list is purposefully concise. Furthermore, it is not an exhaustive list of all available Bible translations. It only represents the most well-known versions. Although my personal bias may occasionally "bleed through" the pages, it is not my intent to subtly suggest which version is best for you. Though there are several I would recommend above others, the ultimate choice must be left to the discretion of the reader. The distinctive features which an individual is looking for may be found in one version while not in another (i.e., the style of language, the flow of thought, the manuscript groups from which it was derived, its study aids, ring of authority, sense of scholarship, its contemporary feel, or the fruit it has exhibited in the lives of others). This list is only meant to serve as a tool in helping to determine which version is best suited for you. With such a wide assortment of versions to choose from, it can be frustrating making up your mind. This list is designed to ease that burden.

Before we proceed, it might be beneficial to clarify the difference between a translation and a paraphrase. A Bible translation is an attempt to communicate in one language what another language, such as Greek or Hebrew, literally says, while a paraphrase says something in different words from those which the author originally used. Another category is what some refer to as an "interpretative translation." This is a cross between an exact translation and a paraphrase; however, for all intents and purposes, it is a meaning-for-meaning paraphrase rather than a word-for-word translation. Christians need to understand this important distinction and use paraphrases and interpretive translations with a measure of caution. Because they represent a subjective interpretation of what the biblical authors actually said, they can occasionally reflect an inaccurate rendering, along with the doctrinal bias, of the interpreter. Therefore, paraphrases should be used as a supplementary tool to sound Bible study, and not be relied upon as the primary source of personal Bible familiarity.

For a far more comprehensive evaluation, I would recommend "The English Bible From the King James Version To the New International Version," by J. Lewis, (Baker Book House).

The King James Version (KJV, 1611)

Background History:

We have already traced the background developments which led up to the production of the King James Version (see previous chapter). The King James Version has been the unsurpassed favorite among Christians for over 375 years.

Evaluation:

The accuracy of translation is good, and the text is extremely faithful to the Greek texts available when it was translated. The beauty in language is excellent and considered by many to be unrivaled. Many prefer the time-tested style, majestic expression, and cadence of this version. The major drawback is its archaic vocabularly of the Elizabethan period which contains many words and phrases which are obsolete and now different in meaning. The widespread opinion of many scholars that it is less accurate than some other modern versions because of the late date of the manuscript texts from which it is derived is a factor which should be taken into consideration.

The Revised Version (1881 and 1885)

Background History:

The discovery of the Codex Alexandrinus sixteen years after the publication of the King James Version added a new dimension to the science of textual criticism. It dated from the fifth century A.D., and was older than any of the Greek texts used in the King James Version. The discovery of the Codex Sinaiticus by Tischendorf in 1844, along with his subsequent translation of the Codex Vaticanus in 1867, resulted in the revolutionary decision to prepare a comprehensive revision of the King James Version utilizing these older texts.

At the convocation of Canterbury in 1870, a resolution was passed to revise the King James Version. In 1870, a team of American scholars were invited to cooperate with the British revision committee on a joint project. About seventy-five of the top biblical scholars of England and America worked on this revision. The major changes primarily affected the New Testament, and were the result of the reliance upon Westcott and Hort's text. The New Testament was published in 1881, and the entire Bible in 1885. Its release was enthusiastically embraced by some, while stubbornly resisted by many others who considered it a sacrilegious attack against the Authorized Version, cherished as the only reliable translation of God's Word by millions. It did not usurp the place of acceptance and esteem enjoyed by the King James Version.

Evaluation:

It is not in common use today and, for all practical purposes, is really not in contention as a version to be considered for general use. Though it incorporated definite revisional improvements, its major fault is its over-dependence upon the Westcott-Hort theory of textual criticism which has received increasing criticism during the twentieth century.

The American Standard Version (ASV, 1901)

Background History:

Though the joint team of British and American revisers cooperated with the publication of the Revised Version, it was primarily a British production. By mutual consent and prior arrangement, the American committee had agreed not to produce their own edition until fourteen years after the release of the Revised Version. The American committee decided to come out with their own version incorporating the changes which had been suggested by them but not included in the text of the Revised Version, along with any additional modifications. The American Standard Version was published in 1901.

Evaluation:

Like the Revised Version, it is not in common use today. It is basically an excellent translation with improvements over the Revised Version, but its language was still archaic in places. It also was unable to take advantage of the additional manuscript discoveries of the twentieth century, and the modern advances in textual criticism.

The Revised Standard Version (RSV, 1952)

Background History:

About a half a century later, revisional work was done on the American Standard Version. In 1946, the New Testament was completed and, in 1952, the entire Bible was finished. This version was called the Revised Standard Version. It was not a new translation, but a revision. One of its major accomplishments was to update the obsolete language used in its predecessors (RV, ASV).

Evaluation:

Though this version was a significant improvement over the Revised and American Standard Version and was able to take advantage of the great strides in textual studies along with the additional discoveries of Greek manuscripts, its accuracy is somewhat deficient. The translators took too much liberty, at times, with conjectural renderings which do not accurately reflect the interpretation of the text. One of the most outstanding is its rendering of the Messianic prophecy of Isaiah 7:14 which substituted the words "young woman" in the place of "virgin." Many conservative Christians consider these and similar revisions to be too liberalistic and, therefore, unacceptable. Though it basically succeeded in modernizing the language to make it more contemporary, it does fall short in some places. However, the Revised Standard Version, for the most part, is a fairly readable version enjoyed by many. On its evaluation, Bruce gave the following comments:

. . . it has found widespread acceptance in the years since its appearance in a great variety of Christian communities, theologically conservative as well as theologically liberal. No change in Christian doctrine is involved or implied in the readings and renderings of the R.S.V.; every article of the historic faith of the Church can be established as readily and as plainly from it as from the older versions in whose tradition it stands.[1]

The New American Standard Bible (NASB, 1971)

Background History:

This version was an outgrowth of the desire to revise the American Standard Version, which was an endangered species as far as the reading public was concerned. To preserve this valuable translation, a non-profit organization, called the Lockman Foundation, assumed the burden of producing an updated revision of this version. Their objective was to adhere as faithfully as possibly to the original languages, and to produce a clear and readable version based upon a contemporary usage of language. The translators paid special attention to the Greek tenses to help clarify the meaning. They also replaced such archaic personal pronouns as "thou,"

---

1 F.F. Bruce, **The English Bible**, p. 199.

"thee," and "thy" with the more contemporary "you" and "your," except when referring to God. It also incorporated a helpful cross-reference system to assist the student in personal study.

Evaluation:

Its accuracy is excellent because it closely adheres to the original texts. Its readability is also good. But because it is an exacting, literal translation, it doesn't achieve the literary beauty or naturalness in style that the King James Version possesses. However, it is a version which is highly recommended by many.

The New International Version (NIV, 1978)

Background History:

This version represents a completely new and distinctive translation of the entire Bible. Its translators made use of the best Hebrew, Aramaic, and Greek texts available. They strove to present a modern speech translation which did not just represent a word-for-word translation but an accurate reflection of the very thought and meaning of the biblical writers. The scholars involved took extraordinary care in their revisional efforts which resulted in an extremely accurate and reliable translation which should inspire the confidence of its readers.

Evaluation:

Its primary value lies in its readability. The accuracy of this translation is excellent and adheres more closely to the Greek than most translations. It doesn't possess the literary beauty of the King James Version, but it does have a freshness in contemporary style and language. Its clarity of expression is excellent. Its only drawback is the fact that since it is an interpretative translation which endeavors to capture the essential thought of the original authors in a readable style rather than present a verbatim translation, the element of paraphrasing occasionally creeps into the text. In this case, the student has no way of determining when a text represents its intended meaning or the translators' personal interpretation. However, the New International Version's overall quality is quite good and has guaranteed its continuing popularity. It is definitely a recommended version.

The New King James Version (NKJV, 1982)

Background History:

Though the King James Version is still immensely popular, much of its Elizabethan English has been outdated for many years. Therefore, the need to update the clarity and language of the King James Version to make it more palatable to the reading tastes of the general public prompted a revisional overhaul. The team of revisers strove to preserve the time-honored dignity, forceful grandeur, and purity of the King James Version. They also endeavored to maintain the original thought flow, with the result that the reader will notice that the sequence and identity of words, phrases, and clauses of the new edition, while much clearer, are so close to the traditional version that it retains its familiar ring. It is, therefore, very easy for those who prefer the King James Version, but desire a more readable text, to make a smooth transition to this contemporary version.

Evaluation:

Since it still basically relies upon the Textus Receptus rather than the more recent body of available manuscripts, its primary criticism comes from those who prefer this older body of manuscripts as more reliable. However, as we have previously seen, this debate is not over and all the evidence is not yet in to make a conclusive judgment concerning this controversy. Where the various manuscript families differ from the Textus Receptus, the variants are recorded in the center column on each page to aid the serious student. Its accuracy is good, and represents a definite improvement over the King James Version. It still retains the beauty of style like the original version, but the combination of the old with the newer language improvements promises to make this version a popular translation in the coming years.

The Living Bible (1971)

Background History:

This Bible represented another attempt to produce a modern speech version in English. It was primarily the brainchild of Kenneth Taylor, the Director of the Moody Literature Mission. It was published in stages, beginning in 1962 with the release of the New Testament letters entitled "The Living Letters." After this came "The Living Prophecies" (1965), "The Living Gospels" (1965), "The Living New Testament" (1967), "The Living Psalms" (1967), "The Living Lessons of Life and Love" (1968), "The Living Books of Moses" (1969), and "The Living History of Israel" (1970). It was completed in 1971. It is not a translation but a paraphrase, which means that it reflects the author's thoughts and interpretation and may or may not represent the intended meaning. Even Taylor himself cautioned, "Whenever the author's exact words are not translated from the Greek there is the possibility that the translator, however honest, may be giving the English reader something that the original writer did not mean to say."[2]

---

2 Norman L. Geisler and William E. Nix, **A General Introduction to the Bible**, p. 444.

Evaluation:

Though its style is simple and easy to read, it has some weaknesses. Its accuracy is inferior because it does not adhere to the original manuscripts. Furthermore, in its attempt to communicate the biblical narrative in a simplified style, it tends to dilute, oversimplify, and even delete some things from the texts. Its primary value lies in its ability to communicate the Bible's message in an understandable and straightforward manner. For this reason, it has been popular to many. While it is a helpful supplementary version and can be used as an elementary introduction to the Bible, it is not recommended as a primary reading source or study Bible.

The Good News Bible (1976)

Background History:

The Good News Bible was the result of the American Bible Society's desire to produce a fresh, readable version in English. The original title to the New Testament was "Good News for Modern Man: The New Testament in Today's English Version." It has the distinctive quality of employing the concept of "dynamic equivalence," which means that instead of translating what the author really said, his words are modified to bring out the essential essence of what he meant in order to make the biblical message more relatable to contemporary readers. Other features include the simplification of vocabulary, and the addition of line-art illustrations.

Evaluation:

Its value lies in its emphasis on simplification and readability, but serious limitations exist. The use of "dynamic equivalence" gives rise to the constant danger of oversimplification and the unintentional adulteration of the intended meaning. For this reason, it represents an elementary narrative of the Bible, but it can not be recommended as a primary reading source for the scriptures.

The Modern Language Bible (1969)
or the Berkeley Version (1945, 1959)

Background History:

In 1945, a new version of the New Testament was released. It was the result of the translating efforts of one lone scholar. His name was Dr. Gerrit Verkuyl of Berkeley, California, hence the title. Under his supervision, a team of translators completed the Old Testament in 1959. After Verkuyl's death, the entire Berkeley Bible was extensively revised, updated, and re-released in 1969 under the title "The Modern Language Bible—The New Berkeley Version in Modern English." It has been described as a more conservative counterpart of the Revised Standard Version. It represents a faithful, literal translation of both the Greek and Hebrew texts.

Evaluation:

One of the beneficial features of the Modern Language Bible is its many beneficial footnotes accompanying the text which are both informative and inspirational. It also faithfully represents the Messianic prophecies of the Old Testament. Its main drawback lies in the fact that since it is such a literal translation of the Greek and Hebrew, it occasionally presents too literal a rendering of the text to be readable. However, it is, overall, an excellent version.

The Phillips New Testament Version (1963)

Background History:

This version of the New Testament was the result of Pastor J.B. Phillips' desire to present a fresh translation tailored for the reading tastes of modern men. The "Letters to Young Churches" was published in 1947. Following its release, he translated the Gospels (1952), Acts (1955), and the Book of Revelation (1957). The complete New Testament, entitled

"The New Testament in Modern English," was completed in 1958 and in 1973 it was revised. It has proven itself to be one of the most popular modern speech translations ever published. Its unique quality is a reflection of Phillips' personal view of the scriptures:

> For the most part I am convinced that they had no idea that they were writing Holy Scripture. They would be, or indeed perhaps are, amazed to learn what meanings are sometimes read back into their simple utterances!
>
> Paul, for instance, writing in haste and urgency to some of his wayward and difficult Christians, was not tremendously concerned about dotting the i's and crossing the t's of his message. I doubt very much whether he was even concerned about being completely consistent with what he had already written.
>
> Consequently, it seems to me quite beside the point to study his writings microscopically, as it were, and deduce hidden meanings of which almost certainly he was unaware. His letters are alive, and they are moving—in both senses of the word—and their meaning can no more be appreciated by cold minute examination than can the beauty of a bird's flight be appreciated by dissection after its death. We have to take these living New Testament documents in their context.

Evaluation:

Strictly speaking, the Phillips Version is not a translation but a paraphrase. It represents a meaning-for-meaning translation rather than a word-for-word translation. Because it is a paraphrase rather than a precise translation, the general caution applies. However, it is an excellent paraphrase. On its merit, Geisler and Nix commented:

> More properly a paraphrase, a "meaning-for-meaning" translation rather than a 'word-for-word' translation. The former involves more interpretation than the latter, and

this may be regarded as the only real weakness in Phillips' translation. Nevertheless, the strength and freshness of this work have recaptured the spirit and heart of the first century writers for twentieth century readers in a unique way.[3]

The Amplified Bible (1965)

Background History:

The Amplified Bible was published in 1965. It is unique from all other translations in that it endeavors to supplement the Greek and Hebrew translations to English with additional shades of meaning, explanations, and clarifications of the words within the text. While other versions have utilized explanatory marginal notes or footnotes to accomplish this, the Amplified Bible actually inserts it within the body of the text.

Evaluation:

Its principal value is found in its ability to enlarge upon the meanings within the scripture texts. However, it has major drawbacks as far as a primary study or reading Bible is concerned. Its constant amplifications on the text break up the flow of thought and make it choppy and unreadable to the average reader for any extended length. Because it includes an amplification of the text, it parallels the same problem which often arises with paraphrases. Occasionally, the interpreter's subjective bias gets injected into the text. Though it is not recommended as a valuable reading Bible, it can be an extremely useful study aid to be used along with a good mainline translation.

---

3 Norman L. Geisler and William E. Nix, **A General Introduction to the Bible,** p. 442.

The New English Bible (1970)

Background History:

This version was the result of a cooperative effort between several major denominational groups in England, Scotland, Wales, and Ireland. This work was not just another addition to the long list of English Bible revisions but an entirely new translation. It was intended as an authoritative English translation which took advantage of the modern advances in textual criticism, linguistics, and history. It was also designed as a readable version which eliminated obsolete styles of vocabulary and language. Rather than incorporate a word-for-word translation, it adopted a meaning-for-meaning rendering of the Hebrew and Greek texts into English. Another unique feature behind the translating efforts of this version is the fact that its translation did not rely solely upon the Westcott-Hort tradition in their rendering of the Greek text, but utilized a selective freedom which permitted them to pick and choose from a variety of textual sources.

Evaluation:

Its major weakness is its attempt to present a meaning-for-meaning translation which inevitably ends up being a paraphrase rather than an exact translation. In the New English Bible's case, there are too many subjective interpretations. Its English words and expressions limit its appeal to American readers and, for this reason, it has not been popular in the United States. Its sole value lies in its colorful style which is attractive to some readers.

The Jerusalem Bible (1956)

Background History:

The Jerusalem Bible is an outgrowth of a French version called "La Bible de Jerusalem" which had been translated in Jerusalem. The French edition was published in 1956 with extensive notes accompanying the text. The Jerusalem Bible incorporates these notes in an English translation. As with so many other versions, it was the intent of the author to provide a translation in a contemporary language format. It is a Roman Catholic Bible whose distinction lies in the fact that it is translated from the original languages rather than the Latin Vulgate from which all previous Catholic translations were derived.

Evaluation:

Its value lies in its readability and extensive marginal notes which provide the reader with an abundance of biblical helps. Its major drawback is due to these same notes which often carry a distinctively Roman Catholic bias which occasionally interprets the scriptures to suit its doctrinal perspective. While it is an excellent translation, its Roman Catholic emphasis is objectionable to most discerning Protestants. Another weakness is its inclusion of the apocryphal books as sacred canon.

The New American Bible (1970)

Background History:

This is the most recent of Roman Catholic translations. Like the Jerusalem Bible, this version departed from the Latin Vulgate texts and made use of the original languages. It represents the American counterpart to the English Jerusalem Bible, and is the first complete American Catholic Bible.

Evaluation:

It is basically an excellent translation with a contemporary readability. However, it has serious drawbacks. The introductions to the various books are too liberalistic, and the marginal notes carry a definite Roman Catholic doctrinal bias which is objectionable to most Protestants. It also includes the apocryphal books on an equal status with the canonical Old Testament.

Additional Twentieth Century Versions

Other lesser known versions include a variety of twentieth century translations. Most of these were the product of individual scholarship, and were the result of the scholar's burden to translate the scriptures into the language of modern man. Though not widely recognized or used, they may appeal to the more serious Bible student who desires to round out his Bible library with quality supplements. These include: **Weymouth's New Testament - The New Testament in Modern English** (1903); **The Moffatt Translation** (New Testament, 1913; Old Testament, 1924); **The Goodspeed Version** (1927); **The Basic English Bible** (New Testament, 1940; Old Testament, 1949); **The Authentic New Testament;** G.W. Wade's **The Documents of the New Testament** (1934); and, Charles B. Williams' **The New Testament In the Language of the People.**

Section III

How to Study Your Bible

INTRODUCTION

Lost and Found

At the age of seventeen, W. P. Mackay left his home in Scotland to attend college. Before he left, his mother gave him her Bible in which she had written his name and a verse of scripture. During his college years, Mackay's life sank into worldliness and carnality. His backslidden state deeply grieved his godly mother. At one point, he sank so low he pawned his mother's Bible to get money for whiskey. However, his mother prayed for him until her death. Eventually, Mackay became a successful doctor in a city hospital. One day, he was called upon to attend to a dying patient who asked for his "book." After the man died, Mackay was curious to know what book could be so precious, so he searched through the belongings of the man. He was surprised to find the very Bible he had pawned years before. He went to his office and gazed again at the familiar writing, noticing many pages with underscored verses his mother had prayed he would read. After many hours of soul searching, Mackay knelt and prayed to God for mercy. W. P. Mackay, the physician, later became a minister. The book he once treated so lightly became his most precious possession.

How many others need a similar experience? Though most Christians have never actually discarded the Bible in such a profane manner, they've never discovered just how precious a possession this book really is.

Our Relationship with the Word

Each of us needs to take spiritual inventory concerning our relationship with the Word of God, especially in light of the times in which we live. Contemporary Christians should recognize that we live in a unique period in church history. We live in an age when unparalleled spiritual blessings are at our disposal. We can draw upon the sacrifices of many saints who have gone before us. Because of the blood, sweat, and tears of millions who have labored and even laid down their lives, we have at our disposal one of the most precious gifts ever given to mankind—the Bible. However, the tragic fact is that many born-again believers manifest an almost total neglect for this precious resource. Widespread indifference and even apathy toward the Word of God exists even in the most biblically-based fellowships. Sadly enough, some Christians are more interested in magazines, newspapers, romantic novels, watching T. V., and listening to the radio than in their Bible. For whatever the reasons, many Christians spend more time reading the newspaper than they do the Word of God. When we consider the billions of Bibles in circulation in relationship to the lack of proper attention given to its contents by believer and unbeliever alike, we might take seriously David Nygren's humorous observation that "If all the neglected Bibles were dusted simultaneously, we would have a record dust storm and the sun would go into eclipse for a whole week."

238

In spite of the fact that Bible-believing Christians embrace the reality that the Bible is the infallible Word of God, many are unconsciously guilty of neglecting this precious resource. Though genuine Christians defend the Bible, respect the Bible, and even revere the Bible as God's authoritative revelation to mankind, many are demonstrating a casual disinterest in its contents through a habitual pattern of disuse simply because they have never established an intimate relationship with the Bible on a consistent, ongoing basis.

The Causes of Neglect

The reasons for this widespread neglect boil down to either slothfulness, spiritual apathy, or a lack of sufficient instruction. In all fairness, the vast majority of Christians who have never achieved a meaningful relationship with God's Word have failed to do so because of a lack of know-how. This is not to say that they have never tried, nor does it imply that they don't sincerely long for such a relationship.

Many have tried again and again, but their attempts have been repeatedly aborted. They have vowed their vows, made fresh resolutions, and determined to discipline themselves, only to find their resolve dashed upon the rocks of disappointment. Because they lack the constructive guidelines for developing a healthy habit of personal devotions in the Word of God, they inevitably slip into a quiet pattern of neglect, disillusionment, and frustration which perpetuates their state of biblical illiteracy.

Others would like to establish such a vital relationship with God's Word but not only do they not know where to begin, the Word of God itself is so perplexing to them that their reaction is similar to the Israelites' first encounter with the manna (a type of God's Word) in the wilderness when they said, ''What is it?'' (Exod. 16:15). Their condition reminds me of the dilemma of the Ethiopian eunuch who was sincerely trying to wade through the 53rd chapter of Isaiah and comprehend its meaning. When God directed Philip the evangelist to his side, he overheard him reading out of the scroll of Isaiah. At that point, he asked him the very pertinent question, "Do you understand what you are reading?" to which the Ethiopian eunuch replied, "How can I, unless someone explains it to me?" (Acts 8). His candid answer reflects the secret confession of many. It is for this very reason that this section is devoted to providing practical, common-sense, equipping insights so that the average Christian can understand what he is reading, and learn to relish the riches of that experience.

Another lesser category of Christians have never established a pleasurable and rewarding relationship with the Bible simply because they have failed to challenge a spirit of slothfulness and indifference. Sometimes, this is a problem arising from an individual's personal apathy and spiritual lukewarmness; at other times, it results from the distorted view of Christianity to which they have been exposed.

The message being promoted by some does not accurately characterize the true nature of Christianity. It reminds me of the story I once heard about the new vacuum cleaner salesman on his first day of door-to-door sales. When he reported back to work at the end of the day, his boss asked him how many he sold. He said, "I made 200 sales." When the boss told him to quit joking around, the salesman proudly produced 200 invoices. With that, the manager went to work on his calculator and declared excitedly, "At $250.00 a machine, you've earned a year's commission in one day!" But the salesman came back and said, "Oh I didn't sell them at $250.00 each, I only sold them for a dollar!" So it is with those who softsell a bargain brand of Christianity which doesn't reflect the actual price or product. Multitudes are willing to partake of this appealing form of Christianity because it does not cost much and demands little.

Those who cheapen the Christian experience by presenting a lazy man's version, which only stresses the benefits and blessings while ignoring the dimension of commitment and discipleship, have done a great disservice to God's people. Any emphasis, subtle or overt, which downplays or undermines the importance of establishing a vital relationship with the Word of God robs the individual of a potential realm which can enhance the overall quality of his or her new-found life in Christ.

What Does the Bible Say?

Because of this, the scriptures have a lot to say about our need for developing one of the most fundamental disciplines for establishing that quality of relationship with Christ. That relationship is inseparably linked to the study of God's Word. The Bible repeatedly reinforces the importance of establishing consistent, daily disciplines in the Word of God. Jesus specifically challenged us to "search the scriptures" (John 5:39, KJV), and Isaiah the prophet exhorted us to "search from the book of the Lord and read" (Isaiah 34:16, NKJV). The Apostle Paul commended the Christians in Berea because they "were more fair-minded than those in Thessalonica, in that they received the word with all readiness, and searched the Scriptures daily to find out whether these things were so" (Acts 17:11, NKJV). He underscored the significance of our personal need to study the Word of God when he exhorted us to "Study to shew thyself approved unto God, a workman that needeth not to be ashamed, rightly dividing the word of truth" (II Timothy 2:15, KJV). He also instructed Timothy to "give attention to reading, to exhortation, (and) to doctrine" (I Timothy 4:13, NKJV). Throughout the length and breadth of the Bible, the need to draw nearer to the scriptures is stressed.

In Closing

Finally, when viewed against the backdrop of millions who have sacrificed their all to protect and preserve the Bible for our behalf lies the fact that a sovereign God took great care, over the course of centuries, to communicate His divine revelations to mankind in the form of the written word. But unless men read that Word and avail themselves of its truths, the gap between what God has endeavored to communicate and our ability to receive can never be adequately bridged. It is not enough to surmise what God says or speculate about His eternal truths— we must know, and one of the most effective ways of accomplishing this is through the medium of the sacred scriptures.

The contents of this section can help build that bridge. It can do so by helping transform the readers' relationship with their Bible from what may be a dull, drab, boring experience, into one which is exciting, satisfying, and thoroughly rewarding! Others have discovered this, and so can you. In closing, let us consider the challenging reflections of George Muller, the great prayer warrior, concerning the relationship he developed with the Book of Books:

> The vision of our spiritual life will be in exact proportion to the place held by the Bible in our life and thoughts. I solemnly state this from the experience of fifty-four years. . . . The first three years after conversion I neglected the word of God. Since I began to search diligently the blessing has been wonderful. I have read the Bible through one hundred times, and always with increasing delight. Each time it seems like a new book to me. . . . I believe that the one chief reason that I have been kept in happy useful service is that I have been a lover of Holy Scripture. It has been my habit to read the Bible through four times a year; in a prayerful spirit, to apply it to my heart, and practice what I find there. I have been for sixty-nine years a happy man; happy, happy, happy. . . . Great has been the blessing from consecutive, diligent, daily study. I look upon it as a lost day when I have not had good time over the word of God.

May each of us be able to one day echo the same sentiments.

1

WHY WE SHOULD STUDY THE BIBLE

A Hidden Treasure

I remember reading a story about an elderly man who made a surprising discovery while leafing through an old family Bible. It seems that one of his aunts had died and left her Bible to him. Part of the instructions of the will read, "To my beloved Steven Marsh I bequeth my family Bible and all it contains, along with the residue of my estate after my funeral expenses and just and lawful debts are paid." After her estate had been settled, he received a few hundred dollars and the old family Bible. The money was soon spent, and his circumstances eventually forced Mr. Marsh to live on a small pension. For over thirty years he lived in poverty until one day when he was rummaging through his attic. In a trunk, he came upon that family Bible which he had inherited years before. When he opened it, he was shocked to find over $5,000 in cash concealed within its pages.

Within his reach was a treasure for the taking if he had only opened the pages of the Book. What a lesson for each of us. Though we shouldn't expect to find financial rewards simply by opening our Bible, we can confidently expect to discover a treasure trove of spiritual blessings which can profit every area of our lives.

The Bible declares that "All scripture is given by inspiration of God, and is profitable" (II Timothy 3:16, KJV). The primary reason why we should regularly study the Bible is because of its measurable profit to our lives.

The Bible is an inexhaustible goldmine of spiritual blessings just waiting to be extracted by each of us. Arthur T. Pierson said,

> No other book proves such an exhaustless mine of precious treasures to those who are content to delve deep into it. It is a field for endless study and ceaseless discovery; and the humblest believer may find hid treasure never before dug up by any other, and therefore peculiarly his own.[1]

This is one reason why Henry Halley, the respected Bible lover, declared, "The Bible is the most precious possession of the human race."

I don't know about you, but treasure hunting has always fascinated me. Stories of buried treasure, gold doubloons, and lost mines have always intrigued me. The exploits of Mel Fisher, the famous treasure seeker, are especially exciting. His seventeen-year ordeal in trying to locate the sunken wreck of the Spanish galleon Atocha recently paid off. His team of salvagers finally found it strewn across a shallow reef forty miles off the Florida Keys. There, for several centuries, had lain an estimated 400 million dollars in silver and gold! Who isn't captivated by such stories and yet, the eternal treasures of God's Word far surpass any temporal treasures which men

---

1 Arthur T. Pierson, cited from **Explore the Book**, by J. Sidlow Baxter, p. 926.

may seek after. What possible comparison can we reasonably make between the riches of this world and those which will last forever?

The scriptures contain a vast deposit of truth which can potentially enrich our lives if we are willing to prospect its pages. Some of its riches are "easy pickins"—they are like gold nuggets scattered on the surface. Others are like deep veins of pure gold which can only be dug out through effort and study. But whatever its source, the Bible offers a mother lode of countless benefits to those who diligently seek to extract its wealth. The Bible is a veritable cornucopia of spiritual blessing which yields its harvest to those who are willing to partake. When we invest ourselves in a common sense pattern of Bible reading and study, we are guaranteed to reap a lifetime of dividends.

Many reasons can be presented in order to demonstrate the profit in developing daily disciplines in the Word of God. The following pages briefly showcase some of the most beneficial by-products of studying the scriptures. Though they occasionally overlap, they each represent a distinctive dimension of blessing.

It Brings Us into an Intimacy with Christ

Dr. S.D. Gordon relates a story about an aged Christian woman whose memory was beginning to fade. She had formed an intimate relationship with the Bible over the years and had memorized much of it. However, as her memory diminished, she was only able to retain one passage, "I know whom I have believed, and am persuaded that he is able to keep that which I have committed unto him against that day" (II Tim. 1:12, KJV). Gradually, her condition deteriorated until she could only recite the words, "that which I have committed unto him." Finally, as she lingered on the threshold of eternity, one of the relatives who was standing by her bedside noticed the old woman's lips moving. When they bent down to hear what she was saying, they heard her mumbling over and over again the final fragment of scripture from that verse, "him, him, him." The entire

245

Bible had faded from her memory except that one word upon which the whole Bible stands—Him!

The study of God's Word is a direct conduit to intimacy with Christ. Because He is the living Word, the written Word is merely a reflection of Christ. As we draw closer to the Bible, we inevitably draw closer to Christ. As Martin Luther noted, "As we go to the cradle to find the baby, so we go to the scriptures only to find Christ."

Pontius Pilate once confronted Christ with the same enigma of life which has troubled mankind throughout the course of human history. He asked Him, "What is truth?" (John 18:38). Though Jesus did not offer a response, He had already answered that question earlier when He declared, "I am the way and the TRUTH and the life" (John 14:6). The real question is not so much "What is truth?" but "Who is truth?" Jesus is the truth. He is the way to truth; He is the wellspring of life. The Word ushers us into more than an intimate intellectual or conceptual relationship with truth—it leads us into an intimate relationship with the fountainhead of truth—Jesus Christ.

If we desire a deeper personal relationship with Jesus, we must embrace the Book. So often, we become so involved in the responsibilities of ministry, Christian service, and spiritual duties that our relationship with Christ is put on the back burner. This is not to say that our busyness about the kingdom is wrong, but without an ongoing relationship with Jesus, all we have is religious activity without the person which makes Christianity what it was intended to be. This is brought out in the story of Martha and Mary (Luke 10:38-42). In this story, we find a contrast between the actions of Martha and her sister, Mary. Martha was frantically scurrying about the house preparing the meal and conscientiously fulfilling her ministerial responsibilities while Mary was relaxing at Jesus' feet, listening to His word. Martha finally got so irritated at her sister that she snapped at the Lord. At this point, Jesus gave her a loving reproof by saying, "Martha, Martha, you are worried and upset about many things, but only one thing is needed. Mary has chosen what is better" (Luke 10:41, 42). The one thing Martha had neglected in all her service and responsibilities before the Lord was to sit at His feet and hear His word. She was neglecting that essential dimension, "that better part" (KJV), of developing an intimacy with Christ through His Word.

Many Christians have unconsciously fallen into this "Martha syndrome" and wonder why the quality of their personal relationship with Christ is not what it should be. When we neglect our relationship with the Bible, our intimacy with Christ inevitably suffers. For this reason, Jerome stated that "Ignorance of the scriptures is ignorance of Christ." One of the fundamental ways of correcting this condition is through establishing a consistency in the study of God's Word.

It Imparts Spiritual Freedom and Liberty

Jesus promised us that, "If you abide in My word, you are My disciples indeed. And you shall know the truth, and the truth shall make you free" (John 8:31, 32, NKJV). The Word of God is the great liberator which emancipates us from spiritual, mental, and emotional bondage and oppression. Its truths are like master keys which, alone, can open the prison door and set the captive free.

There are other secular works and religious writings which claim to be able to set men and women free, but their boasts are empty. It's true that they may contain a measure of truth, but half truths, like half bricks, are more dangerous because they fly farther. While they promise liberty, they end up producing bondage. Their detrimental influence is much like rat poisoning. Though 98% of it is good, wholesome cornmeal, it is laced with a dose of arsenic which can have a lethal effect on all those who partake.

However, the Word of God is pure and unadulterated. It does not contain a misleading sampling of truth mixed with error. It contains "the truth, the whole truth, and nothing but the truth" and for this reason, it can truly impart freedom and liberty to those in bondage.

It Provides Spiritual Cleansing

In Ephesians, Paul speaks about being sanctified and cleansed "by the washing with water through the word" that He may present His church to Himself as a "radiant church, without stain, or wrinkle or any other blemish, but holy and blameless" (Eph. 5:26, 27). Jesus also stated, "You are already clean because of the word which I have spoken to you" (John 15:3). God's Word is a cleansing agent which washes and refreshes our minds and our hearts.

Paul revealed that through the "washing with water through the word," the church of Jesus Christ would be purified from all stains, wrinkles, and blemishes. Stains are external marks which we pick up from our contact with the world. They refer to any outward actions, conduct, conversation, or relationships with others which defile us and are contrary to holiness.

God's Word is a spiritual spot remover that can eliminate even the hardest to remove stains. But its cleansing action goes deeper than that. It is possible to clean up a man's act outwardly through legalistic restraint. Men are capable of religiously sanitizing their lives in a superficial manner—the Pharisees proved that. But God not only desires to clean the outside of the cup, He ultimately desires to cleanse the inside, as well. When Paul referred to blemishes and wrinkles, he was talking about facial eruptions and age lines which result from an inner condition. Acne results from corruption within our system; wrinkles come from dry, tired skin—it results as old age sets in. The water of God's Word purifies our inward parts and cleans up the blemishes. It also refreshes and renews us, and causes the vitality and youthfulness of our Christian experience to continue.

Passing through the pages of God's Word is like passing through a quality car wash. It rinses and removes the external road grime of life, but it does more than just cosmetically clean the exterior. It reaches into the interior, into the crevices between the seats, into the hidden places of the glove compartment, into the secret places of our heart. It doesn't just cleanse a man outwardly—it cleanses the very core of his being. The Word of God has a laundering effect which purifies our thought life, emotions, attitudes, temperament, motives, and the very intents of the heart (Heb. 4:12).

It Establishes a Protective Safeguard Against Sin

As a combat soldier in Vietnam, one of the standard pieces of equipment which we were issued was called a flak jacket. It was a protective vest which we wore around our chests. It was designed to protect our vital organs from shrapnel splinters and other flying fragments which could have lethal effects. Some of those who discarded them because they were too cumbersome learned to regret their choice. It was the protective shield of that vest which saved many a man in the heat of combat or incoming fire. In a spiritual sense, the Bible also serves in the same capacity.

When I was a young Christian, I was given a Bible with the following words of John Bunyan written in the front: "Sin will keep you from the Bible, but this Bible will keep you from sin." Over the years, I have discovered the potency of this admonition. The Bible establishes the godly cautions and restraints required to insure the fear of the Lord and protect our life from erring into sin. It is like a built-in alarm system which alerts us to the possible intrusion of sin into our life.

The Word of God declares, "How can a young man keep his way pure? By living according to your word. I seek you with all my heart; do not let me stray from your commands. I have hidden your word in my heart that I might not sin against you" (Ps. 119:9-11). When we consciously deposit the Word of God within the sanctuary of our heart, it establishes a protective safeguard against sin. It erects a spiritual hedge and protective umbrella against the influence of temptation and solicitation to sin.

It Equips Us

One of the loudest battle cries of the Protestant Reformation was "sola scriptura," or "Scripture alone!"). The Reformers recognized the truth that "All scripture is God-breathed, and is useful for teaching, rebuking, correcting, and training in righteousness, so that the man of God may be thoroughly equipped for every good work" (II Tim. 3:16, 17). In the face of spiritual perversion, superstition, and the empty, man-made traditions of men which had plunged the church into the abyss of the Dark Ages, the Reformers saw the scriptures as the only sufficient source of truth and moral knowledge to usher men back into the light. Though Bible critics may mock the Bible as mankind's only sufficient rule of faith and practice, it, alone, contains all that is required to adequately equip a man for life.

What is more, this revelation of the Reformers has not grown obsolete with time. God's truths are just as pertinent and timely today as they were when they were first written. As Edith Deen simply put it, "The Bible never grows old." The technological advances of modern man, coupled with the quantum leaps in knowledge, have not supplanted the Bible as the ultimate source of truth and knowledge. With all of humanity's learning, we are still no better equipped today to meet the pressures of life than we were a thousand years ago. Our sophistication and increased knowledge have not diminished the relevancy of the Word for today. With all of mankind's accumulated learning, we are still making no real headway against the age-old problem of sin. We are utterly incapable of erradicating hatred, jealousy, selfishness, crime, war, sexual perversion, and man's general inhumanity to man. Apart from the counsel and instruction of God's Word, man's attempt to overcome the spiritual perversion of this age is as futile as a man trying to drive back the ocean's tide with a push broom!

Human knowledge and secular education, as beneficial as it is, can never adequately replace the Word of God. Man can never be truly equipped for life without its instruction. As Wm. Phelps once stated, "A knowledge of the Bible without a college education is more valuable than a college education without a knowledge of the Bible." "All the knowledge you want is comprised in one book, the Bible" (John Wesley). Nobody wants to be caught offguard or find that they are unprepared for the challenges before them. Being unprepared can not only be embarrassing, it can be disastrous. The ill-fated Donner party discovered this the hard way. America was shocked by its lack of preparation at Pearl Harbor, and our country was humiliated by the attempted rescue mission of our embassy hostages in Tehran which had to be aborted at the last moment because of the lack of foresight to properly prepare the commando team with the right equipment. However, humiliation and tragedy can be avoided in the Christian experience through the sufficiency of God's Word.

The Bible stands supreme as the sufficient source of caution, counsel, correction, insight, and instruction to comprehensively prepare us for the inevitabilities of life. Like a well-stocked Sears catalog, the Bible offers us the needed inventory to equip us for every realm of the human experience. It gives us all the answers which we need to victoriously respond to the challenges we encounter, and equips us to fulfill the scriptural admonition to "always be prepared to give the reason for the hope that you have" (I Peter 3:15). It enables us to be men and women for all seasons.

It Gives Divine Direction and Guidance

How many of us have been lost in a strange city, unable to figure out where we are or where we are going. The solution which most of us have arrived at is simple. We merely go to the nearest gas station, pop a few coins in a vending machine, and select the appropriate road map to show us our way. This is precisely what the scriptures provide. They are the infallible road map of life.

Someone once said that the Bible is a book like the needle to the North Pole. Many books supposedly point the way, but the

Bible points the true way. It is a divine compass heading which provides mankind with an absolutely reliable bearing for life.

The Bible declares that "Your word is a lamp to my feet and a light for my path. . . . Direct my footsteps according to your word" (Psalms 119:105, 133). The scriptures illuminate our path and help us negotiate our way through the spiritual darkness of this age. The Bible is a lighthouse whose constant beacon safely guides us over the treacherous shoals of life. It, alone, gives us guidance and clarity of direction in every dimension of the human experience. Martin Luther confirmed: "I am well satisfied with the gift of the Holy Scriptures, which give me abundant instruction and all that I need to know both for this life and for that which is to come."

It Imparts Peace

I remember hearing a sermon story about a group of art lovers who were being taken on a guided tour of a famous art museum. As they made their way down the corridors, pausing to reflect upon each picture they passed, they came to a large painting which immediately arrested the curiosity of the group. It was a dramatically illustrated painting of a rocky coastline gripped in the midst of a violent storm. Ominous clouds covered the sky, enormous breakers churned up the sea, and sheets of rain assaulted the cliffs overlooking the ocean. What caught the party's attention was the title: it simply said "Peace." It seemed so inappropriate until one individual asked the tour guide why in the world the artist gave the painting this title. In response, the guide instructed the group to step closer. He then pointed to a section of the jagged cliff. There, in a small crevice, sheltered in safety from the storm, sat a small bird waiting out the tempest in perfect peace.

This is precisely what the Word of God provides. Its truths create shelters of peace even in the midst of the most violent storms of life. The assurances and promises of God's Word minister peace, confidence, and security in the most trouble-some of times.

"Great peace have they who love your law, and nothing can make them stumble" (Ps. 119:165). If we love God's Word and take heed to its counsel, it has an unconditional guarantee to surround our hearts and minds with peace. When we depart from its counsel, we are inevitably seized by the storms of life and overcome with mental and emotional anxiety. Life is often like a hurricane. The only place of refuge is in the "eye" of the storm. Here the seas are tranquil, the wind blows softly, and the sun shines. But venture out of the eye of the hurricane and you encounter violent seas, gale force winds of 150 knots, and torrential rains. The secret of maintaining that constant dimension of peace is to remain in the center of God's Word.

It Builds Our Faith

The scriptures tell us that "faith comes by hearing, and hearing by the word of God" (Rom. 10:17, NKJV). The Word of God stimulates, promotes, and strengthens our faith. It represents the major source for building faith in our life. Many Christians long for a greater capacity of faith, but it doesn't arise because they are overlooking the relationship between the Bible and faith. There is a direct equation—an intimate relationship with God's Word produces faith. D.L. Moody, one of the great evangelists of the nineteenth century, stumbled upon this revelation and provided this revealing testimony:

> I prayed for faith, and thought that some day faith would come down and strike me like lightning. But faith did not seem to come. One day I read in the tenth chapter of Romans "now faith cometh by hearing, and hearing by the word of God." I had closed my Bible, and prayed for faith. I now opened my Bible, and began to study, and faith has been growing ever since.

This is not to say that the mere reception of scriptural sound waves striking the eardrum will automatically produce faith in

253

the hearer. We could listen to Alexander Scourby for the rest of our lives and never experience an ounce of faith. We must, as Jesus exhorted, not only hear the Word, but take heed how we hear. However, if we take heed to God's Word with an open and receptive heart, we provide the fertile seedbed for faith to inevitably spring forth. If we commit ourselves to consistently exercising ourselves in the precepts of the Word, we will, like diligent body builders, enlarge and strengthen the biceps of our faith.

It Imparts Wisdom, Insight, and Understanding

"The entrance of your words gives light; it gives understanding to the simple" (Psalms 119:130). The Bible quickens our minds and spiritual discernment. It provides the necessary wisdom, insights, and understanding for every area of our life.

The wisdom contained in the Bible can provide the lowliest Christian with far greater insights and understanding than the most intellectually brilliant and learned men of this world who have no saving knowledge of Jesus Christ. For centuries, scholars, scientists, and philosophers have been trying to fathom the depths of meaning behind life. They have wrestled with the great philosophical enigmas of history: "Who am I?"; "Where did I come from?"; "Where am I going?" Apart from the answers contained in the scriptures, they are destined to continue their fruitless quest. But the simplest saint knows the answers because the Word has revealed them. Not only do the scriptures give understanding to these basic questions, they also provide the wisdom and insight needed to see life clearly, and victoriously face all the dilemmas of life.

It Imparts Comfort and Consolation in Times of Trial

The power of God's Word to impart comfort was reinforced in my life as a young soldier on my way to Vietnam. While in transit, my plane had a brief layover in San Francisco. I was only there for a few minutes, but had just enough time to say good-bye to my uncle who met me at the airport. When the boarding announcement came over the loud speaker, my uncle started crying and said, "I want to give you something that will help you when you get overseas." He reached into his pocket and pulled out a well-worn copy of a Gideon's pocket New Testament and Psalms. He told me that he had carried it through Korea as a scared young Marine, and it had ministered to him in times of need. I thanked him and said I would use it myself. In the months that passed, I often resorted to its pages, especially the passages which had been underlined. One of these, in particular, became a special comfort to me in times of fear and distress:

> I will say of the Lord, "He is my refuge and my fortress, my God, in whom I trust."
>
> Surely he will save you from the fowler's snare and from the deadly pestilence. He will cover you with his feathers, and under his wings you will find refuge; his faithfulness will be your shield and rampart.
>
> You will not fear the terror of night, nor the arrow that flies by day, nor the pestilence that stalks in the darkness, nor the plague that destroys at midday.
>
> A thousand may fall at your side, ten thousand at your right hand, but it will not come near you.
>
> You will only observe with your eyes and see the punishment of the wicked.
>
> If you make the Most High your dwelling—even the Lord, who is my refuge—then no harm will befall you, no disaster will come near your tent.
>
> —Psalms 91:2-10

Millions have found this same source of comfort in times of testing. They have found the scripture true which states, "This is my comfort in my affliction, for your word has given me life"

255

(Ps. 119:50, NKJV). They have experienced the reality that the Word of God eases our turmoil, and supplies soothing comfort to our hearts and minds.

It Imparts Hope and Encouragement

The assurances of God's Word can produce hope even in the midst of seemingly hopeless situations. This was quickened to me a few years ago while reading the story of Peter's imprisonment in Acts 12. Herod had already had James murdered, and was planning a repeat performance with Peter. Peter had been apprehended and placed in maximum security to await his execution in the morning. Sixteen guards were assigned to watch his cell, with Peter shackled to two of them.

What amazed me most about this story was Peter's casual, almost nonchalant conduct. Most men, while awaiting certain death, with the sobering reminder of the reality of James' execution, guarded by sixteen soldiers who were under the penalty of death if they let you escape, with no way out, would not have reacted the way Peter did. Most men would have been pleading for mercy, nervously pacing the cell, or sitting up all night in anxious anticipation. But not Peter. He spent a restful night sleeping.

This was not because he had become so overwhelmed with the stress of mental exhaustion that he fell asleep or that he had resigned himself to the inevitable. He was able to sleep through this ordeal because he possessed such a depth of confident hope, and that hope came from the Word of God. Peter knew he wouldn't be executed because Jesus had revealed to him that he would die when he was old and crippled (John 21:18). Because Peter reflected upon the Word of God, hope was birthed in his heart and he was encouraged with the outcome of his situation. So, too, when we take time to reflect upon the counsel of God's Word, hope and encouragement can be imparted to us, as well: "For everything that was written in the past was written to teach us, so that through endurance and the encouragement of the scriptures we might have hope" (Rom. 15:4).

It Imparts Stability and Strength

The Word of God reinforces the strength and stability of our life. This is forcefully illustrated in the parable of the two men who each built a house (Luke 6:47-49). In this parable, Jesus indicated that the man who "hears my words and puts them into practice" is like a wise man who anchored the underpinings of his house upon a rock. The man who didn't was the fool who built his house upon a bed of sand. When the storms arose, the wise man's house stood firm, while the foolish man's collapsed. The strength and stability of our lives is dependent upon what we base our life upon. If our foundation is God's Word, we have stability and strength. If not, we are like a tumbleweed with no roots and no stability.

The rock and sand both originate from the same source. The only difference is the fact that sand is pulverized rock. Since the rock metaphorically represents the soundness of God's Word, the sand must represent that which is contrary to God's Word (the words of men, diluted doctrine, human philosophies, man-made tradition, religious falsehood, the wisdom of man, worldly values, etc.). When we build upon the absolute reliability of God's Word, we have security. When we build on those things which the sand represents, we will ultimately reap instability and destruction.

It Causes Us to Be Approved

Our constant exposure to God's Word helps guarantee that the quality of God's workmanship will not be disappointed. God's ultimate desire is that our lives be conformed into the image of Christ (Rom. 8:29). For this reason, the scripture exhorts us to "Study to shew thyself approved unto God, a workman that needeth not to be ashamed, rightly dividing the word of truth" (II Tim. 2:15, KJV).

God is very fussy about the final product. Without seeming sacrilegious, God is much like "Inspector 12" in the underwear commercial. God is not going to let some inferior product slip through His quality control. Like Inspector 12, "It isn't ready until He says it's ready!" The scriptures enable our life, labor, and efforts, both the outward results as well as the inward mechanics, to be found acceptable before God and others.

Someone once said that the Bible is the only book you don't truly read—it reads you. It reads our life condition like a book and reveals our positive virtues, as well as the areas which need to be corrected. God's Word constantly scans the condition of our heart, and inspects every facet of our life to insure that the end result of His craftsmanship will meet the high standards of excellency He has ordained for each one of us.

2

GUIDELINES FOR SUCCESSFUL BIBLE STUDY

It is not within the intended scope of this book to catapult the reader into the more complex and comprehensive systems of Bible study. This section represents a "back to basics" approach to personal Bible study. It offers an elementary introduction which should enable the average Christian to establish a successful relationship with the Word of God. It not only presents the practical, proven guidelines for developing a consistent habit of basic Bible devotions, but it also provides the commonsense study tips for removing those proverbial "flies in the ointment" which are notoriously counterproductive and guaranteed to undermine consistency in our relationship with the Word of God. Even the average Christian who lacks a mastery of the original languages, a working knowledge of hermeneutical principles, or a seminary degree will be more than able to understand the "meat and potatoes" of Bible truth if he will incorporate the following guidelines for personal Bible study. This is the God-given heritage and privilege of every individual Christian, even if he lacks extensive intellect and learning.

We Must Establish a Consistent Daily Pattern of Bible Reading

Unless we strive to establish a consistent, daily pattern of Bible reading, we will quickly slip into an erratic relationship with God's Word. Paul commended the Berean Christians because they "examined the Scriptures EVERY DAY" (Acts 17:11). The failure to establish this fundamental guideline is probably the greatest single hindrance to successful Bible study. Unless we consistently commune with the scriptures, our relationship with the Bible will inevitably deteriorate to the point where it loses any sense of meaningfulness for our daily life. As with human relationships, if we fail to communicate and draw close to one another on a regular basis, the quality of our relationships grow cold and we become increasingly alienated from each other. In James we read, "Draw near to God and He will draw near to you" (James 4:8, NKJV). This exhortation highlights an important promise concerning our relationship with Christ. If we take the initiative to draw near to God, He will reciprocate. This principle also holds true with God's Word. If we make the effort to draw close to His Word, we will see our relationship with the Bible enhanced and enriched. However, if we fail to draw near to God's Word, it will remain cold and aloof.

Successful Bible reading and study is absolutely dependent upon this fundamental first step. We must structure our schedules and redeem our time in order to achieve success. This is an essential requirement which we must cultivate in order to build a healthy and profitable pattern of Bible study and reading.

Read the Bible Through Consistently

Our reading should not only be daily, it must also be consistent. If we play "scripture roulette" by skipping around in a spasmodic, haphazard, undisciplined manner, we will only reinforce inconsistency and doom any hopes for a meaningful relationship with God's Word to disappointment. As someone once said, "Hit-and-run Bible reading can often become hit and miss."

We should endeavor to read each book through before moving on to another book or switching to another Testament. We must discipline ourselves against any erratic, free-floating patterns of reading which can undermine a consistency in the Word. If we fail to do so, our pick and choose habit of Bible reading will inevitably result in an anemic relationship with the Bible. Amos Wells provided this gentle admonition concerning the need for reading the Bible through consistently:

> I supposed I knew my Bible,
>   Reading piecemeal, hit or miss,
> Now a bit of John or Matthew,
>   Now a snatch of Genesis,
> Certain chapter of Isaiah,
>   Certain Psalms (the twenty-third),
> Twelfth of Romans, First of Proverbs -
>   Yes, I thought I knew the Word!
> But I found that thorough reading
>   Was a different thing to do,
> And the way was unfamiliar
>   When I read the Bible through.
> You who like to play at Bible,
>   Dip and dabble, here and there,
> Just before you kneel, aweary,
>   And yawn through a hurried prayer;
> You who treat the Crown of Writings
>   As you treat no other book -
> Just a paragraph disjointed,
>   Just a crude impatient look -
> Try a worthier procedure,
>   Try a broad and steady view;
> You will kneel in a very rapture
>   When you read the Bible through.

Don't Begin with Elaborate Patterns of Bible Study

Though there are excellent works available for more advanced forms of Bible study, many are so complicated, laborious, and time-consuming that they are actually counterproductive. More serious methods of Bible study are often so intense that only the most serious of Bible students can comprehend them and benefit from their insights. Rather than lead the average Christian into a rewarding relationship with God's Word, their complexities intimidate and confuse. Before we move onto the more involved systems of study, we should first endeavor to master the basics of daily devotions in the scriptures.

Even our daily reading schedule should be as simple as possible. Whether we consecutively read the Bible through in a year or alternate between books in the Old and New Testaments, we should adopt a yearly reading schedule which is easy to follow and keep track of (for recommended reading schedules, see Appendix A). The important thing is to select a reading plan which is best suited for you and structured to encourage consistency.

Furthermore, where we begin is important. We want to make sure that we don't get off on the wrong foot. This is particularly true for newer Christians. Many younger Christians make the mistake of selecting the worst possible books for launching forth into the scriptures. The tragic result is they often bog down and become discouraged with the mistaken first impression that the entire Bible is confusing. I have met scores of Christians whose relationship with God's Word was needlessly aborted simply because they started in the wrong place. I recommend that new Christians begin their Bible reading with the more palatable and easy to digest books such as the Gospels or epistles. They should not start out with the more difficult books such as Revelation or the prophets. They should start out with the milk of the Word before trying to chew on the meatier portions.

Select the Right Bible Version

Many Christians have difficulty developing regular disciplines in the Bible simply because they get off to a wrong start. Their Bible version is confusing and incomprehensible. When it comes to the type of version some Christians are struggling with, the old adage, "It's Greek to me," is quite appropriate. The primary reason is because the language is obsolete and incomprehensible. For example, if the King James Version is difficult to read, you should consider other quality translations such as the New King James Version, the New American Standard Bible, or the New International Version (see Section II, Chapter 6 for an evaluation of Bible versions).

The size of binding and print can also be a subtle hindrance to consistent Bible reading. While Bibles come in a variety of shapes and sizes, not all are helpful as a primary reading source. Pocket Bibles are convenient for carrying in your pocket, stashing in your desk, or placing in the glove compartment. They are useful in situations where carrying a larger Bible around would be cumbersome. However, pocket Bibles, or smaller versions, are not recommended as a mainline reading or study Bible. Christians should select a Bible which is large enough to handle easily, and contains a comfortable and easy to read type size. The print on some versions is so small that it causes eye strain and is physically wearying to the reader. If a Bible's type size is too small, it will serve as a subtle turn-off to consistent Bible reading.

Set a Reasonable Reading Pace

Some Christians establish a self-destructive pattern of Bible reading by biting off more than they can chew. They establish a self-defeating schedule which requires an unrealistic amount of daily reading which they cannot hope to handle on a consistent basis. Some believers unconsciously approach their Bible reading with a marathon mentality when, in reality, they are only equipped with a sprint ability. God is not so much concerned with the quantity of what we read as He is with the quality. He wants our contact with His Word to be a rewarding experience and not a drudgery. He wants our Bible reading disciplines to be long-lived and not short-lived. As we grow in the Word, our hunger and capacity for greater exposure will also increase. He doesn't set any limits on the amount we can read, but common sense dictates that we start off conservatively and exercise moderation in all things. We can always build up to a greater amount of daily Bible reading. But to begin with, a minimal amount of reading is preferable. A recommended amount of chapters which the average Christian can consistently maintain on a regular reading basis is two or three per day.

Read Your Bible Even When You Don't Feel Like It

If we read the Bible only when we feel like it, we will end up with an inconsistent and infrequent pattern of study. The Bible makes it clear that "we live by faith, not by sight" (II Cor. 5:7). As Christians, we should not, ultimately, govern the actions of our life by sight or circumstances. We are not to walk according to our emotions or feelings. We don't just serve God, resist temptation, love others, believe God, pay our bills, or act responsibly only when we feel like it—at least, we shouldn't. This is no less true of our need to maintain such spiritual disciplines as prayer, giving, or Bible devotions. Just because we don't experience an emotional quickening every time we read God's Word doesn't mean our time was wasted or we have not truly benefited.

Daily devotions in the scriptures is a discipline which demands diligence, determination, and a measure of sacrifice. However, the rewards for our labor will far outweigh any effort on our part.

Read at the Right Place and Right Time

Each of our metabolisms is different. We each have our high points and down times during the day. Some of us are more alert in the morning, while others hit their stride during the evening. But an important key is, if at all possible, to establish your Bible reading time during your peak periods of the day. We should take advantage of those time frames when our minds are most alert. For most people, this will be during the morning before the distractions and cares of the day's activities have taken their toll. Our minds are usually refreshed and uncluttered in the morning. Others may find the evening hours, when the responsibilities of the day are behind them, the children are in bed, and you have a period of quiet time to yourself, to be the most convenient time to read God's Word.

We should not only set aside a specific time to read, but we should also set aside a specific place to read. This may be in the comfort of your home, office, or some other secluded spot which affords an atmosphere conducive to Bible reading and study. Trying to read in a place where there are constant distractions and interruptions is obviously not very helpful. This is not to suggest that we should only read the Bible in pre-arranged places or predetermined times. Just as we are encouraged to be "instant in prayer" (Rom. 12:12, KJV), we should also be encouraged to partake of God's Word at any time. God's Word goes well with any time or season. However, by establishing definite times and places, we help ensure the discipline of consistency. If we don't set aside a specific time or place, we will inevitably lapse into an irregular pattern of Bible reading and study.

Keep a Bible Diary or Notebook

I have often reflected upon a passing encounter I had during my college days with one of my professors. I accidently bumped into him in the hallway as I was going to one of my classes. The incident lead to a brief conversation about some point of truth which he had covered in his class. I told him what a profound revelation it had been to my life. At that point, in his half joking, half serious style, he reached into his coat pocket and pulled out a small scratch pad and pen and said, "You know, Bill, after all these years of study, I have finally received one of the greatest revelations of my life, and that is to remember to always carry a pen and some paper to write upon. I can't tell you how many important thoughts and insights I've lost because I didn't write them down." We both laughed and then went our way. However, over the ensuing years I have found, through practical experience, that he was more serious than I first thought. I have, likewise, discovered the wisdom behind this common sense discipline.

We should get in the habit of recording the insights which we glean from our daily reading and study. We can do this by keeping a daily log, by chapter, verse, or book, for future reference. This can be especially helpful in the future when we retrace the same scripture sections during our yearly safari through the Bible. This record of insights can refresh us in those previous truths, and serve as a catalyst for stimulating fresh insights. When we write down these observations and truths, it helps clarify and reinforce the revelations we have received. It gives a dimension of permanency to the learning experience, and fosters a tangible sense of accomplishment and progress.

We should also not be afraid to mark our Bibles. Some Bibles, such as larger print or wide margin versions, are more suited for this. One of the practical ways of preserving the truths we have received in the course of our reading is to carefully underline or highlight important verses, key words, and phrases. There are a variety of colored highlighters which are well suited for this. We can also record notes, individual observations, and additional scripture references in the margin. Keeping a record of notes, both within the text of our Bible, as well as in a separate notebook or personalized file system, is one of the fundamental first steps to more advanced forms of systematic Bible study.

Meditate upon God's Word

We must learn to develop more than just a superficial relationship with the Word of God. If we limit our exposure to the

Bible to a casual contact, we will only reap a limited amount of blessing. John Owen once said that, "In the divine Scriptures, there are shallows and there are deeps; shallows where the lamb may wade, and deeps where the elephant may swim." We can't merely content ourselves with wading in the shallows. The shallows have their benefits, but we must sometimes take the dive into those deeper pools in order to experience the fulness of God's Word. Meditation takes us beyond scratching the surface of God's Word to probing its sublime depths.

Meditation involves both consideration and concentration. It requires that we carefully endeavor to hear what the scriptures are saying. In Luke, Jesus warned us to "take heed how you hear" (Luke 8:18, NKJV). It is possible to listen and not really hear what's being communicated, or to hear and not really listen. Meditation is a discipline which helps us hear, and hear accurately. It helps us tune into the wave length of God's Word. It helps us focus our mental faculties to properly receive what God is trying to communicate to us. Meditation requires a greater degree of discipline on our part. It involves our taking the time to pause and thoughtfully consider what God is saying to us.

God commends the man whose "delight is in the law of the Lord, and on his law he meditates day and night" (Psalms 1:2). The word "meditate" is related to the expression, "chew the cud." It metaphorically characterizes the similarities between the behavior of a cow chewing its cud and the believer meditating on God's Word. Our meditation should be like the action of a cow which chews a lump of grass, swallows it, brings it up again, and chews on it some more before repeating the process.

The problem with many of us is that we have developed poor eating habits, not only in the types of food we eat, but in our manner of eating. The fast-food, fast-paced mentality of our day often carries over to our spiritual eating habits. Often, we are in such a "get there yesterday" mentality that we hastily gulp down the Word of God, on the run, without savoring its flavors or reflecting upon its meaning. If all we have with the

267

Word of God is a rushed relationship which is more interested in hurriedly consuming our daily quota than carefully considering what we have been reading, we are guaranteed to perpetuate an anemic relationship with the scriptures. Quality depends upon disciplining ourselves to reconsider and thoughtfully ponder upon what we have read throughout the course of the day.

Paul essentially encouraged Timothy to do this when he stated, "reflect on what I am saying, for the Lord will give you insight into all this" (II Tim. 2:7). As we reflect upon the Word, the Lord gives deeper insights. In II Timothy 2:15, he highlighted the importance of meditation when he stated, "Study (be diligent, meditate upon, concentrate) to shew thyselve approved unto God, a workman that needeth not to be ashamed, rightly dividing the word of truth" (KJV).

The process of meditation is the pathway to deeper insights and understanding. David even went so far as to state that meditation had made him wiser than all his teachers: "I have more insight than all my teachers, for I meditate on your statutes" (Ps. 119:99). Meditation helps us comprehend the truths we have read, and absorb them into our life situations. Meditation transforms our reading from a superficial, religious exercise into a deeply rewarding experience. When we take the time to contemplate the potential depth of meaning contained within even the most humble of passages, we can appreciate the insights of Martin Luther who said, "In scripture, every little daisy is a meadow."

We Must Personalize the Word of God

Reading the Bible must involve more than our "getting into the Word"—it must involve "the Word getting into us." Robert Horn declared, "If the Bible is to get into us we must get into the Bible." As we have seen with Bible meditation, getting into the Word demands a deeper level of consideration than just reading the printed word. Our meditation should include the added dimension of personalizing the truths we have received, and considering how they practically relate to our lives. Meditation generates knowledge and wisdom, but personalizing the scriptures gives us the needed understanding to apply the truths received. Personalizing the scriptures takes our study out of the realm of the abstract and conceptual and into the realm of personal intimacy, awareness, and relatability. Personalizing the Word helps it become flesh to us, and transforms our reading into a vital, living experience.

There are some simple keys for stimulating successful personalization of the scriptures. Our meditation will come alive if we will remember to consider the familiar who?, what?, where?, when?, why?, and how?:

1. **Who** were the people involved? **Who** wasn't involved?
2. **What** happened? **What** were the ideas expressed? **What** is the main point of the passage(s)? **What** did it mean to the original readers? **What** were the results? If it happened in the Old Testament, **what** is its New Testament meaning or equivalent? **What** was it typically foreshadowing? **What** spiritual lesson does it have for New Testament believers? **What** is an equivalent situation today to that of the original readers?
3. **Where** did the events take place? **Where** was the setting?
4. **When** did the events take place? **When** were they prophesied to take place? **When** was the passage(s) written? **When** will the promise or information be fulfilled?
5. **Why** was it written? **Why** did it happen?
6. **How** does the information relate to me? **How** does it compare with other passages? **How** does it relate to the overall context of the chapter in which it is located, the book, the Testament, the entire Bible?

Some additional guidelines focus upon the following questions:

1. Was there a **sin** for me to avoid?

2. Was there a **promise** to claim?
3. Was there an **example** to follow?
4. Was there a **command** to obey?
5. Was there a new **truth** learned which can help me mature as a Christian?

If we will implement these simple study tips, we will soon see our meditation and personalizing of the scriptures transform our study of God's Word into a richly rewarding adventure.

We Should Use Bible Helps and Reference Books

Additional study aids can assist us in our Bible study. However, they should never serve to supplant our own personal devotions but supplement our study. If we lean too heavily upon outside aids, we run the risk of undermining the potential benefits which God intends for each of us to derive from the personalized study of God's Word. As one author noted,

> . . . there is a definite harm in using reference books the wrong way—particularly by substituting them for personal study. This is like eating pre-chewed or predigested food. No doubt we can get some benefit from such food, but think of what we miss: the benefit to the body of doing our own chewing, the enjoyment of good-tasting food, etc. In Bible study the loss that comes from simply reading what others have learned is even greater. No blessing and joy can surpass what we get from studying the Bible and learning directly from the Lord.[1]

However, when used in a balanced "buddy system" with the Bible, they can be an extremely helpful complement.

Such helps as Bible handbooks, a Bible dictionary, a concordance, a quality commentary, a book on Bible customs and

---

1 T. Norton Sterrett, **How To Understand Your Bible,** p. 33.

manners, and a good study Bible such as the "Thompson Chain Reference Bible" or the "Open Bible" are extremely helpful tools. Using these aids alongside of our daily reading can help provide further insights into the scriptures. They contain a wealth of facts and information which can enrich our Bible knowledge, as well as enhance our overall understanding. A small reference library is a wise investment (see Appendix B).

We should also consider supplementing our reading with other Bible translations, paraphrases, and parallel versions such as "The Living Bible," "Phillips," "The Amplified Bible," and "The Parallel New Testament."

We Must Pray

Maybe you've heard the oft-told story about the sinking ocean liner. As its bow was gradually slipping beneath the water line, those that were unable to get on a life raft were huddled on the fan tail waiting for the end to come. The captain stepped forward and said, "Let us pray." At that point, someone in the crowd replied, "Has it come to that?" Many launch forth into their Bible reading endeavors without considering the need to "come to that." Bible reading, without prayer, can be a dry experience. Prayer brings the refreshing waters of the Holy Spirit into our learning experience. Prayer is an essential prerequisite to Bible reading. Our Bible study will become much more fulfilling if we will take a brief moment to simply ask God to anoint our minds and minister revelation, insight, clarity, and understanding. Prayer will also quicken our discernment, memory, and recall. This is why David entreated the Lord, "Open my eyes that I may see wonderful things in your law" (Ps. 119:18).

Don't Give Up

The Bible declares that "though a righteous man falls seven times, he rises again" (Prov. 24:16). If, in your endeavors to establish consistency you miss a day, don't give up! It takes

271

time to reinforce consistent study habits. If you miss a day or two in your reading, don't become discouraged and disillusioned. Simply rise up and resume your reading schedule where you left off and get back on track to a rewarding relationship with the Word of God.

3

THE NEED FOR APPLICATION

More Than Knowledge

The Bible will do us no good sitting on the proverbial shelf gathering dust. Neither will owning an expensive leather Bible or consistently carrying it around without availing ourselves of its truths automatically profit us or guarantee spiritual growth. Its life-changing power is not mysteriously absorbed through osmosis. We must actively give ourselves to studying its contents. However, the ultimate goal of Bible reading and study is not the accumulation of facts and information. The Word of God must be applied to our life. As D.L. Moody noted, "The scriptures were not given to increase our knowledge but to change lives."

Our western world is currently experiencing a radical revolution which is transforming the face of society. We are rapidly moving away from an industrial-based society to an informational base. The advances in computer technology, along with a shift to a media-oriented society, has placed a premium upon the accumulation and distribution of knowledge. While there are definite benefits associated with this transformation, there are also inherent dangers, especially in regards to our Christian relationship to life. There is a subtle danger that Christians will become more interested in the accumulation of knowledge about Christianity than in applying that knowledge. We must never lose sight of the fact that Christ has not primarily called us into a theological, conceptual, or intellectual relationship. This is not to discount these essential aspects, but unless our knowledge is translated into action, it is utterly worthless. Unless our scriptural head knowledge filters down to heart and life experience, the Word has only been intellectualized and not actualized.

Putting It Into Practice

This reminds me of a story about a young agricultural student fresh out of college. He had recently been hired by the Bureau of Farm Management and assigned to the field to bring farmers up-to-date on the latest principles of farming. When the young man arrived at the farm of one seasoned farmer, he pulled a bunch of pamphlets and circulars out of his briefcase and began to instruct the old farmer on all the new techniques. The farmer patiently heard him out and then replied, "Sonny, my problem is not a lack of knowledge. I already have more knowledge than I can ever hope to use. My problem is putting that knowledge into practice." This humorous story says a lot about the similar need of many Christians.

What Christianity needs most is the putting into practice of the knowledge we receive from the scriptures. This is one of the greatest potential risks threatening the quality and reality of our Christian experience. It's true that God's people can be destroyed from a lack of knowledge (Hosea 4:6), but multitudes are destroyed even with knowledge. The world is filled with spiritually-educated derelicts who can credit their condition to the fact that they have never submitted to the Lordship of Christ and the mandates of His Word. It's true that we need to grow in the boundless knowledge of the Bible, but it must not be isolated to our heads but released through our lives.

A Great Responsibility

Someone once said that, "It is a great responsibility owning a Bible." The reason is simple: the Bible challenges us to respond. Its truths demand action; its revelations require responsibility; its principles necessitate practice. True mastery of the Word is not determined in the classroom or private study. It is, ultimately, determined by our response in the world in which we live.

Bible reading is a good first step, but it is not the final destination. It is a means to an end. Reading schedules, timetables, study methods and techniques will not benefit us if we fail to apply the Word to our life situations. Our meditation and personalization of the scriptures should lead us to become "doers of the word, and not hearers only (thus) deceiving yourselves" (James 1:22, NKJV). Reading the Bible without practicing its precepts is like the habitual dieter who avidly reads every new diet book and follows every new diet craze. He may know every diet program, all the nutritional guidelines, and all the related health tips, but unless he puts into practice the insights he has acquired, he will not lose weight. We must exercise ourselves above and beyond merely skimming the pages of the Bible. We must be as James said, "doers" and not just "hearers." We must apply ourselves wholly to the scriptures, and the scriptures wholly to ourselves. Studying the Word of God without applying it will be about as effective for our life as rubbing an aspirin tablet on our forehead will be for relieving a headache.

We must not only give ourselves to the Bible and believe the Bible, but we must obediently behave it! Our prayers for spiritual insight and understanding must be coupled with the resolute desire and steadfast determination to obediently respond to the truths we receive through our Bible reading and study, for it is at the point of obedience that the Word of God is truly energized and becomes "flesh" in us.

The Result of Neglecting God's Word

The negative consequences of neglecting God's Word are many, but the primary result can be summed up with the words "spiritual weakness." A failure to consistently partake of the Word of God parallels the effects of failing to eat food in the natural. The Word likens itself to milk, meat, and bread for good reasons. It is God's divine provision for spiritual sustenance. The true worth of the Word lies in its nutritional value. As W. H. Houghton stated, "The Bible calls itself food. The value of food is not in the discussion it arouses but in the nourishment it imparts." Vance Harner also added, "The storehouse of God's Word was never meant for mere scrutiny, not primarily for study, but for sustenance!" When we neglect the regular sustenance of God's Word, we soon suffer the detrimental side effects.

So essential is God's Word to our spiritual well-being that Job declared, "I have treasured the words of his mouth more than my necessary food" (Job 23:12, NKJV). All of us would claim that food is absolutely essential to preserving our physical health, but few can honestly confess that the nourishment of God's Word is "more necessary" to our life. A failure to recognize the necessity of this fact invariably leads to spiritual weakness.

Many Christians are spiritually unhealthy, unproductive, anemic, and malnourished simply because they do not eat the Word on a regular basis. Many Christians have spiritual eating disorders similar to those found in the world. Some are spiritually anorexic. They are trying to live on a ration diet rather than partake of the bounty which God has provided. Others are bolemic. They have a gorge and purge relationship with the Bible. They have an inconsistent relationship which goes through intermittent seasons of commitment and neglect, feast and famine. A majority of the problems and perplexities we suffer are the direct by-product of trying to subsist on a starvation diet. Spiritual weakness, inefficiency, and inability are often linked to insufficient spiritual nourishment.

Others are weak because of poor eating habits. The Bible was never intended to be a spiritual smorgasbord which caters to the selective eating habits of picky Christians. We are not exhorted to read only those portions of the Word which appeal to our tastebuds. We should partake of all portions of the scriptures, both the sweet and sour, hot and cold, vegetables and dessert. Only in this manner can we enjoy the well-rounded nourishment of God's balanced diet. If we only eat those sections that are appealing to our palates, we will, in time, suffer nutritional deficiencies. There are many sicknesses which can result from dietary deficiencies such as scurvy, rickets, and weak eyesight. The same holds true of our spiritual health. As we continue to neglect the scriptures, our spiritual health deteriorates and we find ourselves suffering from a lack of vision, a loss of wisdom and discernment, emotional weakness, and an absence of zeal, peace, and joy. Many of the spiritual, mental, emotional ailments afflicting our life are the direct result of neglecting a proper intake of God's Word.

Many Christians have developed poor eating habits and eating disorders because they have never learned to enjoy the taste of God's Word. God's Word is an acquired taste. The more you eat, the more you like. David had discovered this and so declared, "How sweet are your words to my taste!" (Ps. 119:103, NKJV). If we continue eating God's Word, we will soon begin to relish its taste. "The longer you read the Bible, the more you will like it; it will grow sweeter and sweeter" (William Romaine). But if we continue in a pattern of inconsistency, we will never learn to tolerate its many flavors. As someone once stated, "The man who samples the word of God occasionally, never acquires much of a taste for it."

277

This again brings us back to the basic necessity of partaking on a regular basis. The Israelites had to gather manna each day in order to survive. Jesus also revealed that "Man shall not live by bread alone, but by every word that proceeds from the mouth of God" (Matt. 4:4, NKJV). In order to live and thrive we must, likewise, gather a portion of the Word each day. Sound spiritual health absolutely depends upon a wholesome spiritual diet of God's Word.

Appendix A

YEARLY BIBLE READING SCHEDULES

THE NEW TESTAMENT, PSALMS, PROVERBS, ECCLESIASTES, & SONG OF SOLOMON IN A YEAR

Week	Suggested Reading	Week	Suggested Reading
Jan. 1-7	Luke 1-4 Psalms 1-3; Prov. 1	Apr. 2-8	James & I Thess. 1,2 Psalms 38-40; Prov. 14
Jan. 8-14	Luke 5-7 Psalms 4-6; Prov. 2	Apr. 9-15	I Thess. 3-5; II Thess. Psalms 41-43; Prov. 15
Jan. 15-21	Luke 8-11 Psalms 7-9; Prov. 3	Apr. 16-22	Mark 1-4 Psalms 44-46; Prov. 16
Jan. 22-28	Luke 12-14 Psalms 10-12; Prov. 4	Apr. 23-29	Mark 5-8 Psalms 47-49; Prov. 17
Jan. 29- Feb. 4	Luke 15-18 Psalms 13-16; Prov. 5	Apr. 30- May 6	Mark 9-12 Psalms 50-52; Prov. 18
Feb. 5-11	Luke 19-21 Psalms 17, 18; Prov. 6	May 7-13	Mark 13-16 Psalms 53-55; Prov. 19
Feb. 12-18	Luke 22-24 Psalms 19-21; Prov. 7	May 14-20	Romans 1-7 Psalms 56-58; Prov. 20
Feb. 19-25	Acts 1-5 Psalms 22-24; Prov. 8	May 21-27	Romans 8-12 Psalms 59-61; Prov. 21
Feb. 26- Mar. 4	Acts 6-8 Psalms 25-27; Prov. 9	May 28- June 3	Rom. 13-16; I Cor. 1,2 Psalms 62-64; Prov. 22
Mar. 5-11	Acts 9-14 Psalms 28-30; Prov. 10	June 4-10	I Cor. 3-8 Psalms 65-67; Prov. 23
Mar. 12-18	Acts 15-18 Psalms 31-33; Prov. 11	June 11-17	I Cor. 9-13 Psalms 68,69; Prov. 24
Mar. 19-25	Acts 19-23 Psalms 34, 35; Prov. 12	June 18-24	I Cor. 14-16; II Cor. 1,2 Psalms 70-72; Prov. 25
Mar. 26- Apr. 1	Acts 24-28 Psalms 36,37; Prov. 13	June 25- July 1	II Cor. 3-8 Psalms 73,74; Prov. 26

Week	Suggested Reading	Week	Suggested Reading
July 2-8	II Cor. 9-13 Psalms 75-77; Prov. 27	Oct. 8-14	Hebrews 9-13 Psalms 112-115; Eccl. 10
July 9-15	Galatians Psalm 78; Prov. 28	Oct. 15-21	John 1-4 Psalms 116-118; Eccl. 11
July 16-22	Matt. 1-6 Psalms 79-81; Prov. 29	Oct. 22-28	John 5-7 Psalms 119; Eccl. 12
July 23-29	Matt. 7-11 Psalms 82-84; Prov. 30	Oct. 29- Nov. 4	John 8-10 Psalms 120-123; Song 1
July 30- Aug. 5	Matt. 12-15 Psalms 85-87; Prov. 31	Nov. 5-11	John 11-13 Psalms 124-127; Song 2
Aug. 6-12	Matt. 16-20 Psalms 88,89; Eccl. 1	Nov. 12-18	John 14-17 Psalms 128-131; Song 3
Aug. 13-19	Matt. 21-24 Psalms 90-92; Eccl. 2	Nov. 19-25	John 18-21 Psalms 132-135; Song 4
Aug. 20-26	Matt. 25-28 Psalms 93-95; Eccl. 3	Nov. 26- Dec. 2	I, II, III John Psalms 136-138; Song 5
Aug. 27- Sept. 2	Ephesians; Phil. 1,2 Psalms 96-98; Eccl. 4	Dec. 3-9	Revelation 1-7 Psalms 139-141; Song 6
Sept. 3-9	Phil. 3,4; Col.; Philemon Psalms 99-102; Eccl. 5	Dec. 10-16	Revelation 8-14 Psalms 142-144; Song 7
Sept. 10-16	I Timothy Psalms 103,104; Eccl. 6	Dec. 17-23	Revelation 15-22 Psalms 145-147; Song 8
Sept. 17-23	II Timothy; Titus Psalms 105,106; Eccl. 7	Dec. 24-31	Read favorite New Testament book and
Sept. 24-30	I & II Peter; Jude Psalms 107,108; Eccl. 8		prepare to start again! Psalms 148-150
Oct. 1-7	Hebrews 1-8 Psalms 109-111; Eccl. 9		

THE ENTIRE BIBLE IN ONE YEAR*

	January		February		March
Day	**Suggested Reading**	**Day**	**Suggested Reading**	**Day**	**Suggested Reading**
1	Gen. 1,2	1	Exod. 14-17	1	Deut. 4-6
2	Gen. 3-5	2	Exod. 18-20	2	Deut. 7-9
3	Gen. 6-9	3	Exod. 21-24	3	Deut. 10-12
4	Gen. 10,11	4	Exod. 25-27	4	Deut. 13-16
5	Gen. 12-15	5	Exod. 28-31	5	Deut. 17-19
6	Gen. 16-19	6	Exod. 32-34	6	Deut. 20-22
7	Gen. 20-22	7	Exod. 35-37	7	Deut. 23-25
8	Gen. 23-26	8	Exod. 38-40	8	Deut. 26-28
9	Gen. 27-29	9	Lev. 1-4	9	Deut. 29-31
10	Gen. 30-32	10	Lev. 5-7	10	Deut. 32-34
11	Gen. 33-36	11	Lev. 8-10	11	Josh. 1-3
12	Gen. 37-39	12	Lev. 11-13	12	Josh. 4-6
13	Gen. 40-42	13	Lev. 14-16	13	Josh. 7-9
14	Gen. 43-46	14	Lev. 17-19	14	Josh. 10-12
15	Gen. 47-50	15	Lev. 20-23	15	Josh. 13-15
16	Job 1-4	16	Lev. 24-27	16	Josh. 16-18
17	Job 5-7	17	Num. 1-3	17	Josh. 19-21
18	Job 8-10	18	Num. 4-6	18	Josh. 22-24
19	Job 11-13	19	Num. 7-10	19	Judg. 1-4
20	Job 14-17	20	Num. 11-14	20	Judg. 5-8
21	Job 18-20	21	Num. 15-17	21	Judg. 9-12
22	Job 21-24	22	Num. 18-20	22	Judg. 13-15
23	Job 25-27	23	Num. 21-24	23	Judg. 16-18
24	Job 28-31	24	Num. 25-27	24	Judg. 19-21
25	Job 32-34	25	Num. 28-30	25	Ruth 1-4
26	Job 35-37	26	Num. 31-33	26	I Sam. 1-3
27	Job 38-42	27	Num. 34-36	27	I Sam. 4-7
28	Exod. 1-4	28	Deut. 1-3	28	I Sam. 8-10
29	Exod. 5-7			29	I Sam. 11-13
30	Exod. 8-10			30	I Sam. 14-16
31	Exod. 11-13			31	I Sam. 17-20

*Leslie B. Flynn, **Charisma Magazine**, January 1985.

April		May		June	
Day	Suggested Reading	Day	Suggested Reading	Day	Suggested Reading
1	I Sam. 21-24	1	Ps. 61-63	1	Prov. 1-3
2	I Sam. 25-28	2	Ps. 64-66	2	Prov. 4-7
3	I Sam. 29-31	3	Ps. 67-69	3	Prov. 8-11
4	II Sam. 1-4	4	Ps. 70-72	4	Prov. 12-14
5	II Sam. 5-8	5	Ps. 73-75	5	Prov. 15-18
6	II Sam. 9-12	6	Ps. 76-78	6	Prov. 19-21
7	II Sam. 13-15	7	Ps. 79-81	7	Prov. 22-24
8	II Sam. 16-18	8	Ps. 82-84	8	Prov. 25-28
9	II Sam. 19-21	9	Ps. 85-87	9	Prov. 29-31
10	II Sam. 22-24	10	Ps. 88-90	10	Eccl. 1-3
11	Ps. 1-3	11	Ps. 91-93	11	Eccl. 4-6
12	Ps. 4-6	12	Ps. 94-96	12	Eccl. 7-9
13	Ps. 7-9	13	Ps. 97-99	13	Eccl. 10-12
14	Ps. 10-12	14	Ps. 100-102	14	Songs 1-4
15	Ps. 13-15	15	Ps. 103-105	15	Songs 5-8
16	Ps. 16-18	16	Ps. 106-108	16	I Kings 5-7
17	Ps. 19-21	17	Ps. 109-111	17	I Kings 8-10
18	Ps. 22-24	18	Ps. 112-114	18	I Kings 11-13
19	Ps. 25-27	19	Ps. 115-118	19	I Kings 14-16
20	Ps. 28-30	20	Ps. 119	20	I Kings 17-19
21	Ps. 31-33	21	Ps. 120-123	21	I Kings 20-22
22	Ps. 34-36	22	Ps. 124-126	22	II Kings 1-3
23	Ps. 37-39	23	Ps. 127-129	23	II Kings 4-6
24	Ps. 40-42	24	Ps. 130-132	24	II Kings 7-10
25	Ps. 43-45	25	Ps. 133-135	25	II Kings 11-14:20
26	Ps. 46-48	26	Ps. 136-138	26	Joel 1-3
27	Ps. 49-51	27	Ps. 139-141	27	II Kings 14:21-25; Jonah 1-4
28	Ps. 52-54	28	Ps. 142-144	28	II Kings 14:26-29; Amos 1-3
29	Ps. 55-57	29	Ps. 145-147	29	Amos 4-6
30	Ps. 58-60	30	Ps. 148-150	30	Amos 7-9
		31	I Kings 1-4		

July	August	September
Suggested	Suggested	Suggested
Day Reading	Day Reading	Day Reading
1 II Kings 15-17	1 II Kings 20,21	1 II Chron. 4-6
2 Hosea 1-4	2 Zeph. 1-3	2 II Chron. 7-9
3 Hosea 5-7	3 Hab. 1-3	3 II Chron. 10-13
4 Hosea 8-10	4 II Kings 22-25	4 II Chron. 14-16
5 Hosea 11-14	5 Obad.	5 II Chron. 17-19
6 II Kings 18,19	Jer. 1,2	6 II Chron. 20-22
7 Isa. 1-3	6 Jer. 3-5	7 II Chron. 23-25
8 Isa. 4-6	7 Jer. 6-8	8 II Chron. 26-29
9 Isa. 7-9	8 Jer. 9-12	9 II Chron. 30-32
10 Isa. 10-12	9 Jer. 13-16	10 II Chron. 33-36
11 Isa. 13-15	10 Jer. 17-20	11 Ezek. 1-3
12 Isa. 16-18	11 Jer. 21-23	12 Ezek. 4-7
13 Isa. 19-21	12 Jer. 24-26	13 Ezek. 8-11
14 Isa. 22-24	13 Jer. 27-29	14 Ezek. 12-14
15 Isa. 25-27	14 Jer. 30-32	15 Ezek. 15-18
16 Isa. 28-30	15 Jer. 33-36	16 Ezek. 19-21
17 Isa. 31-33	16 Jer. 37-39	17 Ezek. 22-24
18 Isa. 34-36	17 Jer. 40-42	18 Ezek. 25-27
19 Isa. 37-39	18 Jer. 43-46	19 Ezek. 28-30
20 Isa. 40-42	19 Jer. 47-49	20 Ezek. 31-33
21 Isa. 43-45	20 Jer. 50-52	21 Ezek. 34-36
22 Isa. 46-48	21 Lam. 1-5	22 Ezek. 37-39
23 Isa. 49-51	22 I Chron. 1-3	23 Ezek. 40-42
24 Isa. 52-54	23 I Chron. 4-6	24 Ezek. 43-45
25 Isa. 55-57	24 I Chron. 7-9	25 Ezek. 46-48
26 Isa. 58-60	25 I Chron. 10-13	26 Dan. 1-3
27 Isa. 61-63	26 I Chron. 14-16	27 Dan. 4-6
28 Isa. 64-66	27 I Chron. 17-19	28 Dan. 7-9
29 Mic. 1-4	28 I Chron. 20-23	29 Dan. 10-12
30 Mic. 5-7	29 I Chron. 24-26	30 Esth. 1-3
31 Nah. 1-3	30 I Chron. 27-29	
	31 II Chron. 1-3	

October Day	Suggested Reading	November Day	Suggested Reading	December Day	Suggested Reading
1	Esth. 4-7	1	Luke 14-17	1	Rom. 5-8
2	Esth. 8-10	2	Luke 18-21	2	Rom. 9-11
3	Ezra 1-4	3	Luke 22-24	3	Rom. 12-16
4	Hag. 1,2	4	John 1-3	4	Acts 20:3-22:30
	Zech. 1,2	5	John 4-6	5	Acts 23-25
5	Zech. 3-6	6	John 7-10	6	Acts 26-28
6	Zech. 7-10	7	John 11-13	7	Eph. 1-3
7	Zech. 11-14	8	John 14-17	8	Eph. 4-6
8	Ezra 5-7	9	John 18-21	9	Phil. 1-4
9	Ezra 8-10	10	Acts 1,2	10	Col. 1-4
10	Neh. 1-3	11	Acts 3-5	11	Heb. 1-4
11	Neh. 4-6	12	Acts 6-9	12	Heb. 5-7
12	Neh. 7-9	13	Acts 10-12	13	Heb. 8-10
13	Neh. 10-13	14	Acts 13,14	14	Heb. 11-13
14	Mal. 1-4	15	James 1,2	15	Philem.
15	Matt. 1-4	16	James 3-5		I Peter 1,2
16	Matt. 5-7	17	Gal. 1-3	16	I Peter 3-5
17	Matt. 8-11	18	Gal. 4-6	17	II Peter 1-3
18	Matt. 12-15	19	Acts 15-18:11	18	I Tim. 1-3
19	Matt. 16-19	20	I Thess. 1-5	19	I Tim. 4-6
20	Matt. 20-22	21	II Thess. 1-3	20	Titus 1-3
21	Matt. 23-25		Acts 18:12-19:10	21	II Tim. 1-4
22	Matt. 26-28	22	I Cor. 1-4	22	I John 1,2
23	Mark 1-3	23	I Cor. 5-8	23	I John 3-5
24	Mark 4-6	24	I Cor. 9-12	24	II John
25	Mark 7-10	25	I Cor. 13-16		III John
26	Mark 11-13	26	Acts 19:11-20:1		Jude
27	Mark 14-16		II Cor. 1-3	25	Rev. 1-3
28	Luke 1-3	27	II Cor. 4-6	26	Rev. 4-6
29	Luke 4-6	28	II Cor. 7-9	27	Rev. 7-9
30	Luke 7-9	29	II Cor. 10-13	28	Rev. 10-12
31	Luke 10-13	30	Acts 20:2	29	Rev. 13-15
			Rom. 1-4	30	Rev. 16-18
				31	Rev. 19-22

A MORNING AND EVENING SCHEDULE
THROUGH THE ENTIRE BIBLE IN A YEAR*

JANUARY

Date	Morning MATT.	Evening GEN.
1	1	1,2,3
2	2	4,5,6
3	3	7,8,9
4	4	10,11,12
5	5:1-26	13,14,15
6	5:27-48	16,17
7	6:1-18	18,19
8	6:19-34	20,21,22
9	7	23,24
10	8:1-17	25,26
11	8:18-34	27,28
12	9:1-17	29,30
13	9:18-38	31,32
14	10:1-20	33,34,35
15	10:21-42	36,37,38
16	11	39,40
17	12:1-23	41,42
18	12:24-50	43,44,45
19	13:1-30	46,47,48
20	13:31-58	49,50
		EXOD.
21	14:1-21	1,2,3
22	14:22-36	4,5,6
23	15:1-20	7,8
24	15:21-39	9,10,11
25	16	12,13
26	17	14,15
27	18:1-20	16,17,18
28	18:21-35	19,20
29	19	21,22
30	20:1-16	23,24
31	20:17-34	25,26

FEBRUARY

Date	Morning MATT.	Evening EXOD.
1	21:1-22	27,28
2	21:23-46	29,30
3	22:1-22	31,32,33
4	22:23-46	34,35
5	23:1-22	36,37,38
6	23:23-39	39,40
		LEV.
7	24:1-28	1,2,3
8	24:29-51	4,5
9	25:1-30	6,7
10	25:31-46	8,9,10
11	26:1-25	11,12
12	26:26-50	13
13	26:51-75	14
14	27:1-26	15,16
15	27:27-50	17,18
16	27:51-66	19,20
17	28	21,22
	MARK	
18	1:1-22	23,24
19	1:23-45	25
20	2	26,27
		NUM.
21	3:1-19	1,2
22	3:20-35	3,4
23	4:1-20	5,6
24	4:21-41	7,8
25	5:1-20	9,10,11
26	5:21-43	12,13,14
27	6:1-29	15,16
28	6:30-56	17,18,19
29	7:1-13	20,21,22

MARCH

Date	Morning MARK	Evening NUM.
1	7:14-37	23,24,25
2	8:1-21	26,27
3	8:22-38	28,29,30
4	9:1-29	31,32,33
5	9:30-50	34,35,36
		DEUT.
6	10:1-31	1,2
7	10:32-52	3,4
8	11:1-18	5,6,7
9	11:19-33	8,9,10
10	12:1-27	11,12,13
11	12:28-44	14,15,16
12	13:1-20	17,18,19
13	13:21-37	20,21,22
14	14:1-26	23,24,25
15	14:27-53	26,27
16	14:54-72	28,29
17	15:1-25	30,31
18	15:26-47	32,33,34
		JOSH.
19	16	1,2,3
	LUKE	
20	1:1-20	4,5,6
21	1:21-38	7,8,9
22	1:39-56	10,11,12
23	1:57-80	13,14,15
24	2:1-24	16,17,18
25	2:25-52	19,20,21
26	3	22,23,24
		JUDG.
27	4:1-30	1,2,3
28	4:31-44	4,5,6
29	5:1-16	7,8
30	5:17-39	9,10
31	6:1-26	11,12

APRIL

Date	Morning LUKE	Evening JUDG.
1	6:27-49	13,14,15
2	7:1-30	16,17,18
3	7:31-50	19,20,21
		RUTH
4	8:1-25	1,2,3,4
		I SAM.
5	8:26-56	1,2,3
6	9:1-17	4,5,6
7	9:18-36	7,8,9
8	9:37-62	10,11,12
9	10:1-24	13,14
10	10:25-42	15,16
11	11:1-28	17,18
12	11:29-54	19,20,21
13	12:1-31	22,23,24
14	12:32-59	25,26
15	13:1-22	27,28,29
16	13:23-35	30,31
		II SAM.
17	14:1-24	1,2
18	14:25-35	3,4,5
19	15:1-10	6,7,8
20	15:11-32	9,10,11
21	16	12,13
22	17:1-19	14,15
23	17:20-37	16,17,18
24	18:1-23	19,20
25	18:24-43	21,22
26	19:1-27	23,24
		I KINGS
27	19:28-48	1,2
28	20:1-26	3,4,5
29	20:27-47	6,7
30	21:1-19	8,9

MAY

Date	Morning LUKE	Evening I KINGS
1	21:20-38	10,11
2	22:1-20	12,13
3	22:21-46	14,15
4	22:47-71	16,17,18
5	23:1-25	19,20
6	23:26-56	21,22
		II KINGS
7	24:1-35	1,2,3
8	24:36-53	4,5,6
	JOHN	
9	1:1-28	7,8,9
10	1:29-51	10,11,12
11	2	13,14
12	3:1-18	15,16
13	3:19-38	17,18
14	4:1-30	19,20,21
15	4:31-54	22,23
16	5:1-24	24,25
		I CHR.
17	5:25-47	1,2,3
18	6:1-21	4,5,6
19	6:22-44	7,8,9
20	6:45-71	10,11,12
21	7:1-27	13,14,15
22	7:28-53	16,17,18
23	8:1-27	19,20,21
24	8:28-59	22,23,24
25	9:1-23	25,26,27
26	9:24-41	28,29
		II CHR.
27	10:1-23	1,2,3
28	10:24-42	4,5,6
29	11:1-29	7,8,9
30	11:30-57	10,11,12
31	12:1-26	13,14

JUNE

Date	Morning JOHN	Evening II CHR.
1	12:27-50	15,16
2	13:1-20	17,18
3	13:21-38	19,20
4	14	21,22
5	15	23,24
6	16	25,26,27
7	17	28,29
8	18:1-18	30,31
9	18:19-40	32,33
10	19:1-22	34,35,36
		EZRA
11	19:23-42	1,2
12	20	3,4,5
13	21	6,7,8
	ACTS	
14	1	9,10
		NEH.
15	2:1-21	1,2,3
16	2:22-47	4,5,6
17	3	7,8,9
18	4:1-22	10,11
19	4:23-37	12,13
		ESTH.
20	5:1-21	1,2
21	5:22-42	3,4,5
22	6	6,7,8
23	7:1-21	9,10
		JOB
24	7:22-43	1,2
25	7:44-60	3,4
26	8:1-25	5,6,7
27	8:26-40	8,9,10
28	9:1-21	11,12,13
29	9:22-43	14,15,16
30	10:1-23	17,18,19

JULY

Date	Morning	Evening
	ACTS	**JOB**
1	10:24-48	20,21
2	11	22,23,24
3	12	25,26,27
4	13:1-25	28,29
5	13:26-52	30,31
6	14	32,33
7	15:1-21	34,35
8	15:22-41	36,37
9	16:1-21	38,39,40
10	16:22-40	41,42
		PS.
11	17:1-15	1,2,3
12	17:16-34	4,5,6
13	18	7,8,9
14	19:1-20	10,11,12
15	19:21-41	13,14,15
16	20:1-16	16,17
17	20:17-38	18,19
18	21:1-17	20,21,22
19	21:18-40	23,24,25
20	22	26,27,28
21	23:1-15	29,30
22	23:16-35	31,32
23	24	33,34
24	25	35,36
25	26	37,38,39
26	27:1-26	40,41,42
27	27:27-44	43,44,45
28	28	46,47,48
	ROM.	
29	1	49,50
30	2	51,52,53
31	3	54,55,56

AUGUST

Date	Morning	Evening
	ROM.	**PS.**
1	4	57,58,59
2	5	60,61,62
3	6	63,64,65
4	7	66,67
5	8:1-21	68,69
6	8:22-39	70,71
7	9:1-15	72,73
8	9:16-33	74,75,76
9	10	77,78
10	11:1-18	79,80
11	11:19-36	81,82,83
12	12	84,85,86
13	13	87,88
14	14	89,90
15	15:1-13	91,92,93
16	15:14-33	94,95,96
17	16	97,98,99
	I COR.	
18	1	100,101,102
19	2	103,104
20	3	105,106
21	4	107,108,109
22	5	110,111,112
23	6	113,114,115
24	7:1-19	116,117,118
25	7:20-40	119:1-88
26	8	119:89-176
27	9	120,121,122
28	10:1-18	123,124,125
29	10:19-33	126,127,128
30	11:1-16	129,130,131
31	11:17-34	132,133,134

SEPTEMBER

Date	Morning	Evening
	I COR.	**PS.**
1	12	135,136
2	13	137,138,139
3	14:1-20	140,141,142
4	14:21-40	143,144,145
5	15:1-28	146,147
6	15:29-58	148,149,150
		PROV.
7	16	1,2
	II COR.	
8	1	3,4,5
9	2	6,7
10	3	8,9
11	4	10,11,12
12	5	13,14,15
13	6	16,17,18
14	7	19,20,21
15	8	22,23,24
16	9	25,26
17	10	27,28,29
18	11:1-15	30,31
		ECCL.
19	11:16-33	1,2,3
20	12	4,5,6
21	13	7,8,9
	GAL.	
22	1	10,11,12
		SONG
23	2	1,2,3
24	3	4,5
25	4	6,7,8
		ISA.
26	5	1,2
27	6	3,4
	EPH.	
28	1	5,6
29	2	7,8
30	3	9,10

OCTOBER

Date	Morning	Evening
	EPH.	**ISA.**
1	4	11,12,13
2	5:1-16	14,15,16
3	5:17-33	17,18,19
4	6	20,21,22
	PHIL.	
5	1	23,24,25
6	2	26,27
7	3	28,29
8	4	30,31
	COL.	
9	1	32,33
10	2	34,35,36
11	3	37,38
12	4	39,40
	I THESS.	
13	1	41,42
14	2	43,44
15	3	45,46
16	4	47,48,49
17	5	50,51,52
	II THESS.	
18	1	53,54,55
19	2	56,57,58
20	3	59,60,61
	I TIM.	
21	1	62,63,64
22	2	65,66
		JER.
23	3	1,2
24	4	3,4,5
25	5	6,7,8
26	6	9,10,11
	II TIM.	
27	1	12,13,14
28	2	15,16,17
29	3	18,19
30	4	20,21
	TITUS	
31	1	22,23

NOVEMBER

Date	Morning	Evening
	TITUS	**JER.**
1	2	24,25,26
2	3	27,28,29
3	PHILEM.	30,31
	HEB.	
4	1	32,33
5	2	34,35,36
6	3	37,38,39
7	4	40,41,42
8	5	43,44,45
9	6	46,47
10	7	48,49
11	8	50
12	9	51,52
		LAM.
13	10:1-18	1,2
14	10:19-39	3,4,5
		EZEK.
15	11:1-19	1,2
16	11:20-40	3,4
17	12	5,6,7
18	13	8,9,10
	JAMES	
19	1	11,12,13
20	2	14,15
21	3	16,17
22	4	18,19
23	5	20,21
	I PETER	
24	1	22,23
25	2	24,25,26
26	3	27,28,29
27	4	30,31,32
28	5	33,34
	II PETER	
29	1	35,36
30	2	37,38,39

DECEMBER

Date	Morning	Evening
	II PETER	**EZEK.**
1	3	40,41
	I JOHN	
2	1	42,43,44
3	2	45,46
4	3	47,48
		DAN.
5	4	1,2
6	5	3,4
7	II JOHN	5,6,7
8	III JOHN	8,9,10
9	JUDE	11,12
	REV.	**HOS.**
10	1	1,2,3,4
11	2	5,6,7,8
12	3	9,10,11
13	4	12,13,14
		JOEL
14	5	
		AMOS
15	6	1,2,3
16	7	4,5,6
17	8	7,8,9
		OBAD.
18	9	
		JON.
19	10	
		MIC.
20	11	1,2,3
21	12	4,5
22	13	6,7
		NAH.
23	14	
		HAB.
24	15	
		ZEPH.
25	16	
		HAG.
26	17	
		ZECH.
27	18	1,2,3,4
28	19	5,6,7,8
29	20	9,10,11,12
30	21	13,14
		MAL.
31	22	

THE OLD TESTAMENT IN TWO YEARS*

Month	Suggested Reading	Month	Suggested Reading
Books of Moses		**Judah's Middle Prophets**	
1	Genesis 1-30	14	Micah
2	Genesis 31-50		Isaiah 1-26
	Exodus 1-9	15	Isaiah 27-55
3	Exodus 10-40	16	Isaiah 56-66
4	Leviticus 1-27	**History**	
5	Numbers 1-27	16 (cont.)	II Kings 1-24
6	Numbers 28-36	**Pre-Captivity Prophets**	
	Deuteronomy 1-22	17	Nahum
7	Deuteronomy 23, 24		Habakkuk
History of Israel			Zephaniah
7 (cont.)	Joshua 1-15		Jeremiah 1-22
8	Joshua 16-24	18	Jeremiah 23-52
	Judges 1-21		Lamentations
9	Ruth	**History**	
	I Samuel 1-31	19	I Chronicles 1-29
10	II Samuel 1-24	**Captivity Prophets**	
Wisdom Literature		20	Ezekiel 1-31
11	Job 1-32	21	Ezekiel 32-48
12	Job 33-42		Daniel 1-6
History		22	Daniel 7-12
12 (cont.)	I Kings 1-15	**History**	
13	I Kings 16-22	22 (cont.)	II Chronicles 1-28
Early Prophets		23	II Chronicles 29-36
13 (cont.)	Hosea	**Restoration Writings**	
	Joel	23 (cont.)	Ezra
	Amos		Nehemiah
	Obadiah	24	Esther
	Jonah		Haggai
			Zechariah
			Malachi

*Psalms, Proverbs, Ecclesiastes and Song of Solomon are not included in this reading schedule.

Appendix B

RECOMMENDED REFERENCE BOOKS

The scripture declares, "Of making many books there is no end" (Eccl. 12:12). This is not only true of secular works but also of Christian publications, as well. Christians have a seemingly endless selection of quality reference books and study aids from which to choose. However, I have endeavored to offer only a limited list of recommended reference books so as not to overwhelm the Bible student. This concise list is broken down into basic topical categories. Those books recommended as a first choice are indicated with an asterisk. Books which are suited for the more advanced student are marked with a " + ." I have also added a basic beginner's reference library.

Basic Reference Library

1. *Thompson's Chain Reference Bible* (KJV or NIV), B.B. Kirkbride Bible Co.
2. Vine, Unger & White - *Expository Dictionary of Biblical Words,* Thomas Nelson Publishers.
3. *Strong's Exhaustive Concordance,* Thomas Nelson Publishers.
4. *Zondervan Pictorial Bible Dictionary,* Merrill C. Tenney, Zondervan.
5. *Unger's Bible Handbook,* Merrill F. Unger, Moody Press.
6. *Matthew Henry's Commentary on the Whole Bible* (1 volume), Leslie F. Church, Zondervan.
7. *Survey of Old Testament Introduction,* Gleason Archer, Moody Press.
8. *Bible History of the Old Testament,* Alfred Edersheim, Eerdmans.
9. *New Testament Survey,* Merrill C. Tenney, Eerdmans.
10. *Survey of Israel's History,* Leon Wood, Zondervan.
11. *Christianity Through the Centuries,* Earle E. Cairns, Zondervan.
12. *Explore the Book,* J. Sidlow Baxter, Zondervan.
13. *Wycliffe Historical Geography of Bible Lands,* Charles F. Pfeiffer, Moody Press.
14. *The Life and Epistles of St. Paul,* Conybeare & Howson, Eerdmans.

THE BOOK OF BOOKS

Study Bibles and Supplementary Bibles

* 1. *Thompson's Chain Reference Bible* (KJV or NIV), B.B. Kirkbride Bible Co.
2. *The Layman's Parallel New Testament* (KJV, Amplified, Living New Testament, & Revised Standard), Zondervan.
3. *The Reese Chronological Bible* (KJV), Edward Reese, Bethany House Publishers.

Concordances

* 1. *Strong's Exhaustive Concordance* (KJV), James Strong, Thomas Nelson Publishers.
2. *Cruden's Complete Concordance,* Alexander Cruden.
3. *New American Standard Exhaustive Concordance,* Robert Thomas, A.J. Holman Co.

Meaning of Words

* 1. *An Expository Dictionary of Biblical Words,* W.E. Vine, Merrill F. Unger and William White, Thomas Nelson Publishers.
+ 2. *Dictionary of New Testament Theology* (3 volumes), Colin Brown, Zondervan.
3. *New Testament Words,* William Barclay, Westminster Press.
* 4. *Word Studies in the Greek New Testament,* Kenneth Wuest, Eerdmans.
+ 5. *Word Studies in the New Testament,* M.R. Vincent, Eerdmans.
* 6. *Wilson's Old Testament Word Studies,* William Wilson, Macdonald Publishing Co.
7. *Theological Wordbook of the Old Testament,* R. Harrison, Gleason L. Archer, and Bruce K. Waltke, Moody Press.
+ 8. *Greek-English Lexicon of the New Testament,* Joseph H. Thayer.
+ 9. *Word Pictures in the New Testament,* A.T. Robertson, Broadman Press.

Bible Dictionaries, Handbooks, and Atlases

* 1. *Zondervan Pictorial Bible Dictionary,* Merrill C. Tenney, Zondervan.
2. *Unger's Bible Dictionary,* Merrill F. Unger, Moody Press.
* 3. *Unger's Bible Handbook,* Merrill F. Unger, Moody Press.
4. *Eerdman's Handbook to the Bible,* David Alexander, Eerdmans.
5. *Halley's Bible Handbook,* Henry H. Halley, Zondervan.
* 6. *Baker's Bible Atlas,* Charles F. Pfeiffer, Baker.
7. *Student Map Manual Historical Geography of Bible Lands,* J. Monson, Zondervan.
* 8. *Macmillan Bible Atlas,* Y. Aharoni and Aui-Yonahi, Macmillan Publishing Co.

RECOMMENDED REFERENCE BOOKS

Bible Introduction

Old Testament:

1. *Survey of Old Testament,* Gleason Archer, Moody Press.
* 2. *An Introduction to the Old Testament,* Edward J. Young, Eerdmans.
3. *Bible History of the Old Testament,* Alfred Edersheim, Eerdmans.
* 4. *Survey of Israel's History,* Leon Wood, Zondervan.

New Testament:

* 1. *New Testament Survey,* Merrill C. Tenney, Eerdmans.
+ 2. *New Testament Introduction,* Donald Guthrie, InterVarsity Press.
3. *New Testament Times,* Merrill C. Tenney, Zondervan.
+ 4. *A Guide to the Gospels,* Graham W. Scroggie, Fleming H. Revell Co.
* 5. *The Life and Times of Jesus the Messiah,* Alfred Edersheim, Eerdmans.
* 6. *The Life and Epistles of St. Paul,* Conybeare and Howson, Eerdmans.

The Entire Bible:

* 1. *Explore the Book,* J. Sidlow Baxter, Zondervan.
* 2. *Wycliffe Historical Geography of Bible Lands,* Charles F. Pfeiffer, Moody Press.

Bible Manners and Customs

* 1. *The Bible Almanac,* J.I. Packer, Merrill C. Tenney and William White, Thomas Nelson Publishers.
2. *Manners and Customs of the Bible,* Fred H. Wight, Moody Press.

Archaeology

* 1. *An Introduction to Bible Archaeology,* Howard F. Vos, Moody Press.
2. *Archaeology in Bible Lands,* Howard F. Vos, Moody Press.
3. *The Biblical World: A Dictionary of Biblical Archaeology,* Charles F. Pfeiffer, Baker.

Commentaries

One Volume:

1. *Matthew Henry's Commentary on the Whole Bible,* Leslie F. Church, Zondervan.
2. *The New Layman's Bible Commentary,* G.C.D. Howley, F.F. Bruce, and H.L. Ellison, Zondervan.

291

THE BOOK OF BOOKS

Series:

1. *Clarke's Commentary* (3 volumes), Adam Clarke, Abingdon Press.
* 2. *Commentaries on the New Testament Books* (17 volumes), Charles R. Eerdman, The Westminster Press.
3. *Tyndale New Testament Commentary Series,* R.V.G. Tasker, Eerdmans.
+ 4. *Barnes Notes* (14 volumes), Baker.
+ 5. *Calvin's Commentaries* (22 volumes), Baker.
+ 6. *Keil and Delitzsch's Commentary on the Old Testament* (10 volumes), C.F. Keil and F. Delitzsch, Eerdmans.

Bible Apologetics

* 1. *Evidence That Demands a Verdict,* Josh McDowell, Campus Crusade for Christ.
* 2. *Many Infallible Proofs,* Henry M. Morris, Creation Life Publishers.
* 3. *Know Why You Believe,* Paul E. Little, Victor Books.
* 4. *Science Speaks,* Peter W. Stoner, Moody Press.
5. *Protestant Christian Evidences,* Bernard Ramm, Moody Press.

For a more thorough coverage of reference books, I recommend the following works:

1. *The Minister's Library,* Cyril J. Barber, Baker.
* 2. *A Basic Library for Bible Students,* Warren W. Wiersbee, Baker.
3. *Commenting on Commentaries,* Charles H. Spurgeon, Baker.

BIBLIOGRAPHY

Albright, William F. *Archaeology and the Religions of Israel.* Baltimore, Maryland: Johns Hopkins University Press, 1956.
_____. *The Archaeology of Palestine.* Hammondsworth, Middelsex: Pelican Books, 1960.
Archer, Gleason. *A Survey of Old Testament Introduction.* Chicago, Ill.: Moody, 1974.
_____. *Encyclopedia of Bible Difficulties.* Grand Rapids, Mich.: Zondervan, 1982.
Boettner, Lorraine. *Roman Catholicism.* Phillipsburg, New Jersey: Presbyterian & Reformed Pub. Co., 1962.
Boice, James Montgomery. *Does Inerrancy Matter?* Oakland, Calif.: International Council on Biblical Inerrancy, 1979.
Board of Managers American Bible Society, *American Bible Society Record,* May 1986, Vol. 131, No. 5. New York, New York.
Boyd, Robert T. *A Pictorial Guide to Biblical Archaeology.* Eugene, Oregon: Harvest House Pub., 1969.
Bruce, F.F. *The Books and the Parchments.* New York, New York: Fleming H. Revell, 1963.
_____. *The New Testament Documents: Are They Reliable?* Downers Grove, Ill.: InterVarsity Press, 1943.
Burrows, Millar. *What Mean These Stones?* New York, New York: Meridian Books, 1956.
Camargo, Gonzalo Baez. *Archaeological Commentary on the Bible.* Garden City, New York: Doubleday, 1984.
Carson, D.A. *The King James Version Debate.* Grand Rapids, Mich.: Baker, 1979.
Cottrell, Jack. *The Authority of the Bible.* Grand Rapids, Mich.: Baker, 1978.
Crouch, Owen. *What the Bible Says About the Bible.* Joplin, Mo.: College Press Publishing Company, 1981.
Dorsett, S. Braybrook and Scott, John B. *Gleanings from the Apocrypha.* London, England: Covenant Publishing Co., 1946.
Geisler, Norman L. and Nix, William E. *A General Introduction to the Bible.* Chicago, Ill.: Moody Press, 1958.
Glueck, Nelson. *Rivers in the Desert.* Philadelphia, Penn.: Jewish Publications Society of America, 1969.
Green, William. *General Introduction to the Old Testament.* New York, New York: C. Scribner's Sons, 1899.

Greenleaf, Simon. *Testimony of the Evangelists, Examined by the Rules of Evidence Administered in Courts of Justice.* Grand Rapids, Mich.: Baker Book House (reprint from 1847 edition), 1965.

Haley, John W. *Alleged Discrepancies of the Bible.* Grand Rapids, Mich.: Baker, reprinted 1977.

Hall, Terry. *Getting More from Your Bible.* Wheaton, Ill.: Victor Books, 1984.

Halley, Henry H. *Halley's Bible Handbook.* Grand Rapids, Mich.: Zondervan, 1927.

Johnson, Carl G. *So the Bible Is Full of Contradictions?* Grand Rapids, Mich.: New Hope Press, 1983.

Josephus, Flavius. translated by William Whiston. Grand Rapids, Mich.: Baker, n.d.

Kelly, Balmer H., et al. *The Laymen's Bible Commentary* (Introduction). Atlanta, Georgia: Knox Press, 1959.

Kenyon, Frederick G. *The Bible and the Ancient Manuscripts.* New York, New York: Harper and Brothers, 1941.

_____. *The Bible and Archaeology.* New York, New York: Harper and Row, 1940.

_____. *The Bible and Modern Scholarship.* London, England: John Murray, 1948.

Lea, John W. *The Greatest Book in the World.* Philadelphia, Penn.: N.P., 1929.

Lewis, J. *The English Bible from KJV to NIV.* Grand Rapids, Mich.: Baker.

Lightfoot, J.B. *The Apostolic Fathers.* Grand Rapids, Mich.: Baker, 1956.

Lindsell, Harold. *The Battle for the Bible.* Grand Rapids, Mich.: Zondervan, 1976.

Little, Paul E. *Know Why You Believe.* Wheaton, Ill.: Victor Books, 1967.

Martin, Ray. *Quotations from Jesus and His Followers.* Fort Washington, Penn.: Christian Literature Crusade, 1962.

McDowell, Josh. *Answers to Tough Questions.* Arrowhead Springs, Ca.: Campus Crusade for Christ, 1980.

_____. *Evidence That Demands a Verdict.* Arrowhead Springs, Ca.: Campus Crusade for Christ, 1972.

_____. *More Evidence That Demands a Verdict.* Arrowhead Springs, Ca.: Campus Crusade for Christ, 1975.

_____. *Reasons Skeptics Should Consider Christianity.* Arrowhead Springs, Ca.: Campus Crusade for Christ, 1981.

Metzger, Bruce. *The Test of the New Testament.* New York and Oxford: Oxford University Press, 1968.

Montgomery, John W. *History and Christianity.* Downers Grove, Ill.: InterVarsity Press, 1971.

Morris, Henry M. *Explore the Word.* San Diego, Ca.: Creation Life Publishers, 1978.

_____. *Many Infallible Proofs.* El Cajon, Ca.: Master Books, 1974.

_____. *Men of Science, Men of God.* San Diego, Ca.: Master Books, 1982.

_____. *That You Might Believe.* San Diego, Ca.: Creation Life Pub., 1978.

_____. *The Bible and Modern Science*. Chicago, Ill.: Moody Press, 1951.

_____. *The Bible Has the Answer*. Grand Rapids, Mich.: Baker, 1971.

Mounce, Robert H. *Answers to Questions About the Bible. Grand Rapids,* Mich.: Baker, 1979.

Pinnock, Clark H. *A Defense of Biblical Infallibility*. Nutley, New Jersey: Presbyterian and Reformed Pub. Co., 1967.

Ramm, Bernard. *Protestant Christian Evidences*. Chicago, Ill.: Moody Press, 1957.

Ramsay, William. *St. Paul the Traveller and the Roman Citizen*. Grand Rapids, Mich.: Baker, 1962.

_____. *The Bearing of Recent Discoveries on the Trustworthiness of the New Testament*. Grand Rapids, Mich.: Baker, 1953.

Reid, James. *God, the Atom, and the Universe*. Grand Rapids, Mich.: Zonderan, 1968.

Riedel, Eunice, et al. *The Book of the Bible*. New York, New York: Bantam Books, 1979.

Rowell, Earle A. *Prophecy Speaks*. Tacoma Park, Wash.: Review and Herald, 1933.

Saucy, Robert L. *Is the Bible Reliable?* Wheaton, Ill.: Victor Books, 1978.

Smith, Wilbur M. *Therefore Stand: Christian Apologetics. Grand Rapids,* Mich.: Baker, 1965.

Smith, Wilder A.E. *The Reliability of the Bible*. San Diego, Ca.: Master Books, 1983.

Sterrett, T. Norton. *How to Understand Your Bible*. Downers Grove, Ill.: InterVarsity Press, 1973.

Stoner, Peter W. *Science Speaks*. Chicago, Ill.: Moody Press, 1958.

The Navigator Bible Studies Handbook. Colorado Springs, Colo.: Navpress, 1975.

Thompson, J.A. *The Bible and Archaeology*. Grand Rapids, Mich.: Eerdmans, 1962.

Torrey, R.A. *Difficulties in the Bible*. Chicago, Ill.: Moody Press, n.d.

_____. *The Bible and Its Christ*. New York, New York: Fleming H. Revell, 1904-06.

Underwood, Jonathan. *A History of the English Bible*. Cincinnati, Ohio: Standard Pub. Co., 1955.

Unger, Merrill F. *Archaeology and the New Testament. Grand Rapids,* Mich.: Zondervan, 1962.

_____. *Archaeology and the Old Testament*. Grand Rapids, Mich.: Zondervan, 1981.

Vos, Howard F. *An Introduction to Bible Archaeology*. Chicago, Ill.: Moody Press, 1956.

Warfield, Benjamin B. *Introduction to Textual Criticism of the New Testament*. London, England: Hodder and Stoughton, 1907.

Young, Edward J. *Thy Word Is Truth*. Grand Rapids, Mich.: Eerdmans, 1957.

295